GLOBAL COMPETITION IN FINANCIAL SERVICES

The American Enterprise Institute
Trade in Services Series

COMPETING IN A CHANGING WORLD ECONOMY PROJECT

Deregulation and Globalization: Liberalizing International Trade in Air Services — *Daniel M. Kasper*

Global Competition in Financial Services: Market Structure, Protection, and Trade Liberalization — *Ingo Walter*

International Trade in Business Services: Accounting, Advertising, Law, and Management Consulting — *Thierry J. Noyelle and Anna B. Dutka*

International Trade in Construction, Design, and Engineering Services — *James R. Lee and David Walters*

International Trade in Films and Television Programs — *Steven S. Wildman and Stephen E. Siwek*

International Trade in Ocean Shipping Services: The United States and the World — *Lawrence J. White*

When Countries Talk: International Trade in Telecommunications Services — *Jonathan David Aronson and Peter F. Cowhey*

International Trade in Services: An Overview and Blueprint for Negotiations — *Geza Feketekuty*

Global Competition in Financial Services

Market Structure, Protection, and Trade Liberalization

Ingo Walter

An American Enterprise Institute/Ballinger Publication

Ballinger Publishing Company, Cambridge, Massachusetts
A Subsidiary of Harper & Row, Publishers, Inc.

"American Enterprise Institute" and ⬱ are registered service marks of the American Enterprise Institute for Public Policy Research.

International Standard Book Number: 0-88730-234-3

Library of Congress Catalog Card Number: 87-30858

Printed in the United States of America.

Library of Congress Cataloging-in-Publication Data

Walter, Ingo.
   Global competition in financial services : market structure, protection, and trade liberalization / Ingo Walter.
      p.   cm. — (American Enterprise Institute series on trade in services)
      "An American Enterprise Institute/Ballinger publication."
      Bibliography: p.
      Includes index.
      ISBN 0-88730-234-3
   1. Financial institutions. 2. Banks and banking. International. 3. Commercial policy.
4. Competition. International. 5. International finance. I. Title. II. Series.
HG173.W35   1988
332.1—dc19   87-30858
                                                                                                             CIP

CONTENTS

LIST OF FIGURES

LIST OF TABLES

EDITOR'S FOREWORD

The American Enterprise Institute's *Trade in Services Series* represents an important step toward creating the policy alternatives necessary to enhance the international competitiveness of American services.

The series is part of a larger, continuing AEI project, *Competing in a Changing World Economy*. Launched in 1983, this project has produced a wealth of publications, seminars, and conferences, analyzing the most significant policy challenges confronting U.S. policymakers in the areas of international trade and finance, science and technology policy, and human capital development.

Early in the project, we concluded that the United States would be successful in its drive to initiate a new round of trade negotiations with the other major trading nations, under the auspices of the General Agreement on Tariffs and Trade (GATT). We also chose to concentrate our resources on the new issues that would be placed on the table in that round: trade in services, intellectual property, and trade-related investment. In September 1986, at Punta del Este, Uruguay, the United States and the other members of GATT did indeed reach an agreement to launch a new multilateral round of trade negotiations, the Uruguay Round. Trade in services, along with intellectual property and investment issues, was included on the agenda. Hence, over the next several years negotiators in Geneva and top policy officials in all the major trading nations will face the formidable task of forging trading rules for these new issues.

In the area of services, a number of countries, including the United States, have produced individual, national studies of service trade liberalization. Yet government and private-sector officials agree that these studies are only a first step, and that substantial research remains to be done in key service sectors before major policy questions can be answered regarding a new service trade regime.

Designed to fill this policy gap, *Trade in Services* brings together eleven outstanding writers who have committed their expertise to analyzing the seven key service sector industries:

- Aviation—Daniel M. Kasper, Harbridge House

- Banking—Ingo Walter, Graduate School of Business Administration, New York University

- Construction—James R. Lee, American University, and David Walters, Staff Economist, Office of the U.S. Trade Representative

- Professional services—Thierry J. Noyelle and Anna B. Dutka, Conservation of Human Resources, Columbia University

- Shipping—Lawrence J. White, Member, Federal Home Loan Bank Board, on leave from the Graduate School of Business Administration, New York University

- Telecommunications: Information and Data Processing— Jonathan David Aronson, School of International Relations, University of Southern California, and Peter F. Cowhey, Department of Political Science, University of California at San Diego

- Telecommunications: Motion Pictures, Television, and Prerecorded Entertainment—Steven S. Wildman and Stephen E. Siwek, Economists Incorporated

In addition, Geza Feketekuty, of the Office of the U.S. Trade Representative, has written an overview volume for the series.

All of the books in the series embody two main goals: first, to analyze the dynamics of international competition for each of the seven industries, identifying existing and potential barriers to trade; and second, to formulate and assess policy approaches for opening service markets through an umbrella service agreement and subsequent individual sector agreements in GATT.

A related goal is to disseminate the results of our research through conferences and seminars, televised forums, and a variety of publication formats. We aim to make our findings known to government officials, trade experts, the business and financial communities, and concerned members of the public. To that end, during 1987 we convened major conferences in London, Geneva, and Washington, and in early 1988 the team of authors traveled to Tokyo and Singapore. Thus, as with all AEI projects, we have sought to ensure that the studies not only make a significant contribution to scholarship but also become an important factor in the decision making and negotiating processes.

In addition to the authors, who have produced outstanding books, we would like to thank John H. Jackson, Hessel E. Yntema Professor of Law at the University of Michigan, and Gardner Patterson, who for many years served in the GATT Secretariat. Both of these men provided invaluable help and guidance as advisers to the project.

—Claude E. Barfield
Coordinator
Competing in a Changing World Economy

PREFACE

International trade and competition in financial services is a rather difficult topic to analyze in terms of competition and market structure, and even more so in terms of the incidence and significance of competitive distortions in this sector of the global economy.

The problems begin immediately. Precisely *what* is being traded? How is the volume, direction, and composition of trade in this sector to be defined and measured? What are the criteria that drive global trade flows in this industry, and what determines the sectoral pattern of competitive advantage and disadvantage on the part of institutions and countries? How is protectionism to be defined in an industry that embodies a distinctive "public good" character, and therefore has usually been (and is likely to continue to be) heavily regulated? What rules appear to make sense in setting a "level playing field" for financial services in the context of national money and capital markets, and how can agreement and enforcement of these rules be achieved?

All of these are issues that confront anyone trying to come to grips with this topic. Research tends to be informal and qualitative, and evidence tends to be case-oriented and anecdotal, not least because confidentiality and proprietary know-how play a critical role in competitive relations in the financial services industry. Bankers themselves tend to be reticent in talking specifics, and for good reason.

It is nevertheless possible to reach some rather robust conclusions, both about the international economics of the industry and about the policy dimensions.

This volume develops further and elaborates upon my earlier work on this subject, published as *Barriers to Trade in Banking and Financial Services* (London: Trade Policy Research Centre, 1985), which was written during the summer of 1983. I am grateful to Hugh Corbet and Brian Hindley of the TPRC for allowing me to draw on part of that monograph in preparing the present volume. My research assistant during 1985–86, Fergal Byrne, now with Swiss Bank Corporation International (SBCI) in London, contributed significantly to much of the research. Financial support for the project was provided under the International Financial Services project at the Institut Européen d'Administration des Affaires (INSEAD) in Fontainebleau, France.

I am also grateful to Peter Bernholz, Jagdish Bhagwati, Ernest Bloch, Don Boudreau, Geza Feketekuty, Ian H. Giddy, Herbert Giersch, Wilfried Guth, Peter B. Kenen, Charles P. Kindleberger, Pentti Koivista, Herwig Langohr, Mario Monti, Gardner Patterson, A. Kendall Raine, Jr., David A. Ruth, Arnold Sametz, Anthony Saunders, Richard Self, Roy C. Smith, Eberhard von Wangenheim, Martin Wolff, and others in academia, banking, and government with whom I have discussed these issues over the years or who commented on earlier drafts of this book. Ann Rusolo and Hugh Thomas assisted in preparing the final manuscript. None, of course, is responsible for any remaining errors or shortcomings.

—*Ingo Walter*
New York City
January 15, 1988

INTRODUCTION

Certainly the dominant characteristic of the international financial services industry today is the unprecedented level of competition facing many of the major players. Market and product interpenetration in this sector is proceeding at a ferocious rate, driven by rapid financial innovation, securitization of international capital flows, and continued evolution of offshore capital markets. All have induced major competitive and structural changes in the industry. It is also an environment in which countries are rebalancing the static and dynamic efficiency properties against the stability characteristics of their domestic financial systems, and individual institutions are reexamining their corporate strategies and their chances for survival in the competitive environment of the 1990s. And it is an environment in which distortions of competitive conditions have taken on greatly increased importance. How level, in other words, is the playing field?

A measure of the rapid change that has occurred in patterns of international financing is given by the data in Table 1–1, which compares the situation 1981–82 with that in 1985. Figure 1–1 traces these developments through time. In particular, the extent of securitization of financial flows and the movement away from conventional and syndicated lending is very clear, in large part due to the international debt crisis. The volume raised on international capital markets increased from $175.6 billion in 1982 to $367 billion in 1986. Of this total, in 1986 securitized forms of financing accounted for 87 percent as compared with 13 percent for loans. This contrasts with 44 percent and 56 percent, respectively, in 1982.

Table 1–1.   The Emergence of New Instruments (%).

	1981–82	1985
Syndicated bank credits		
Eurocurrency		
Commercial	53.4	12.7
Managed	—	2.7
Foreign	3.2	2.7
Bonds		
Straights	27.0	36.1
Floating-rate notes	7.8	23.7
Equity related	2.1	4.4
Zero coupon	0.8	2.6
Other Facilities		
Note issuance and similar facilities	2.9	12.4
Other backup facilities	2.8	2.7
Total (billions)	$170	$242

Source: OECD, March 1986.

Less developed countries (LDC) did virtually all of their borrowing through syndicated loans, their paper being largely unacceptable in the securities markets. With the collapse of "voluntary" lending (as opposed to forced debt restructurings) to many LDCs, the share of syndicated loans in international capital markets likewise declined, to be replaced in large measure with securities issued by firms and government entities in developed countries. This is made clear by the figures presented in Table 1–2, showing the greatly increased concentration of international financing on highly creditworthy Organization for Economic Cooperation and Development (OECD) borrowers and issuers. One consequence has been intensified competition among banks and securities firms competing for the available business, and the emergence of a true buyers' market for the most sought after borrowers.

In addition to their rapid change, financial services constitute one of the most structurally complex industries in the world economy. It is also one of the most heavily regulated as a

Figure 1–1. International Financial Flows, by Type.

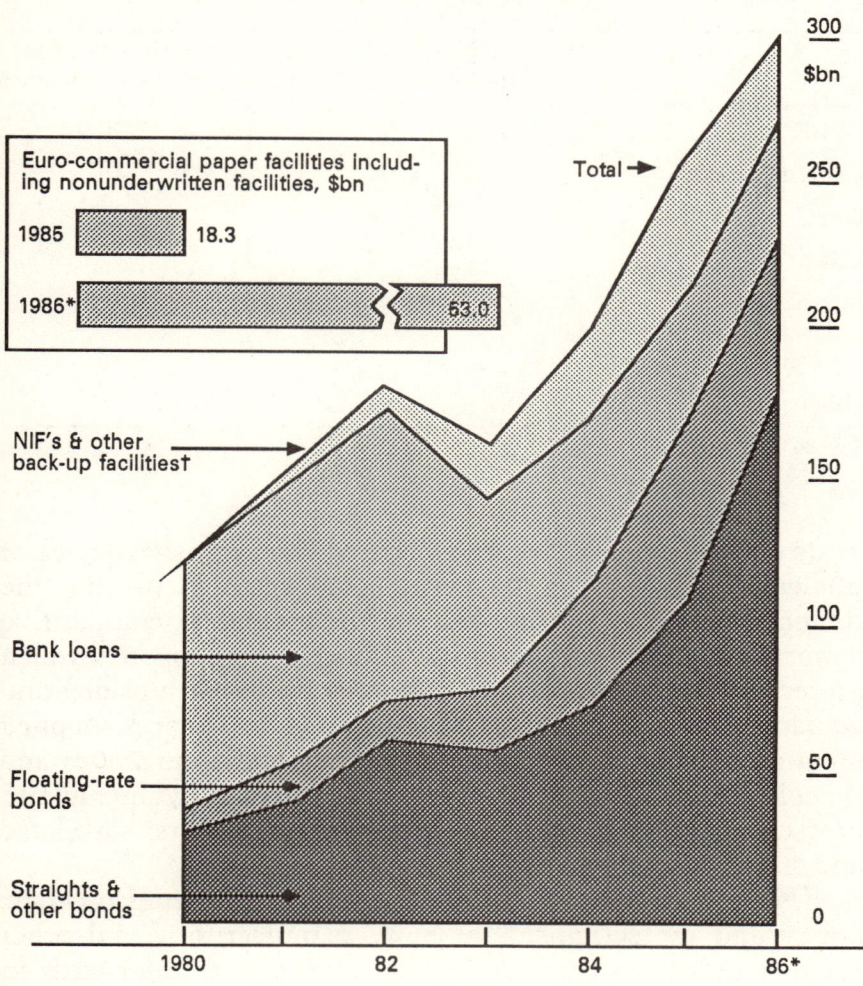

Key: * denotes January–September date at annual rate.
    † excludes Euro-commercial paper.

Source: *The Economist*, March 21, 1987. Copyright 1987, *The Economist*, distributed by Special Features. Data from OECD.

consequence of the fiduciary nature of much of its activities, its pivotal role in the execution of money and credit policies, as well

Table 1–2. Composition of Borrowers by Instruments, 1985 (%).

	External Bond Markets	Bank Credits	Other Facilities (NIFs, RUFs, etc.)
OECD	86.6	42.2	90.5
Eastern Europe	—	10.9	—
OPEC	0.6	5.8·	2.2
LDCs	4.0	36.2	6.9
International development institutions	7.3	3.6	—
Other	1.5	1.2	0.4

Source: OECD, March 1986.

as its susceptibility to recurring crises. The extensive degree of prudential supervision, regulation, and control covering the financial services sector provides fertile ground for competitive distortions, either in the form of public-sector support through protective measures (direct or indirect) or through subsidies and guarantees (direct or indirect). Today, financial services supplied on a global scale constitute a fast-moving, innovative, and fiercely competitive game, one that is unusually vulnerable to protectionist initiatives on the part of those players, both large and small, who are not able to keep up.

Nevertheless, unlike the rather sad track record on trade policy and protectionism in many manufacturing and other services industries (such as insurance), the picture for trade in financial services (defined as value added, using factors of production found in one country, which is then sold to residents of another country) has in fact been rather bright. Serious problems remain, and new ones will inevitably arise. But the industry has already become heavily internationalized, and parts of it have become truly globalized, with few prospects that this is likely to be reversed in the years ahead.

PURPOSE OF THE BOOK

There has in recent years been a great deal of research on changes in the environment facing competitors in the financial services industry. Issues of interest have included the following:

- The increasing pace of disintermediation and securitization of debt

- Financial deregulation at the national level

- Globalization of international capital markets

- Emergence of international equity markets

- Increasing concern of regulators for capital adequacy addressed to problems of country, sectoral, and off-balance-sheet exposures

- Continued exchange-rate and interest-rate volatility

- Increasing competition in banking coming from nonbank competitors

- Growing domestic market penetration by foreign based institutions

- Increased financial sophistication of consumers and users of financial services

- Changing financial needs of corporations

- Sustained growth of offshore finance

- Increased rates of financial innovation and a shortening of the half-life of innovations due to reductions in imitation lags.

All of these pressures have dramatically altered the static and dynamic characteristics of competition in national and international financial environments, and have had significant effects on the strategic thinking of firms in the international financial services industry. Equally, they have encouraged regulators to rethink the balance between financial efficiency and creativity on the one hand, and safety and stability of the financial system on the other. Theirs is a difficult task: to strike an optimum balance for the financial sector in its role as a central agent for national and global economic growth and development.

The intent of this book is to build on the base of previous research,[1] assembling what we now think we know about the structure, conduct, and performance of the global financial services industry and applying that knowledge to the task of liberalizing competition and trade in this critical sector of the world economy.

FLOW OF THE DISCUSSION

We begin, in Chapter 2, with an overview and consideration of "internationalization" in the financial services industry, tracing this phenomenon from its medieval and colonial antecedents to successive modern waves of geographic market interpenetration: U.S. commercial bank penetration of Europe in the 1960s, foreign commercial bank penetration of the United States (alongside massive lending to LDCs) in the 1970s, and U.S. investment bank penetration of Europe together with truly impressive Japanese incursions into major markets in the 1980s. The dual threads of market interpenetration and product interpenetration are developed as the basis for the conceptual and empirical discussion that follows.

Chapter 3 develops a model that establishes a coherent analytical framework for interpreting the critical variables that explain market positioning in the financial services sector internationally. This framework is used in Chapter 4 to assess the strategic behavior of individual institutional players and the underlying sources of institutional and national competitive advantage or disadvantage in the international delivery of financial services.

In Chapter 5, trade in financial services is carefully defined in terms comparable to the definition of international trade in other industries. This definition is then used to outline the dimensions of protection and competitive distortions in this sector.

Chapter 6 discusses the political economy of protection as it affects the financial services industry internationally—its causes, its forms, and its consequences. This discussion is based on accepted political and economic models of rent-seeking and public-choice behavior, and the conversion of economic interests into political power through the lobbying process. Financial institutions are often in an unusually strong position to make this conversion and are able to exploit their position at the center of national economic activity to achieve protectionist goals even at the expense of the national interest.

In Chapter 7, the characteristics of protectionist measures in the global financial services industry are reviewed. They are broken down into tariff-like and quota-like distortions, both as explicit protectionist devices and as "collateral" or "incidental" discrimination arising from prudential and regulatory controls or monetary policies. A broad array of financial services are not in fact sold directly to the ultimate consumer, but rather represent inputs to suppliers of goods and services throughout national economies. Since these industries are in many cases themselves exposed to vigorous international competition, competitive distortions in the financial services sector have to be viewed in a so-called effective protection context. They raise costs and lower the quality of financial services, thereby impairing the competitive performance of clients. The analysis of competitive distortions is then linked back to the basic structural model, in order to identify consequences for global competitive performance that lie beyond the markets directly subject to such distortions.

Chapter 7 also raises the issue of offshore financial markets, which are subject to limited regulation and even more limited scope for protectionism. Unlike other goods and services sectors, part of the financial services industry operates through the Euromarkets in ways that are largely outside the scope of national control. This contributes two unique perspectives that do not exist in other industries. First, offshore markets make it possible to "lead" selected clients out of a protected national environment and transfer their business to the offshore markets, thereby avoiding national restrictions. Second, offshore markets make clear to national authorities the price they are paying, in terms of static and dynamic efficiency losses, for protectionist competitive distortions in the financial services sector at home.

Chapter 8 considers the principal dimensions of trade liberalization as they apply to this sector, including reciprocity and national treatment. These issues are then linked to the GATT Articles of Agreement in order to determine whether the General Agreement on Tariffs and Trade, as an international set of rules that have served reasonably well in facilitating trade liberalization in goods, can make a significant contribution to trade liberalization in the financial services sector as well.

The book concludes with some normative guidelines for market liberalization in the international financial services industry, and its implications for the Uruguay Round of multilateral trade negotiations.

NOTE

1. Ingo Walter, *Barriers to Trade in Banking and Financial Services* (London: Trade Policy Research Centre, 1985).

2
INTERNATIONALIZATION OF THE FINANCIAL SERVICES INDUSTRY

Involvement of banks and other firms in the financial services industry in national economies outside their home countries is nothing new. In historical terms, international activities in the financial services industry can be traced back at least to the ancient Egyptians and Sumerians, who used papyrus letters of credit and clay tablet "checks" to facilitate the flow of international trade. Bills of exchange made their appearance in Babylonia and Assyria as early as the twenty-first century B.C. The merchant banking dynasties of the fifteenth and sixteenth centuries, dominated by the Medicis in Florence and Fuggers in Frankfurt, often engaged in highly sophisticated cross-border operations, many of which were similar to some of today's internationally traded financial products.[1] Similarly the dominant British merchant banks of the nineteenth century developed on the pattern of the Continental investment banks of the time, with extensive equity holdings in extractive and manufacturing enterprises abroad representing an additional sphere of international activity and an important contribution to industrial development.

Besides cross-border lending and investing, even these fore-runners of modern international banking maintained impressive direct links outside their home countries. The Medicis, for example, had numerous correspondent relationships throughout Europe, as well as branches in Rome, Venice, Milan, Paris, Avignon, Bruges, London, and Geneva, each separately capitalized with majority ownership and control in the hands of the Medici family in Florence. Later, while Baring Brothers in London limited itself to strong correspondent banking links abroad and one representative office in the United States, other British merchant banks of the nineteenth century had impressive branch networks, especially in Latin America and South Africa. In the 1860s, five British banks had operations in the state of California alone, while twenty-two operated in the Far East. The Rothschilds set up branches in Paris, London, Vienna, and Frankfurt, while Crédit Mobilier had investment banking affiliates in England, Spain, Germany, Italy, and the Netherlands.

Internationalization has taken on an entirely new meaning in the modern context, of course, and geographic interpenetration of financial institutions with respect to various domestic and offshore markets has become very significant indeed. For example, in 1950 only seven American banks had activities abroad, with a total of 95 branches. By 1970 there were 79 banks with 536 branches, and by 1984 there were more than 150 banks with over 1,000 branches that booked assets in excess of $337 billion.

Table 2–1 indicates the number of foreign banks that had a

Table 2–1. Foreign Banking Presence, by Host Country.[a]

Country	1970	1980	1985
United States[b]	50	579	783
United Kingdom	95	214	336
West Germany[b]	77	213	287
France[b]	58	122	147
Switzerland	97	99	119
Japan[b]	38	85	112
Luxembourg[b]	23	96	106
Belgium	26	51	58
Canada	0	0	58
Netherlands	23	39	44
Italy	4	26	40

Source: Bank for International Settlements, as reported in Morgan Guaranty Trust Company, *World Financial Markets* (November–December 1986): 6.

a. The data are not fully comparable. Except for countries denoted with a superscript [b], the data count foreign banking institutions or families operating through branches or majority-owned subsidiaries (branches only for Italy).

b. Data count banking offices (branches only for Japan), so that foreign organizations represented by more than one entity are double-counted. On June 30, 1985, total represented foreign organizations numbered 350 in the United States, 95 in Germany, and 76 in Japan.

significant presence (branches or majority-owned affiliates) in the major industrial countries in 1970, 1980, and mid-1985, respectively. These data actually understate the degree of internationalization of banks, since forms of involvement other than branches or majority-owned subsidiaries are not captured in the statistics. Nor do the data capture the growing involvement abroad by investment and merchant banks, brokerage houses, and other types of financial services firms. Table 2–2 indicates the size of the overseas presence, in terms of both assets and net earnings, of four major U.S. money-center banks in 1985.

According to a study by Morgan Guaranty[2], foreign banks operating in the United States booked $411 billion in deposits (13 percent of the U.S. total) and $110 billion in business loans (22 percent of the total U.S. market and 50 percent of the New York City market) in 1986. In dollar-denominated acceptance financing, they took 33 percent of the U.S. market. Japanese banks alone captured a 40 percent share of foreign bank assets in the United

Table 2–2. U.S. Banks' Geographic Spread, 1985 (%).

	J.P. Morgan	Citicorp	BankAmerica	Chemical
Assets				
Europe	26	21	16	13
Western Hemisphere	11	12	9	11
Asia	8	14	9	6
Middle East and Africa	2	—	1	2
Total non-United States	47	47	35	33
United States	53	53	65	67
Net Pretax Income				
Europe	55	19	loss	10
Western Hemisphere	0.5	25	loss	20
Asia	8	10	loss	loss
Middle East and Africa	0.5	—	profit	1
Total non-United States	64	54	loss	31
United States	36	46	profit	69

Source: Annual Reports. Middle East and Africa included within Europe by Citicorp; Canada is included in Western Hemisphere by Morgan and in U.S. totals by others, for whom it has represented 3–6 percent of assets and earnings. Banks not providing comparable breakdowns include Chase, Manufacturers Hanover, and Bankers Trust.

States and an 80 percent share of foreign banks' dollar-denominated acceptances. Meanwhile, the 30 Japanese banks in London held over 25 percent of all banking assets booked in the United Kingdom in 1986.

Acquisitions abroad by Japanese financial institutions have reached significant proportions—see Table 2–3 for a list of the principal banking acquisitions in the United States. By 1987 five of the eleven major banks in California were in Japanese hands. Meantime, Dai-Ichi Kangyo Bank bought Chekiang First Bank in Hong Kong in 1986, while Mitsubishi acquired Mercantile Bank in Hong Kong from Citicorp. Fear of a backlash reportedly prompted the Ministry of Finance to discourage for a time further foreign acquisitions by Japanese financial institutions, which evidently stalled several additional moves then under consideration.[3]

At the same time, the share of the United States in global equity markets has been eroded rapidly by the rise of Japan during the 1980s. In 1986 a total of 493 different stocks were being traded daily in at least one market (compared with 240 in 1983), and over $12 billion in new Euroequity issues were undertaken. Global equity capitalization amounted to $5,606 billion (compared with $1,150 billion in 1975), with the U.S. share shrinking from 61.2 percent to 31.8 percent over the same time period. In May 1987 total capitalization of the Tokyo Stock Exchange exceeded that of the New York Stock Exchange. On the other hand, the United States continued to dominate financial futures trading.

Table 2–4 indicates the size of the foreign presence in London, Tokyo, Frankfurt, and New York stock exchanges. Table 2–5 illustrates the extent to which foreign firms have purchased shares in U.S. and U.K. securities firms.

The reasons for the rapid growth in the activities of financial institutions in various onshore and offshore markets lie primarily in the nature of the services provided. It is often (but not always) imperative for a financial institution to have a presence physically close to the client and an active presence in important markets in order to do business effectively. While a certain amount of a business can certainly be done through correspondent relationships and travel, the increasingly complex nature of

Table 2–3. Japanese Bank Acquisitions in the United States, 1981–86.

Date	Acquiring Company/ Acquired Company	Aggregate Consideration (in thousands)	Business of Acquired Company
08/81	The Mitsui Bank Ltd./ Manufacturers Bank	173,000	Commercial bank
02/81	The Sanwa Bank Ltd./ First City Bank of Rosemead	28,000	Commercial bank
06/84	The Mitsubishi Bank, Limited/ BanCal Tri-State Corporation	268,701	Holding company for the Bank of California
12/84	The Sanwa Bank Ltd./ Continental Illinois Leasing Corp. and Cobak Corp. (from Continental Illinois Corp.)	505,000	Middle market leasing and Big Ticket leveraged leasing
01/84	The Fuji Bank, Limited/ Walter E. Heller & Company and Walter E. Heller Overseas Corporation (subs of Walter E. Heller International Corporation)	425,000	Commercial and consumer financing and factoring
07/85	Industrial Bank of Japan/ J. Henry Schroder Bank & Trust Co. (51% interest to increase to 75.1% in 18 months)	110,000	U.S. commercial banking, trust, and leasing subsidiaries of British parent
08/86	Golden State Sanwa Bank (U.S. unit of Sanwa Bank Ltd.)/ Lloyds Bank of California (U.S. unit of Lloyds Bank Plc)	263,000	State bank
12/86	J. Henry Schroder Bank & Trust Co. (unit of Industrial Bank of Japan)/ Aubrey G. Lanston & Co.	234,000	Primary dealer in U.S. Government Securities

Source: Goldman Sachs.

Table 2–4. Stock Exchange Membership by Foreign Based Securities Firms.

Exchange	No. of Foreign Firms	Opened to Foreigners	Cost of a Seat (1987)
New York	36	1977	$625,000
Frankfurt	0/40[a]	1982	$198,000
London	101	1986	$16–80,000
Tokyo	6	1985	$7.5 million

Source: The Economist, April 11, 1987. Copyright 1987, The Economist, distributed by Special Features.

a. No foreign based brokers are allowed. However, foreign based banks that are licensed by the Federal Banking Supervisory Authority in West Berlin may own seats on the Frankfurt exchange.

financial services and client needs has in many ways enhanced the importance of reliable direct connections.

International trade in this sector is defined as financial services produced by factors of production whose ownership resides in one country and sold to residents of another, often through some sort of direct presence of the supplier in the client's country. Even in cases where a foreign based financial institution is engaged in purely local business, some sort of cross-border flows of products, factors of production, or technologies must be taking place as the basis for its ability to survive in the market of the host country.

The value of the services thus traded is measured by *current* flows of commissions, fees, profits, and related returns associated with services sold during the current period. Interest remitted on cross-border lending is the product of *past* sales of services, and is accounted for when the loans are made. The value of financial-service returns wholly earned within the host country, such as local-currency lending or fee and commission income, is reflected in the value of current profit remittances to the parent company abroad.[4]

Internationally traded financial services closely parallel those offered in purely domestic markets. They encompass a great variety of different businesses involving products and

Table 2–5.   Foreign Investment in U.S. and U.K. Securities Firms, as of 1987.

	Percentage Foreign-owned	Foreign Investor
U.S. Securities Firms:		
Wertheim Schroder & Co.	50.0	Schroders P.L.C. (British)
Moseley Securities	39.0	Al Mal Group (Middle East investors)
Drexel Burnham Lambert	27.0	European investor group that includes Pargesa of Switzerland and Groupe Bruxelles Lambert of Belgium
Smith Barney, Harris Upham	22.0	Lama Holdings (Arab investor group)[a]
First Boston	33.0	Crédit Suisse (Swiss)
Lazard Freres & Co.	15.3	Lazard Brothers of London and S. Pearson and Son (British)
Salomon Brothers	14.0	Minorco (controlled by Anglo American Corporation of South Africa)
Shearson Lehman Brothers	13.0	Nippon Life Insurance Company (Japan)
Goldman, Sachs & Co.	12.5	Sumitomo Bank (Japan)[b]
L.F. Rothschild, Unterberg, Towbin	8.0	J. Rothschild Holdings (British)
U.K. Securities Firms:		
Morgan Grenfell	5	Deutsche Bank
Kleinwort Benson	5	American Can
Henry Ansbacher	50	Pargesa Holdings and Groupe Bruxelles Lambert
Guinness Peat	21	UKPI
Hambros	9	Prudential Insurance
Brown Shipley	21	Kredietbank

Source: Individual company reports.

a. Interest held directly. Sold to Primerica Corp. in 1987.

b. Non-voting interest.

markets that have highly differentiated structural and competitive profiles. Some are quite homogeneous and, unless distorted by government policies, have many of the attributes of efficient markets—intense competition, ease of entry and exit, low transaction and information costs, rapid adjustment to change, and very thin profit margins. Others involve substantial monopoly elements, with high degrees of product differentiation, natural barriers to entry and substantial competitive power on the part of individual firms.[5] Internationally traded financial services can be classified into at least six broad "product" categories.

Deposit-taking. There is deposit-taking in onshore markets abroad and in offshore (Euro) markets, demand and time deposits of residents and nonresidents in foreign onshore accounts, as well as Euro-deposits in offshore accounts. Deposits include those of individuals, corporations, governments, and other banks (redeposits). Competition for deposits is often intense. Funding costs are dependent, in part, on the perceived safety and soundness of the institution, its sophistication, the efficiency of its retail deposit-gathering, and customer services reflected in compensating deposit balances.

International Trading and Dealing. Closely related are international trading and dealing in foreign currencies, deposits, forward-exchange contracts, financial futures and options, gold and perhaps other commodities. These activities are intended to position the institution to profit from shifts in markets within acceptable limits of exposure to risk. A major determinant of profitability is the management of sources and uses of funds—mismatching the maturity structure of a part of the institution's assets and liabilities in the light of the shape of the yield curve, expectations about future interest-rate movements and anticipated liquidity needs. Here the financial institution has to anticipate market developments more correctly and consistently than the competition, and to move faster, if it is to earn more than a normal return on its capital. The parties with which it trades in money and foreign exchange, for example, must have different interest-rate and exchange-rate expectations or be slower and less sophisticated (and the institution itself has to be correct more of the time) if it is to excel in this activity. All of this must be accomplished in an environment where each important player has simultaneous access to the same information. It is a fiercely competitive business.

Traditional International Trade and Cash Management Services. The traditional international financial product line encompasses international documentary collections, letters of credit, and acceptance financing. International trade services (ITS) have always been a mainstay of banks involved in global business. In banking they have been considered somewhat routine in nature, with relatively little scope for product differentiation and incremental returns. In recent years, however, there have been a number of innovations, particularly in the areas of process technology, systems, and data transmission, so that international trade services, especially proprietary international cash management services supplied to multinational corporate clients, have become much more attractive for banks.

In addition, standby letters of credit covering the issuance of debt by private firms and public-sector entities, as well as construction and related projects, have become an insurance-related and fee-earning activity that is not based on enlarging the balance sheet and, hence, is very attractive to banks. As a result of renewed interest in international trade and cash management services, competition between banks in this area has once again become heated. In part, this is because some major institutions have a strong interest in making up lost ground in areas that they have long neglected in favor of more lucrative business opportunities.

International Lending. A mainstay of the banking industry is still international lending: secured and unsecured loans to local corporations, banks, governments, multinational enterprises, and individuals domiciled outside the bank's home country either in local or foreign currencies. Competition here varies from being exceedingly intense in the Euromarkets to essentially monopolistic in some of the more protected U.S. domestic markets. Returns tend to vary with the degree of competition prevailing in the local environment, the complexity and riskiness of the deal, and the credit worthiness of the borrower. Dimensions of competitiveness in this area include the initiation and maintenance of contact with borrowers or other customers, the feasibility of credit evaluation, and questions of country risk.[6]

Specialized forms of international lending include syndicated loans and the financing of projects. In loan syndications, the economic rents are to a significant degree associated with lead-management roles: namely, a bank's ability to obtain syndication mandates, to handle legal and information tasks as well as agency functions, and to develop networks of bank contacts and knowledge about their portfolios so that other participants can be brought into a transaction. Not every institution is able to cope successfully with all of these functions, or to carry the often substantial underwriting risks involved, so that the fee-based returns from loan syndication activities can be significant.

This is even more true of the financing of projects generally associated with energy or mineral development activities at least partly without recourse to the project's sponsors, often energy or mining companies.[7] Such lending requires highly technical scientific and engineering capabilities within the bank and the ability to work with technical consultants. It also requires the capacity to assess a broad range of risks that run the gamut from project completion (delays, cost overruns) and *force majeure* to market prospects in natural resources and political change. Barriers to entry are quite high and the structure of the market for lead positions in this business can be described as oligopolistic. International lease financing and ship and aircraft financing are other forms of specialized (asset-based) lending that require particular types of financial expertise and can generate substantial returns.

International Securities Business. Besides trade-related and lending-related activities, there is also a range of services involving underwriting and trading or dealing in domestic and international securities issues (both foreign bonds and Eurobonds and notes) of various maturities, as well as futures, options, and (increasingly) equity shares. The origination, underwriting, and distribution of new securities in the international marketplace can be highly profitable, but, like syndicated lending, requires a high degree of distribution or placing power, extensive issuer contact, and the ability and willingness to take substantial underwriting risks. It also requires a well-developed trading capability in secondary markets. Trading itself increasingly is a global, 24-hour business in many instruments, requiring a strong presence in each time zone.

Other Merchant-Banking Activities. Additional merchant-banking activities include international mergers and acquisitions, interest-rate and currency swaps, parallel loans, private placements, and financial advisory services to institutions and countries. All involve a high degree of proprietary expertise and can therefore generate substantial profits. While commercial and securities-related merchant banking have been substantially separated by law in the United States since 1933 (the Glass-Steagall Act) and in Japan since World War II (Article 65), the same is not true in overseas markets, and American and Japanese commercial banks, among others, have carved out important niches abroad through affiliates and joint ventures. Elsewhere, the distinction between commercial banking and securities business is less sharp or unknown, and some of the major European universal banks are powerful players in international capital markets. So are some of the traditional merchant-banking houses centered in London, the international activities of American investment banks, as well as European and Japanese securities firms.

Finally, there are international personal banking and investment services, fiduciary trust and investment activities for institutional clients, and retail banking abroad. This includes the issue of travelers' checks and travel-related services, stockbrokerage, mutual funds, and meeting the financial needs of the wealthy. Such businesses involve specialized financial services and unique forms of competition and institutional cooperation.

A significant worldwide market position is quite difficult to achieve, and yet is often (as in travelers' checks) indispensible in offering a viable product. Retail banking in national financial markets abroad is often not easy to penetrate, but product differentiation and infusion of new banking technologies can produce substantial returns to successful competitors able to gain access to local markets abroad.

PRODUCT CLASSIFICATION

It is useful to reformulate the foregoing activity-oriented discussion of internationally traded financial services as a product-based classification scheme, based on the principal generic services actually provided to clients in the marketplace. Financial institutions produce five more or less distinct "primary" kinds of services that are sold to clients. All financial services that appear in the market, including the most arcane and complex financial innovations, can be broken down into one or more of these "primary" categories.

Credit Products. Although credit products have become a less significant source of returns for many international financial institutions, they nevertheless remain the core of much of the banking business.

Financial Engineering Products. These comprise the design and delivery of technology-intensive financial services specifically structured to satisfying often complex client objectives at minimum cost. In a world where borrowers, securities issuers, savers, and investors often have distinctive and complex objectives, financial engineering is perhaps the ultimate form of product differentiation. It accounts for a great deal of the value added in domestic and international capital markets. Financial technologies can be either "disembodied" or "embodied." Purely disembodied financial technology normally takes the form of advisory services that institutions undertake for clients, often based in part on client-specific information. Embodied financial technology combines this with one or more financial transactions sold to the client as part of a package.

Risk Management Products. Risk bearing has long been recognized as one of the key functions of financial institutions and is one of the reasons they tend to be heavily regulated. The main forms of exposure include credit risk, interest-rate risk, liquidity risk, foreign exchange risk, country risk, project risk, commodity risk, counterparty risk, settlement risk, and technical risk in areas such as cash transmission. Risk management activities can be broken down into (1) those in which financial institutions themselves assume all or part of the exposure and (2) those in which the institutions provide technology needed to achieve a shifting of risk or themselves take on exposure only on a contingent basis (an off-balance-sheet commitment to buy or sell, borrow, or lend). Effective risk reduction through diversification clearly depends on the "independence" of the various risks represented in an institution's portfolio of exposures.

Financial institutions themselves provide risk management services to others, which range from simple revolving credit lines and forward interest rate agreements (FRAs) to explicit, tightly defined products addressed to a broad range of contingencies.

Market Access Products. Financial institutions can provide value-added services to clients by using their internal networks to transfer information, funds, or securities from one client or geographic area to others. Accomplishing this requires both tangible and intangible networks in the form of state-of-the-art hardware and software.

Arbitrage and Positioning. For their own account, financial institutions engage in certain activities that facilitate and in many cases make possible the supply of the first four types of financial services to clients internationally.

Arbitrage opportunities occur when the same asset is priced differently in different markets (or market segments), often

21

because of information asymmetries. "Pure" arbitrage takes place when an asset is simultaneously bought and sold. By this definition, financial institutions rarely engage in pure arbitrage. Rather, they engage in positioning—buying an asset in one market, holding it for a time (however short), and then reselling it in the same or different market. The institution is thus exposed to "differential risk" since the underlying price differential may evaporate or be reversed during the time needed to complete the transaction. Exposure to differential risk depends both on the time necessary to complete the transaction and on the underlying volatility in the price of the asset and the markets in which it is traded.

Positioning has become an integral part of managing international financial institutions during a time of significant exchange-rate and interest-rate volatility, and in turn drives securities, options, and futures trading and dealing.

This classification of financial services into five generic types of *activities* can be combined with the previous discussion of *products* traded internationally and cross-classified into well over 50 more or less distinct financial services available to various client segments in various markets. These are listed in Table 2–6.

If the variety and complexity of the kinds of international financial services are impressive, so too are the types of institutions that provide them. They range from enormous private and government-owned financial supermarkets selling almost the entire range of products on a global scale, to small, specialist houses or financial boutiques that have carved out a position in international markets for a limited range of services. They also include predominantly domestic institutions that nevertheless have a substantial and frequently quite profitable international business, often conducted through correspondent relationships with foreign institutions. Across this product range competition is frequently fierce. Yet, perhaps more than in some other industries, there is a substantial amount of cooperation as well, particularly in very large or very complex transactions.

Table 2–6. Subclassification of International Financial Services.

Product	Primary Classification			
	1	2	3	4
Deposit-taking				
Time deposits	L			
Demand deposits	L			
Other	L			
Trading and dealing				
Money market				X
Securities				X
Foreign exchange				X
Swaps				X
Futures				X
Options				X
Bullion				X
Other				X
Sale of bank securities				
Certificates of deposit	L			
Ordinary shares	L			
Preferred shares	L			
Floating-rate notes	L			
Short and long-term debt	L			
Lending (local or foreign currency)				
Sovereign	X	X		
Corporate				
Indigenous majors	X	X		
MNC affiliates	X	X		
Parastatals	X	X		
Indigenous middle market	X	X		
Foreign middle market	X	X		
Correspondent				
Indigenous banks	X	X		
Foreign banks	X	X		
Private				
High net worth	X	X		
High net income	X	X		
Retail	X	X		
Specialized financing activities				
Asset-based financing	X	X		
Equity financing	X	X		

23

Table 2–6. continued.

Product	Primary Classification			
	1	2	3	4
Specialized financing activities (continued)				
Project financing	X	X		
Venture capital financing	X	X		
Real estate financing	X	X		
Mergers and acquisitions financing	X	X		
Leveraged buyout financing	X	X		
Securities underwriting				
Sovereign debt			X	X
State debt, revenue, and agency bonds			X	X
Mortgage backed securities			X	X
Insurance			X	X
Equities			X	X
Other			X	X
Securities distribution				
Domestic				X
Fixed income				X
Equities				X
Other				X
International				X
Fixed income				X
Equities				X
Other				X
Advisory Services				
Corporate cash management		X	X	X
Corporate fiscal (tax) planning		X	X	
General corporate financial services		X	X	X
Real estate advisory		X	X	X
Mergers and acquisitions		X	X	
Domestic		X	X	
International		X	X	
Risk management services		X	X	
Interest-rate risk		X	X	
Foreign-exchange risk		X	X	
Country risk		X	X	
Other		X	X	
International trade advisory services		X	X	X
Trust and estate planning		X	X	

Table 2–6. continued.

Product	Primary Classification			
	1	2	3	4
Advisory Services (continued)				
Legal and investment advisory services		X	X	
Tax advisory services		X	X	
General financial advice		X	X	
Consumer services				
Credit cards	X			X
Travelers checks			X	X
Other consumer services	X		X	X
Asset management services				
Private and retail		X	X	
Fiduciary activities		X	X	
Safekeeping and lock box services		X	X	
Mutual funds		X	X	
Corporate and correspondent		X	X	
Safekeeping and lock box services		X	X	
Pension fund management		X	X	
Mutual fund management		X	X	
Brokerage				
Money market				X
Eurocurrencies and foreign exchange				X
Fixed income (government and corporate)				X
Equities				X
Financial futures				X
Options				X
Commodities				X
Gold				X
Insurance				X
Payments mechanism				
Domestic funds transfer				X
International funds transfer				X
Insurance-related services				
Standby letters of credit			X	
NIFs, RUFs, and MOFFs	X		X	
Revolving credits	X		X	
C/P standby facilities	X		X	
Life insurance			X	
Property and casualty			X	

25

Table 2–6. continued.

Product	Primary Classification			
	1	2	3	4
International trade services				
International collections			X	X
Letter of credit business		X	X	X
Bankers acceptances	X		X	X
Countertrade		X		X
Market intelligence				X

Key:
1. Credit products (L = credit extension by counterparties).
2. Financial engineering products.
3. Risk management products.
4. Market access products.

PATTERNS OF INTERNATIONAL MARKET PENETRATION

Why do firms providing financial services go international? There are a number of common sense explanations that, quite apart from competitive distortions imposed by governments, often dictate the kinds of foreign affiliates established abroad by financial institutions.

Following the Customer

As the number and complexity of international financial products multiply it becomes increasingly questionable whether traditional correspondent banking (largely associated with syndicated lending, trade-related financing, and foreign-exchange business) can serve customer needs adequately. Long-term financing, project financing, financial advisory services, and the like have increased the need for physical proximity in order to meet the corporate customer's financial needs. When U.S. based multinational enterprises emerged as a major global economic force in the 1960s and early 1970s, it was only natural that U.S. commercial and investment banks seek to follow their expansion into Canada and Western Europe. Having a presence in a country that is host to an affiliate of a multinational enterprise cements a relationship that already exists at home. Decisions can be made more efficiently than through correspondent banking links. Higher priority is assigned to the client's needs.

Many Amerian banks thus evolved a "customer-following" pattern that built on domestic client relationships by supplying financial services to affiliates of multinational enterprises in countries that received the bulk of foreign direct investment by American firms. In the 1970s and 1980s, when European, Canadian, and later Japanese investment in the United States took over some of the most rapidly growing aspects of multinational corporate operations, foreign banks in turn followed their respective companies into the American market.[8] In essence, customer-following strategies derived from their close financial and institutional links to the major trading houses or manufacturing enterprises.

Following the customer does not go unchallenged. Besides host-government restrictions on the activities of foreign financial firms, indigenous banks also see local multinational affiliates as a fertile area for business development and often rise to the challenge.[9] Conversely, foreign based financial institutions have attempted to use their natural multinational customer base to get a foothold in serving the indigenous corporate community in host countries and eventually, local retail customers as well.

Customer following has occasionally led to managerial tensions within multinational financial institutions themselves. Multinational affiliates are often among the most creditworthy corporate customers in host-country financial markets and, therefore, can command comparatively fine lending terms. Indigenous companies often have to pay higher rates on loans and, within accepted parameters of risk, may present more attractive financing prospects to foreign banks. Moreover, the companies present a potential opportunity to the extent that they themselves subsequently move into foreign business environments where the bank is already present. Yet, neglect of multinational affiliates in local markets can strain bank relations with the parent corporation at home. It has always been difficult to weigh

27

the profitability of the total relationship between banks and multinational enterprises against the alternatives that present themselves in various onshore banking environments abroad. Similar conflicts emerge in nonbank firms offering financial services, but perhaps on a somewhat smaller scale.

Leading the Customer

International banks sometimes lead their multinational customers into foreign markets. A bank that is well established in a national business environment abroad can provide useful information, contacts, advice, and financial services to foreign firms considering entering the foreign market. Leading the client into the foreign market, whether through "green-field" investments or acquisitions, can pay off in terms of new financing opportunities, fee-based service income, and future business with the multinational enterprise worldwide.

Again, foreign banks must compete with indigenous institutions. But in customer-leading activities they frequently seem to have an inside track because of existing banking and advisory relationships with the customer back home and possibly in third countries. Once the financial institution has learned how to engage in customer-leading activities, which often have many of the characteristics of investment banking, it can use its global presence to good advantage in obtaining maximum leverage. Patterns of customer-leading have also emerged in the case of nonbank international investment houses, particularly among U.S. and Japanese securities firms.

Seeking Local Markets

Besides exploiting the synergy that exists between multinational enterprises and financial institutions through customer following and customer leading, there is a third option: seeking direct access to wholesale and retail customers in local markets.

Astute research can reveal the essential competitive structure of national financial markets. Local banks may do a very poor job of deposit-gathering or money-dealing in the domestic financial market. Or they may not be fully competitive in lending, either in transaction efficiency, operations, and systems or in providing ancillary service such as financial advice. Such conditions translate either into the high levels of profitability for local institutions or low levels of productivity, or both. They spell a potentially strong opportunity for foreign based competitors to penetrate the local market and provide better and less costly services to indigenous customers. If the foreigners can transfer product or process technologies, seeking local markets can be highly rewarding.

Such activity is not likely to go unnoticed by indigenous competitors. As long as foreign penetration of their traditional markets is small and not considered a material threat, little may happen. But once a certain threshold is reached, fierce competition can break out, with local institutions adopting many of the financial innovations, business strategies, and managerial tactics imported by their foreign rivals. Clearly, banking customers will be the principal beneficiaries of the heightened efficiency and creativity that accompany the intense competition. Alternatively, the local institutions may seek government protection to exclude or limit the foreign institutions. Or they may try to use their superior power in the marketplace to constrain foreign encroachment in lending or foreign access to funding sources in the local currency. Both responses help to preserve financial inefficiency and banking profits in the local environment.

Local market-seeking activities of foreign banks or other firms providing financial services may be aimed at a number of different groups of customers: corporate, banking, government, and retail. The government market is probably the easiest to penetrate, in terms of foreign currency lending, followed by the indigenous banking sector. The number of local corporations that may be attractive to foreign banks is often extremely limited. Once a bank begins to seek clients beyond a small cadre of prime names that are the targets of virtually every other institution in the market, the list of potential customers—subject to substantial difficulties in evaluating credit risks in the local environment—may become rather short. In the investment business, exchange restrictions preventing residents from placing funds abroad often severely limit the value of foreign firms' financial services in the local market.

An interesting case of foreign market penetration by U.S. institutions in recent years involves credit cards in Western Europe and Japan. With the domestic market virtually saturated, and European and Japanese retail customers only beginning to accept credit cards as a means of payment in the 1980s, the prospects for transferring the necessary product and marketing know-how, as well as processing technologies, seemed very promising indeed.

In Europe, travel and entertainment cards such as American Express and Diners Club have been marketed to up-scale clients for a long time, but only in recent years have bank charge cards made significant inroads. Both faced resistance from local banks, especially in Germany, where institutions place a premium on cross-selling a variety of products to their customers. That this fear was not unfounded was underscored by the American Express purchase of a bank in Frankfurt, as well as the sale of insurance and other financial services through credit cards. Moreover, German retail bank marketing is heavily based on the client's physical presence inside the banking office, which would obviously be made far less necessary by the widespread use of credit cards.

Following several attempts to impede entry by regulatory means and collaboration among banks in refusing credit card participation, the German banks launched their own "Eurocard" as a means of curbing the foreign incursions. The inroads continued, however, and in 1987 the German retailers announced a plan to issue charge cards themselves, to the great consternation of the banks. Given the pressures from competitors, bank resistance to charge cards was viewed as a lost cause, with the response likely to involve creation of a Europe-wide charge card complete with a common clearing and processing system—even as the U.S. based charge card systems redouble their efforts to sign up increasing numbers of European bank issuers.

Japan eased limits on foreign bank card operations in the late 1970s, and both Visa International and MasterCard International began to compete with the local JCB card operations. The number of cards outstanding increased from 23.6 million in 1979 to 85 million in 1985. Each firm approached the market in a different way, with MasterCard franchisees issuing cards under their own names and Visa franchising through a 22-bank consortium called Visa Japan, Inc. Visa also reached a marketing arrangement with Japan's postal savings system, accounting for roughly one-third of personal savings, a move that strained relations with the franchisees represented by Visa Japan, which compete directly for savings with the post office. American Express and Diners Club, meantime, dominated the upper end of the market, each with about 450,000 cards outstanding, and in 1987 Citibank launched a gold card as part of an effort to increase its small foothold in the Japanese retail market. Japanese cardholders are not permitted to access a revolving line of credit through their cards, but rather must pay all balances in full at the end of each billing period. This regulation was being held in place by persistent lobbying on the part of local consumer finance companies, which saw a distinct threat to their customer base.[10]

FORMS OF INVOLVEMENT

How foreign based financial institutions choose to serve national markets depends on the specific types of services to be provided, the degree of control management wants to exercise, as well as local restrictions. These range from travel by bankers, either based at the bank's head office or at a regional center, to representative offices, to consortium banks, minority participation, joint ventures, wholly owned subsidiaries, agencies, and full branches. Table 2–7 lists the various strengths and weaknesses associated with different forms of involvement.

Table 2–7.   Relative Advantages of Alternative Forms of Organization.

	Representative Office	"Shell" Branch	Affiliate	Subsidiary	Branch	Consortium and Joint Venture
Amount of investment required	Modest	Minor/modest	Moderate	Moderate/substantial	Moderate/substantial	Moderate
Control over operation	Direct	Direct	Minor	Substantial/direct	Direct	Minor/moderate
Referral Business	Favorable	None	Minor	Favorable[a]	Favorable	Minor/moderate
New Business	Favorable	None	Limited potential	Favorable[a]	Favorable	Minor/moderate
Flexibility of operation	Relatively inflexible	None	Inflexible	Flexible[b]	Flexible[b]	Some flexibility
Manpower	Some manpower[d]	Minor	Minor	[c]	[c]	Modest

Source: R. M. Pecchioli, *The Internationalization of Banking* (Paris: OECD Secretariat, 1983), p. 19.

a. A subsidiary is likely to refer business to its own parent and is virtually capable as a branch of introducing new business to the group.

b. Under certain circumstances, subsidiaries can undertake business which cannot be undertaken by a branch. In addition, subsidiaries have "independent" management decision-taking power which may give more flexibility than is enjoyed by a branch.

c. Difficult to categorize, since it depends on specific circumstances, the type of subsidiary or branch and the characteristics of the business to be undertaken (for example, retail or wholesale business).

d. In some instances, however, the scale of business carried out by a representative office is such as to require a substantial amount of manpower.

THE REGULATORY DIMENSION

As noted, there is an important regulatory distinction between domestic and offshore financial activities, one that bears on the definition and assessment of protectionism in this sector. Domestic financial activities involve *onshore*, or domestic, markets for financial services that are *fully subject to domestic supervisory, regulatory, and monetary-policy controls*. Whether and how foreign based financial institutions may compete in onshore markets is strictly a matter of national policy. Domestic institutions systematically protected from outside competition are frequently highly profitable. They can use that artificial profitability to cross-subsidize the penetration of other markets for financial services. These may also be relatively uncompetitive and inefficient by international standards.

Offshore financial activities involve *offshore* markets for financial services that are substantially *beyond the reach of national authorities*. They include Eurodollar and Eurobond markets along with the peripheral financial services that complete the Eurocredit business. These are largely untaxed, unregulated, and highly efficient markets—both statically and dynamically—in which any number can play. While it seems fair to say that such characteristics have exposed the international economic and financial system to certain risks from time to time (some of them serious), offshore markets nevertheless set standards of performance in financial efficiency against which all other financial markets must be measured.

It is important to recall that the Eurobond market and more recently the Euroequity market are the outcomes of confused and often muddled behavior on the part of national regulators since the 1960s. Authorities in European Economic Community (EEC) member nations were unable to agree, for example, on the establishment of an integrated European capital market in fulfillment of their obligations under the Treaty of Rome. Individual national authorities permitted increasing freedom of capital movement, yet excluded foreign borrowers and issuers from their national capital markets, driving them offshore. As capital markets moved offshore, in the 1960s and 1970s, there were successively fewer reasons for returning to the various national markets if and as regulations were liberalized. National authorities thus lost much of the game, and their loss was in large measure London's gain.

These same considerations ought to apply to the broader context as well. The highly developed state of the Euromarkets and the deregulated state of most of the major onshore markets (Japan, the United States, and the United Kingdom) threatens to turn the banking centers of other countries in Europe, Asia, and Latin America into financial backwaters. Unless they, too, deregulate and permit world-class players to operate in their markets, value added in the process of capital allocation will move abroad, particularly as it affects the prime names among borrowers and issuers. Equally, they must afford their own financial institutions adequate opportunity to compete in international markets that are appropriate to their specific clients and product strengths.

As an example, although liberalization of the German capital market in the 1980s has proceeded gradually, the importance of the German economy and financial market had already attracted over 250 foreign banks to Frankfurt by the end of 1983. In April 1984, a 25 percent withholding tax on securities was eliminated, removing a major obstacle to the growth of that market. In May 1985, DM certificates of deposit were introduced for the first time, and a number of other DM instruments such as swaps, floating rate notes, and Euronote facilities were permitted. This was followed, in April 1986, with a broadening of the federal debt consortium of primary government bond dealers to include a guaranteed share of new issues for foreign based institutions. Also under consideration was the abolition of the stock exchange turnover tax and a reduction or elimination of the notice period required in advance of new Euro-DM bond issues.

The global environment for the provision of financial services has been and is complex—and, in recent years, subject to rapid change. Shifts in the pattern and volume of international trade, protectionist trends, regional economic integration, changing exchange-rate regimes and balance-of-payments measures, as well as general monetary and fiscal policies, have telling effects on the industry both in the short term and over longer periods of time. Perhaps more than most others, firms dealing in financial services need to react quickly and decisively to perceived threats and opportunities. Success or failure hinges to an extraordinary degree on the value of information and on being able to move faster and more accurately than the competition.

Measures of Monetary Control

The competitive behavior of firms in the business of financial services is to some extent constrained within onshore financial systems. Certain common patterns are apparent in the way these systems have evolved. The most obvious is the integration of banks and other firms providing financial services into the formation and execution of national monetary and fiscal policies, as well as balance-of-payments policies. The tools of monetary control range from sledgehammer techniques such as changes in reserve requirements and mandatory asset ratios, open-market purchases and sales of securities by the central bank or monetary authority, and moral suasion to rather selective credit controls such as margin requirements on borrowings against securities purchases, limits on loans to certain sectors, ceilings on deposit and lending rates, and "corset" restrictions limiting the expansion of loans. Within an overall policy, financial institutions also carry a fiduciary responsibility: they hold assets in trust, as it were, for depositors and investors.

Profitability in the financial services industry depends on astute management of assets and liabilities, which often entails very high leverage ratios, the acceptance of carefully controlled interest-rate, exchange-rate, and liquidity risks, imaginative design and marketing of fee-earning services, and the resolution of agency problems in carrying out satisfactorily the wishes of the ultimate holders of the assets with which they are dealing.

All of these characteristics have combined to make financial services at the national level a "sensitive" industry, both as a central vehicle for the implementation of economic policy and as an industry subject to collective crises and failures by individual firms. The history of the United States, for example, records well over 15,000 bank failures: 5,000 during the Great Depression of the 1930s alone, and an average of 90 annually during the period 1984–86. In 1986, 138 financial institutions failed in the United States.

Mismanagement or outright fraud have left prominent names like Banco Ambrosiano, Bank Bumiputra, Crédit Suisse (Chiasso), Franklin National, Herstatt, Schroder Munchmeyer Hengst, Seafirst, and Continental Illinois among the failed, incapacitated, or injured in recent years. Others, such as Bank-America, have seen their competitive standing seriously impaired. And, because of close interbank financial links, a crisis for one can quickly spread to a crisis for many, producing negative externalities that subsequently result in damage to depositors, commerce and industry, and to the economy at large. Grubel points out that the regulation of banking systems has evolved in response to a tendency in unregulated banking toward endemic financial crises.[11] Similarly Hindley, in an assessment of the benefits that will accrue from greater international competition in the insurance industry, explicitly recognizes the need for fiduciary regulation.[12] All of these are reasons why foreign based financial institutions are viewed with suspicion by some nations' regulatory authorities.[13]

Prudential Control

This book is concerned primarily with the activities of foreign-based financial institutions in national (or onshore) markets, not with offshore lending and other services conducted in the Euromarkets. The two, however, are often difficult to separate, especially with respect to problems of regulation and control.

Governments are well aware of the inherent risks and potential conflicts involved in domestic banking, securities underwriting, and trading and dealing in financial instruments, foreign exchange, precious metals, and the like. Most notably in banking, these risks focus on the solvency of borrowers and the liquidity of institutions. Banking crises always carry with them negative externalities, damage imposed on individuals and institutions outside the firms directly involved and, in some cases, outside the industry itself. It is conventional wisdom that major banking crises can lead to severe damage to employment, income, economic growth, and related goals of society.

In order to protect themselves against such adverse external consequences, countries have built elaborate safety nets designed to provide liquidity to institutions in trouble, insure deposits, and sometimes bail out borrowers to help the bank maintain solvency. The operation of domestic financial safety nets invariably creates problems of efficiency and fairness; for example, how to distinguish between institutions that are TBTF (too big to fail) and those TSTS (too small to save), and how to neutralize competitive distortions that may result from people's expectations about the operation of the safety net.[14] Even more important, the existence of a safety net creates potential "moral hazard" problems where management of financial institutions, knowing that they are likely to be bailed out, will behave in a less risk-averse manner and thus impose substantial contingent liabilities on those who hold up the safety net—the taxpayers and the general public.

To cope with this problem, and to ensure the safety and stability of national financial systems, governments apply various techniques of financial surveillance and control, ranging from careful bank-examination procedures, reserve requirements, mandatory asset ratios, and maximum lending limits to risk-related deposit insurance premiums, disclosure provisions, securities laws, and moral suasion. Countries deal with this problem in different ways. Some simply nationalize all or major parts of the domestic financial services industry. Regulation and control usually damage the efficiency of the domestic financial system, but this loss in efficiency can be regarded as something of an insurance premium and is usually considered to be more than offset by the resulting gain in the safety and stability of the system.

Problems arise, however, when national financial institutions take some of their activities offshore into the Euromarkets and foreign markets. While home countries are supposed to regulate offshore branches and host countries are supposed to regulate subsidiaries and other affiliates, the effectiveness of government regulation and control with regard to these activities remains the subject of intense debate. The oil shocks of 1973 and 1979, dramatic changes in the monetary policies of the United States and rising real rates of interest beginning in 1979, the severe recession of the early 1980s, and economic mismanagement on the part of borrowers along with intense competitive pressures in offshore lending and gaps in risk/return assessments of financial institutions, combined to produce the international banking crisis that began in 1982. The stability of the international financial system as a whole was called into question, while holders of assets began a mass flight to quality.

As central banks and other government authorities sought to stabilize the system through direct, bilateral financial infusions to countries in trouble, short-term lending by the Bank for International Settlements (BIS) and increases in the lending resources of the International Monetary Fund (IMF), the inevitable question of regulation and control of offshore financial activities arose. Legislation, such as the U.S. International Lending Supervision Act of 1983, has been enacted and tighter cooperation among national regulatory authorities has been sought.

Table 2–8 indicates how authorities in various developed countries assess overseas operations of domestic banks and the supervisory authorities of the foreign parent companies of local affiliates. Table 2–9 surveys banking supervision based on global consolidated accounts in member countries of the OECD and others.

While the precise design of an *international* financial safety net that goes beyond the moral obligation of governments to extend their support to offshore problems of domestic financial institutions remains in doubt, any such arrangement will certainly entail greater regulation and control on the part of national authorities and, thus, an erosion of efficiency in the delivery of

Table 2–8. Inspection of Foreign Establishments' Returns.

Country	Methods Used for Verification of Domestic Banks' Establishments Abroad	Country's Attitude Toward Direct Inspection By Parent Authorities
Australia	na	na
Austria	A	na
Belgium	A + H	Allowed (R)
Canada	H A	na
Denmark	H	Allowed (R)
Finland	H	Forbidden
France	H	Forbidden by law (1980)
West Germany	A	Allowed (R)
Greece	na	na
Iceland	na	na
Ireland	I	Allowed (R)
Italy	H	Allowed (R)
Japan	na	na
Luxembourg	H + A	Forbidden
Netherlands	H(R)	Allowed
New Zealand	na	na
Norway	na	na
Portugal	I	Allowed
Spain	H + A	Allowed (R)
Sweden	na	na
Switzerland	A	Forbidden by law
Turkey	na	na
United Kingdom	A	Allowed
United States	I	Allowed

Source: R. M. Pecchioli, *The Internationalization of Banking* (OECD Secretariat, 1983), p. 27.

Key: na = not available, I = on-site inspection, H = head-office inspection, A = external auditors, and R = based on reciprocity.

offshore financial services. Spreads between what borrowers pay and what savers receive will tend to widen, and financial innovation will be impaired. Whether another major oil shock in the 1990s and the accompanying need for financial recycling can again be absorbed by the offshore activities of financial institutions can only be conjectured. Such adverse implications have to be regarded as a price to be paid for greater financial stability.

Table 2–9. Supervision Based on Consolidated Accounts.

Country	Solvency	Liquidity	Risk Concentration	Currency Exposure
Australia	na	na	na	na
Austria	Yes	—	—	—
Belgium	Yes	b	Yes	b
Canada	Yes	Yes	Yes	Yes
Denmark	Yes	Yes[c]	Yes	Yes[c]
Finland	Yes	Yes	—	—
France	Yes	—	Yes	—
West Germany[a]	c	—	c	b
Greece	na	na	na	na
Iceland	na	na	na	na
Ireland	Yes	Yes	—	—
Italy	b	—	—	—
Japan	Yes	Yes	Yes	—
Luxembourg[d]	Yes	Yes	Yes	Yes
Netherlands	Yes	—	Yes	Yes
New Zealand	na	na	na	na
Norway	na	na	na	na
Portugal	—	—	—	—
Spain	b	b	b	b
Sweden	Yes	—	—	—
Switzerland	Yes	—	—	—
Turkey	na	na	na	na
United Kingdom	Yes	—	Yes	e
United States	Yes	Yes	Yes	Yes

Source: R. M. Pecchioli, *The Internationalization of Banking* (Paris: OECD Secretariat, 1983), p. 31.

Key: na = not available and — = not applicable.

a. In West Germany, foreign branches of West German banks are supervised on a fully consolidated basis. With regard to foreign subsidiaries, supervision based on consolidated returns applies to a limited extent (solvency and risk concentration on the basis of a gentleman's agreement).

b. Under consideration.

c. Legal proposal.

d. Branches only.

e. Partial consolidation as supervision of currency exposure extends to foreign branches of banks registered in the United Kingdom, but not to subsidiaries.

Whether financial regulation is in some sense optimal, and the cost of regulation therefore minimized, is arguable. Characteristics of financial efficiency in the larger unregulated offshore markets can often yield useful insights into the nature and magnitude of these losses in efficiency in individual domestic regulatory arrangements, while periodic offshore crises can indicate the nature and magnitude of some of the benefits of a more controlled domestic financial environment. We shall return to this topic in Chapter 7.

SUMMARY

The financial services industry has become global. Some of the financial services, or "products," that it supplies to wholesale and retail clients around the world are highly localized or tailored to the idiosyncratic needs of a particular client or situation. Others are broad-based and generic, capable of being spread across wide markets. The important thing is to realize the extreme complexity of the financial services industry today. In a real sense it is not just one industry, but perhaps 20 or 30, each driven by a distinctive set of criteria for competition. This implies that public policies toward the industry can have consequences that are difficult to anticipate. At the very least, policymakers must invest heavily in acquiring a sound understanding of the industry in order to have reasonable prospects of developing rules that make sense.

NOTES

1. Steven I. Davis, *The Euro-bank*, 2d ed. (London: MacMillan, 1979).
2. Morgan Guaranty Trust Company, "America's Banking Market Goes International," *Morgan Economic Quarterly* (June 1986).
3. Peter Koenig, "Into the Maelstrom," *Euromoney*, June 1987.
4. H. Peter Gray, "Toward a Unified Theory of International Trade, International Production and Foreign Direct Investment," in John

Black and John H. Dunning (eds.), *International Capital Movements* (London: Allen and Unwin, 1982).

5. Ingo Walter, "Competitive Performance and Market Structure in International Financial Services," New York University, 1987. Mimeo.

6. John F. Mathis, (ed.), *Offshore Lending by U.S. Commercial Banks*, 2d ed. (Philadelphia: Bankers' Association for Foreign Trade and Robert Morris Associates, 1982).

7. Ingo Walter, "Financing Energy Projects," New York University, 1987. Mimeo.

8. R.M. Pecchioli, *Internationalization of Banking* (Paris: Organization for Economic Cooperation and Development, 1983).

9. Olivier Pastré, *Multinationals: Banking and Firm Relationships* (Greenwich, Conn.: JAI Press, 1981) and "International Bank-Industry Relations: An Empirical Assessment." *Journal of Banking and Finance* (March 1981).

10. "The U.S. Is Getting Japan Hooked on Plastic," *Business Week*, May 25, 1987.

11. Herbert G. Grubel, "A Theory of Multinational Banking," *Banca Nazionale del Lavoro Quarterly Review* (December 1977).

12. Brian Hindley, *Economic Analysis and Insurance Policy in the Third World*, Thames Essay No. 32 (London: Trade Policy Research Centre, 1982).

13. Anthony Saunders and Ingo Walter, "International Trade in Financial Services: Are Bank Services Special?" paper presented at the Symposium on New Institutional Arrangements for the World Economy, University of Konstanz, 1987. Mimeo.

14. Bank for International Settlements, *Recent Innovations in International Banking* (Basel: BIS, 1986).

3

GLOBAL COMPETITIVE POSITIONING IN FINANCIAL SERVICES

The complex web of markets, services, and institutions that has emerged from the internationalization of the financial services industry is not easily subject to analysis. The model of the industry presented in this chapter focuses on competitive market structure.[1] Not only does the model identify markets capable of producing supernormal profits, but it also specifies the linkages among those markets that are the basis for economies of scale and economies of scope—critical dimensions in the globalization of the financial services industry. The model will be used in subsequent chapters to analyze sources of national and institutional competitive advantage in this sector, as well as the effects of competitive distortions.

THE CLIENT-ARENA PRODUCT MATRIX

Three principal dimensions define the global market for financial services: client, arena, and product. Firms in the global financial services industry have an unusually broad range of choice with respect to each of these dimensions, and different combinations yield different strategic and competitive profiles. Figure 3–1 depicts these dimensions in the form of a matrix composed of C × A × P cells. Each cell has a distinctive competitive structure based on fundamental economic considerations as well as public-policy considerations.

Largely as a result of technological change and deregulation, financial institutions confront increasing potential access to client, arena, and product opportunities. Financial deregulation

Figure 3–1.   International Financial Services Activity Matrix (C-A-P Model).

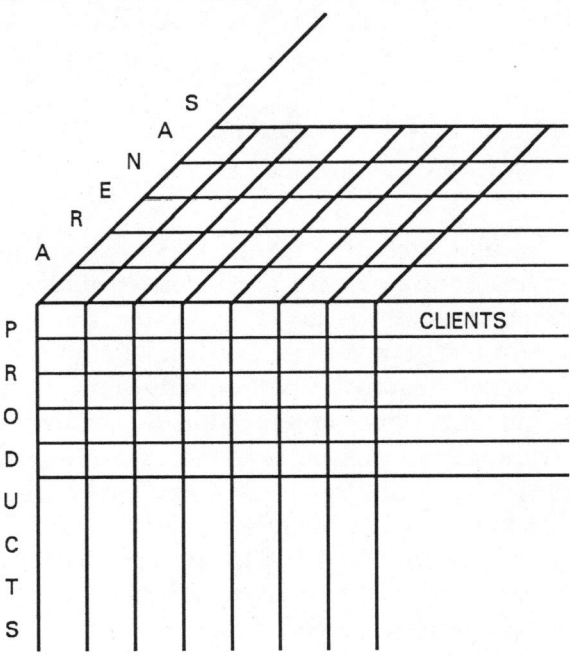

has influenced (1) accessibility of geographic arenas, (2) accessibility of individual client groups by players from different parts of the financial services business, and (3) substitutability among financial products in meeting personal, corporate, or public financial needs.

Client

The conventional division of financial services into wholesale and retail is not of much help in the C-A-P model; instead the following categorization of the major client groups is more appropriate:

Sovereign. National states and their instrumentalities.

Corporate. Nonfinancial corporations regardless of industry classification, ranging from multinational corporations and parastatals to middle-market and small, privately owned companies.

Correspondent. Other financial institutions in the same industry subcategory (for example, correspondent banks).

Private. High net worth and high net income individuals.

Retail. Other individual clients, generally in significant numbers.

The five categories can be subdivided down into narrower segments, each differing with respect to product-related attributes such as currency requirements, liquidity and maturity needs, risk levels, industry, level of service requirements, price sensitivity, and timing. Defining and segmenting markets effectively depend on identifying coherent client groups that are relatively uniform with respect to each of these variables.

Arena

The international market for financial services can be divided into onshore and offshore arenas with respect to geographic location. The "arena" differs from the market "region" in that it encompasses the concepts of regulatory and monetary sovereignty, which are of critical importance in determining international trade in financial services. Each arena is characterized by different risk/return profiles, levels of financial efficiency, regulatory conditions, client needs, and other factors.

Geographic penetration of financial institutions into various domestic and offshore markets is no longer country-specific, and the arena dimension of Figure 3–1 can be taken into the analysis at the global, regional, national, subregional, and location-specific levels. Country-specific analysis remains paramount, nonetheless, due to the importance of national monetary policies, financial regulation, and competition policies, all of which are imposed at the country level. It is only in federal states that the rules of the game are importantly set at the subnational level.

Product

The range of financial services that can be supplied to the various client segments in the various arenas was discussed in Chapter 2. Table 2–4 combines the client and product dimensions and links each combination to the underlying type of activities being undertaken by the institution concerned: credit products, financial engineering products, risk management products, market access products, and products related to positioning. As the need for product differentiation in the marketplace increases, firms in the banking industry create new instruments and techniques tailored to the needs of their clients.[2]

We can now put the three dimensions together once again in Figure 3–2, which uses two "cells" in the matrix to illustrate the markets for consumer installment lending in Germany (A), and interest-rate swaps sold to corporations in Japan (B).

Another illustration can be taken from the global activities of Citicorp Investment Bank as of 1986. Table 3–1 divides the world into broad geographic zones (the *arena* dimension). It indicates which *products* are actively made available in each arena by Citicorp to *clients* consisting of corporations, banks, other institutions, and governments. Citicorp's retail and other businesses are not included in Table 3–1.

CELL CHARACTERISTICS

The inherent attractiveness of each of the cells in Figure 3–2 will depend on the *size and durability* of prospective returns that can be extracted from that cell, adjusted for the perceived risks involved. Each cell has embedded within it a certain value

Figure 3–2. Examples of Cell Identification in the C-A-P Model.

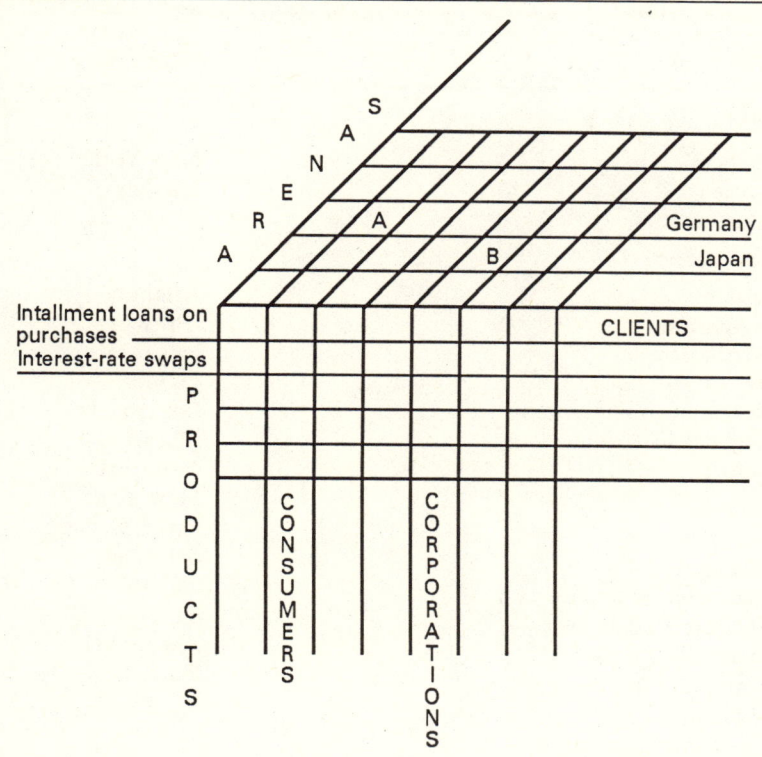

quotient potentially available to all players. The absolute level of the cell-specific returns depends on the level of demand for a particular financial service, its price and cost, and the price elasticity of demand, which in turn is affected primarily by the existence of product substitutes. The actual returns captured by each institution will depend on its competitive positioning. Their durability will be based in part on the ability of new players to enter the cell and the development of substitute products over time. Cell characteristics can be analyzed in terms of conventional competitive-structure criteria, as summarized in Figure 3–3. (See, for example, Porter.[3])

Table 3–1.   Clients, Arenas, Products—Citicorp Investment Bank.

Activities and Products	Activity Locations
Global	
Products	New York
Equities	London
Eurosecurities	
North America	
Activities	Atlanta
Origination	Chicago
Distribution	Houston
Advisory services	London
Investment management	Los Angeles
Mergers and Acquisitions	Miami
Trading	Montreal
Products	New York
Asset sales	San Francisco
Asset trading	San Juan
Bankers' acceptances	Tokyo
Certificates of deposit	Toronto
Commercial paper	Vancouver
Commercial real estate	Zurich
Eurobounds	
Euro-commercial paper	
Exchange-traded futures and options	
Foreign currency swaps	
Foreign exchange	
Forward rate agreements	
FX options	
Guaranteed return portfolio	
Interest-rate swaps, caps and collars	
International exposure management	
International trade paper	
Long rate agreements (LORAs)	
Long-dated forwards	
Mortgage-backed securities	
Municipal bonds and notes	
Municipal reinvestment portfolio	
OTC options	

Table 3–1. continued.

Activities and Products	Activity Locations

North America

Products (continued)
  Private placements
  Project finance
  Repurchase agreements (repos)
  Reverse repos
  Syndicated loans
  Whole mortgages
  U.S. Agency securities
  U.S. treasuries

Latin America

Activities	Latin America Investment
Distribution	Bank
Risk management	Argentina
Principal investing	Brazil
Investment management	Chile
Positioning	Ecuador
Mergers and acquisitions	Mexico
Trading	Panama
	Uruguay
Products	Venezuela
Blocked currency trading	Equity Finance: Venture
Certificates of deposit	Capital
Corporate debt security and	Dallas
equity underwriting	New York
Corporate finance	Palo Alto
Foreign exchange	Equity Finance: Mergers and
Government securities	Acquisitions
Mergers and acquisitions	Chicago
Risk management	Cleveland
Venture capital	Frankfurt
	Hong Kong
	London
	Lausanne
	Milan
	New York
	São Paulo
	Sydney

Table 3–1. continued.

Activities and Products	*Activity Locations*

Europe and the Middle East

Activities	Austria
Origination	Bahrain
Distribution	Belgium
Principal investing	Channel Islands
Positioning	Denmark
Risk management	Finland
Mergers and acquisitions	France
Trading	Germany
Products	Greece
Bonds	Ireland
Commercial paper	Italy
Convertible bonds	Luxembourg
Corporate advisory services	Netherlands
Currency and interest-rate swaps	Norway
Foreign exchange	Pakistan
FX futures	Portugal
FX options	Spain
Management buyouts	Sweden
Money market deposits	Switzerland
Options	Turkey
Stocks	United Arab Emirates
Syndicated loans	United Kingdom
Venture capital	

Asia-Pacific

Activities	Australia
Advisory services	Brunei
Investment management	Hong Kong
Principal investing	India
Risk management	Indonesia
Mergers and acquisitions	Japan
Trading	Korea
Products	Malaysia
Government bonds and	New Zealand
commercial bills	Philippines
Currency and rate risk swaps	Singapore
Floating and fixed-rate Eurobonds	Sri Lanka
and securities	Taiwan
Foreign exchange	Thailand
Futures and options	
Money market instruments	
Private placements	
U.S. treasuries	
Venture capital	

Source: Citicorp Investment Bank, 1986 Annual Review (New York: Citicorp Investment Bank, 1987), pp. 6–7.

Figure 3–3. Application of a Competitive Analysis Framework to Financial Services.

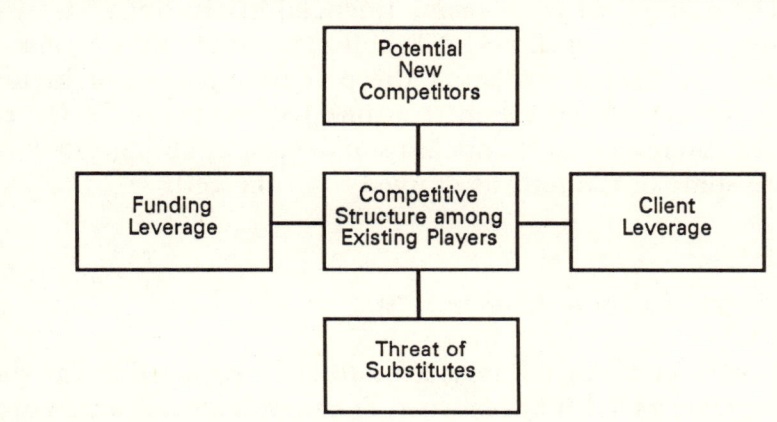

Market Power of Suppliers

Suppliers of the principal inputs for the production of financial services—capital and labor—can absorb some of the available rents in a particular C-A-P cell. Their ability to do so will depend on their market power, which can be expected to vary substantially from one arena to another, somewhat from one product to another, and sometimes from one client to another.

First, depositors and purchasers of securities issued by the financial institution demand returns commensurate with the perceived level of risk. The risk perceived depends heavily on the credit rating of the individual financial institution. To the extent that an institution is perceived to be less creditworthy due to the quality of its assets or its exposure to other types of risk, its market power is eroded as bondholders and depositors demand higher yields for the funds they supply. The removal of regulations on interest payable on various types of deposit accounts clearly raises the market power of capital suppliers and the cost of liabilities for financial institutions. Moreover, the more financially sophisticated the suppliers of funds become, the more

51

aware they are of alternative opportunities and the better able to obtain access to them.

The market for labor facing financial institutions has also changed in some of the C-A-P cells in which they operate. Increases in market power on the part of suppliers of highly skilled labor to financial institutions has occasionally led to dramatic increases in compensation levels, enabling labor to capture some of the returns derived from the cell.

Market Power of Clients

Buyers of financial services naturally seek to attain the highest value added at lowest cost. The more successful they are, the narrower the margins and the lower the rents available to the financial institution in a specific C-A-P cell. Especially in international wholesale markets, buyers of financial services are typically sought after by a large number of institutions competing firecely for their business. Client groups such as multinational corporations and individuals with high net worth and high net income have significantly more monopsony power than client groups for whom competition is markedly less intense. The market power of buyers of financial services can be expected to differ in all three dimensions of the C-A-P matrix—from one client group to another, from one product category to another, and across arenas.

Availability of Product Substitutes

Product substitutes available to clients in a given cell clearly increase the price elasticity of demand, which in turn determines the price-volume vectors that are accessible to the financial institution, and consequently the overall level of returns. The closer the substitutability among financial services, the higher the price elasticity of demand and the lower the level of returns that are available within a given C-A-P cell. One would expect the degree of product substitutability to differ from one client group to the next and across arenas.

The most important factor relating to product substitutes in financial services is information and technology content, so that the creation of product substitutes has become one of the most important and pervasive effects of financial innovation. Innovations that succeed a given cell are those embodying a low degree of product substitutability over a relatively long duration.

Competitive Structure and Strategic Groups

Clearly, the competitive structure of each C-A-P cell is the principal determinant of the excess returns an institution may be able to extract from it. To the extent that competition takes place on the pricing variable, prospective returns are transferred to clients.[4] Competitive structure is conventionally measured using concentration ratios based on the number of firms, distribution of market share among firms, and similar criteria.[5]

Normally, the addition of players to a C-A-P cell would be expected to reduce market concentration, increase the degree of competition, and lead to an erosion of margins as well as a more rapid pace of financial innovation. If the new players are from the same basic strategic group as existing players (as is the case when one more investment bank joins a number of other investment banks competing in a given cell), then the expected outcome would be along conventional lines of intensified competition. But if the new player comes from a completely different strategic perspective (as when the finance affiliate of a major oil company penetrates the same market cell for investment banking services), the competitive outcome may be quite different. Cell penetration by a player from a different strategic group may lead to a greater increase in competition than an incremental player from the same strategic group. This is because of potential diversification benefits, scope for cross-subsidization and staying-power, and incremental horizontal or vertical integration gains that the player from a "foreign" strategic group may be able to capture.

Natural Barriers to Entry and Contestable Markets

The higher the barriers to entry, the lower the threat of new entrants reducing the level of rents available in each C-A-P cell. Natural barriers to entry include capital adequacy, human resources, financial technologies, and economies of scale. (For details see Chapter 4, which deals with the sources of competitive advantage.) Entry barriers also include the role of "contracting costs" avoided by a close relationship between a financial institution and its client, which in turn is related to the avoidance of opportunistic behavior by either party.

Not least, the competitive structure of each cell depends on the degree of *potential* competition. This represents an application of the "contestable markets" concept, which suggests that the existence of potential entrants causes existing players to act *as if* those entrants were already active in the market.[6] Hence margins, product quality, and the degree of innovation in a given cell may exhibit characteristics of intense competition even though the degree of market concentration is in fact quite high.

Price Discrimination and Predation

In penetrating a particular cell or set of cells, it may be to the advantage of a player to "buy into" the market by cross-subsidizing financial services supplied in that cell from returns derived in other cells. For example, a Japanese securities firm benefiting from restricted competition and high, fixed commissions in Tokyo has enormous resources at its disposal to penetrate the London or New York market. This may make sense if the assessed horizontal, vertical, or lateral linkages (see below) are sufficiently positive to justify such pricing, either now or in the future. It may also make sense if the cell characteristics are expected to change, so that an unprofitable presence today is expected to lead to a profitable presence tomorrow. And it may make sense if a player's behavior in buying market share has the potential to drive out competitors and fundamentally alter the structure of the cell in his favor. Such behavior can be termed predatory and is no different from predation in the markets for goods. The institution "dumps" (or threatens to dump) financial services into the cell, forcing out competitors either as a result of the direct effects of the dumping in the face of more limited staying power or because of the indirect effects, working through expectations. Once competitors have been driven from the market, the institution takes advantage of the reduced degree of competition to widen margins and achieve excess returns.

A number of concerns have been expressed about under-pricing as a way for an institution to buy its way into a particular cell.[7] It cannot be assumed that the new entrants will in fact take away significant amounts of business from the established players. It is perhaps equally likely that the new entrant ends up with the cats and dogs, with possibly serious consequences for its own safety and stability. An alternative scenario involves the emergence of a price war, with adverse profitability and stability consequences for all players. In any case, the pricing that may accompany upstarts, whether foreign or domestic, could have a bearing on institutional stability, and is therefore a legitimate concern of the regulators.

Conversely, it may also be possible for an institution with significant market power to keep potential competitors out of attractive cells through explicit or implied threats of predatory behavior.[8] It can make it clear to new entrants that it will respond very aggressively to unfriendly incursions, and that they face a long and painful road to profitability. In this way, new competitors may be discouraged and the cell characteristics kept more monopolistic than would otherwise be the case.

CELL LINKAGES

Financial institutions clearly will want to allocate their available financial, human, and technological resources to those C-A-P cells in Figure 3–1 promising to throw off the highest risk-adjusted returns. In order to do this, they will have to appropriately attribute costs, returns, and risks across cells.

But beyond this, the economics of supplying financial services internationally is jointly subject to *economies of scale* and *economies of scope*. The existence of both types of economies have strategic implications for players in the industry. Economies of scale suggest an emphasis on *deepening* activities within a cell, or across cells in the product dimension.

Economies of scope suggest an emphasis on *broadening* activities across cells; that is, a player can produce a given level of output in a given cell more cheaply or effectively than institutions that are less active across multiple cells. This depends importantly on the benefits and costs of *linking* cells together in a coherent web of joint products.

The gains from linkages among C-A-P cells depend on the possibility that an institution competing in one cell can move into another cell and perform in that second cell more effectively than a competitor lacking a presence in the first cell. The existence of economies of scope and scale is a critical factor driving institutional strategy. Where scale economies dominate, the objective will be to maximize volume of the product within a given C-A-P cell configuration, driving for market penetration. Where scope economies dominate, the drive will be toward aggressive cell proliferation.

Client-Driven Linkages

Client linkages exist when a financial institution serving a particular client or client group can, as a result, supply financial services either to the same client or to another client in the same group more efficiently in the same or different arenas. With respect to a particular client, this linkage is part of the value of the relationship. With respect to a particular client segment, it will clearly be easier for an institution to engage in business with a new client in the same segment than to move to another client segment. It is possible that client-driven linkages will decline as market segmentation in financial services becomes more intense.

Arena-Driven Linkages

Arena-driven linkages are important when an institution can service a particular client or supply a particular service more efficiently in one arena as a result of having an active presence in another arena. The presence of nonfinancial multinational corporation clients in the same arenas as their financial institutions is one important form such linkages can take. By competing across a large number of arenas, a financial institution also has the possibility of decreasing the overall level of risk to which it is exposed and thereby increasing its overall risk-adjusted rate of return.

Product-Driven Linkages

Product-driven linkages exist when an institution can supply a particular financial service in a more competitive manner because it is already producing the same or a similar financial service in different client or arena dimensions. Product specializations would appear to depend upon the degree of uniformity of the resource inputs required, as well as information and technology commonalities. Thus, certain types of skills embodied in key employees may be applied across different clients and arenas at relatively low marginal cost within a given product category, as may certain types of information about the environment, markets, or client needs.

COMPETITIVE AND COOPERATIVE BEHAVIOR

Whether within cells or across cells, one complication in analyzing the competitive behavior of firms in the financial

Figure 3–4. A Behavioral Model of Competition and Cooperation in International Financial Services.

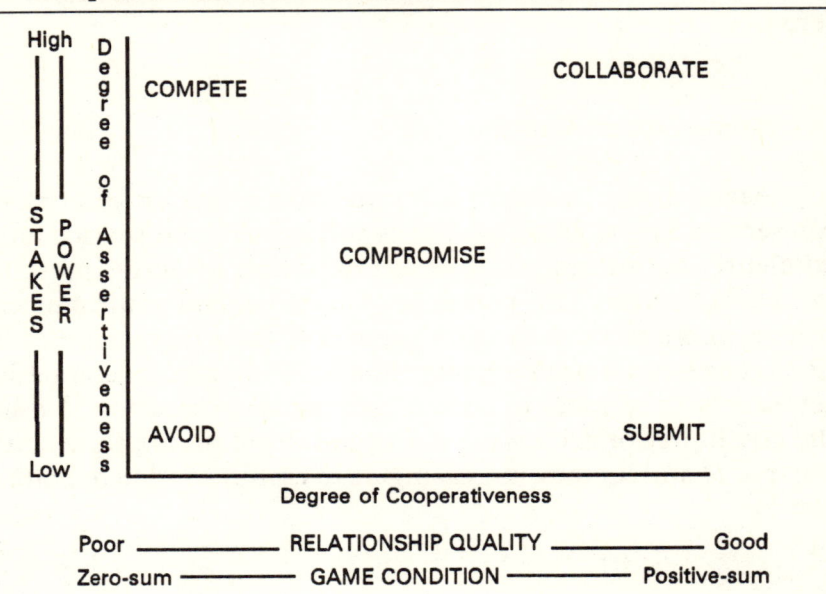

services industry that does not arise to as great an extent in other industries is the need to *cooperate* closely with rivals on individual transactions while at the same time *competing* intensively with them. Examples include securities underwriting and distribution, loan syndication, project finance, and credit card networks.

When does it make sense for an institution to compete and when to cooperate in order to extract maximum returns from the individual cells in the C-A-P matrix? Following Gladwin and Walter, the diagram in Figure 3–4 can be used to model an institution's behavior with respect to a particular cell or a transaction within that cell.[9]

The vertical axis measures the degree of *assertiveness* the institution will tend to bring to bear vis-à-vis the competition. This is a joint product of the perceived stakes the organization has in the game and its competitive power. The higher the stakes and the greater its power to ride over the competition, the more assertive the institution will want to be. Both stakes *and* power have to be high in order for the assertive mode to make sense.

The horizontal axis measures the extent to which the game is perceived as being *zero sum* (what one gains the other loses) or *positive sum* (both can gain), and the quality of the *relationship* with other players, usually a cumulative product of past experience. The more the game is viewed as being positive sum and the better the relationship, the more likely it is that the institution will want to cooperate with others.

The grid in Figure 3–4 can be divided into five zones, based on how these four underlying variables appear in a particular case: compete, collaborate, comply, avoid, and compromise. It is thus likely that one institution will be seen to work closely together with another in a given project in a particular cell even while it is competing vigorously elsewhere, submitting to the dominance of the other institution or avoiding involvement on the same kind of project in a different cell or a different project in the same cell. A large number of combinations are clearly possible in imposing this behavioral grid onto the underlying market matrix in Figure 3–1.

The evolution of international correspondent banking relationships provides an interesting example of cooperative behavior in a fundamentally competitive market structure. Correspondent banking activities include management of local currency accounts, effecting of payments, providing access to the local clearing system, opening and confirming documentary credits arising from international trade transactions, participation in loans and syndicated credits, and custody services in securities business—traditionally paid for largely through correspondent balances. Banks that do not pose a direct threat to their correspondents in their own home markets, either because of their strategic positioning or because of government restrictions, have been in an ideal position to develop correspondent relationships, a classic case of "collaboration," in terms of Figure 3–4.

Things have changed, however. Improvements in communications and automation have provided direct access for banks to services previously accessible only through correspondents.

Disintermediation has altered the value of correspondent banking on the lending side, and high real interest rates have raised the cost of correspondent balances. The result has been a significant "unbundling" of the previously stable correspondent relationship into a less stable and more price-sensitive one centered around a specific set of services that one bank sells to another. Like international finance generally, the drift has been from a relationship-driven to a transactions-driven business. In terms of Figure 3–4, the correspondent banking business has drifted laterally from collaboration to competition.

In loan syndication and securities underwriting the same phenomenon can be observed. Although large securities firms are bitter rivals in battling for underwriting mandates from issuers, they also need to work closely together in providing for effective distribution and market support. Firms will therefore invite each other into underwriting syndicates along reciprocity patterns that develop over time, taking into account relative strengths and weaknesses in distribution to different investor groups. As Tables 3–2 and 3–3 show, syndicates for European and international equities led by different players evidence quite different membership patterns.

The acquisition in March 1987 of a 13 percent share in Shearson Lehman Brothers, the investment banking subsidiary of American Express, by Nippon Life of Japan provided a good example both of technology and capital acquisition and market interpenetration in a collaborative context.

Nippon Life stood to gain diversification and improved access to international financial markets, as well as badly needed financial expertise and knowledge of international markets. It also stood to benefit in competing with the large Japanese securities houses, which had increasingly been siphoning off clients directly into financial markets and bypassing the insurance companies, even as the insurance firms were themselves compelled to continue investing through these same securities houses. With Japanese insurance companies increasingly investing rather than lending and increasing their overseas exposures, enhanced portfolio management expertise was badly needed. And

Table 3–2.   Cooperative Behavior in Eurobond Underwriting.

Rank 1986	Lead Bank	1986 Involvement	
		No.	%
	Crédit Suisse First Boston	55	
1	Deutsche Bank	36	66.7
2	Swiss Bank Corp.	36	66.7
3	Banque Nationale de Paris	32	59.3
4	S.G. Warburg	32	59.3
5	Union Bank of Switzerland	29	53.7
6	Banque Bruxelles Lambert	27	50.0
7	Nomura Securities	25	46.3
8	Banque Paribas	25	46.3
9	Salomon Brothers	24	44.4
10	Morgan Stanley	23	42.6
	Deutsche Bank	49	
1	Commerzbank	28	57.1
2	Dresdner Bank	27	55.1
3	Crédit Suisse First Boston	25	51.0
4	Swiss Bank Corp.	23	46.9
5	Union Bank of Switzerland	22	44.9
6	Morgan Stanley	20	40.8
7	Orion Royal Bank	19	38.8
8	Westdeutsche Landesbank	19	38.8
9	Banque Nationale de Paris	17	34.7
10	Nomura Securities	16	32.7
	Banque Paribas	44	
1	Banque Bruxelles Lambert	32	72.7
2	S.G. Warburg	25	56.8
3	Swiss Bank Corp.	24	54.5
4	Crédit Suisse First Boston	24	54.5
5	Banque Internationale à Luxembourg	20	45.5
6	Morgan Stanley	20	45.5
7	Morgan Guaranty	19	43.2
8	Nikko Securities	19	43.2
9	Crédit Commercial de France	18	40.9
10	Daiwa Securities	17	38.6

Table 3–2.   continued.

Rank 1986	Lead Bank	1986 Involvement No.	%
	Nikko Securities	30	
1	Daiwa Securities	18	62.1
2	Nomura Securities	14	48.3
3	Banque Paribas	13	44.8
4	Merrill Lynch	13	44.8
5	Swiss Bank Corp.	12	41.4
6	Crédit Suisse First Boston	12	41.4
7	Mitsubishi Bank	12	41.4
8	Morgan Stanley	11	37.9
9	S.G. Warburg	10	34.5
10	Union Bank of Switzerland	10	34.5
	Nomura Securities	62	
1	Daiwa Securities	36	58.1
2	Swiss Bank Corp.	35	56.5
3	Union Bank of Switzerland	34	54.8
4	Yamaichi Securities	34	54.8
5	Mitsui Trust & Banking Co.	30	48.4
6	Morgan Stanley	29	46.8
7	Nikko Securities	29	46.8
8	Crédit Suisse First Boston	28	45.2
9	Crédit Lyonnais	28	45.2
10	Long-Term Credit Bank of Japan	24	38.7
	Daiwa Securities	45	
1	Sumitomo Trust and Banking Co.	22	50.0
2	Industrial Bank of Japan	20	45.5
3	Yamaichi Securities	19	43.2
4	Mitsui Trust and Banking Co.	19	43.1
5	Crédit Lyonnais	18	40.9
6	Nikko Securities	18	40.9
7	Yasuda Trust and Co.	18	40.9
8	Sumitomo Bank	18	40.9
9	Bank of Tokyo	17	38.6
10	Crédit Suisse First Boston	16	36.4

Table 3–2.   continued.

Rank 1986	Lead Bank	1986 Involvement	
		No.	%
	Morgan Guaranty	32	
1	Banque Bruxelles Lambert	26	83.9
2	Swiss Bank Corp.	21	67.6
3	Union Bank of Switzerland	20	64.5
4	Orion Royal Bank	18	58.1
5	Nomura Securities	17	54.8
6	Crédit Suisse First Boston	17	54.8
7	Banque Nationale de Paris	15	48.4
8	BankersTrust	14	45.2
9	County Bank	14	45.2
10	S.G. Warburg	13	41.9
	Merrill Lynch	23	
1	Union Bank of Switzerland	16	69.6
2	Banque Bruxelles Lambert	15	65.2
3	Crédit Lyonnais	12	52.2
4	Orion Royal Bank	12	52.2
5	Nomura Securities	12	52.2
6	Daiwa Securities	11	47.8
7	Banque Nationale de Paris	11	47.8
8	Societe Generale	11	47.8
9	Swiss Bank Corp.	11	47.8
10	Bank of America	11	47.8
11	Banque Paripas	11	47.8
	Morgan Stanley	34	
1	Banque Bruxelles Lambert	22	64.7
2	Goldman Sachs	16	47.1
3	Crédit Suisse First Boston	16	47.1
4	Union Bank of Switzerland	15	44.1
5	Banque Paribas	15	44.1
6	Crédit Lyonnais	14	41.2
7	Daiwa Securities	14	41.2
8	Merrill Lynch	13	38.2
9	Morgan Guaranty	13	38.2
10	Salomon Brothers	13	38.2

Table 3–2. continued.

Rank 1986	Lead Bank	1986 Involvement	
		No.	%
	Salomon Brothers	33	
1	Swiss Bank Corp.	29	90.6
2	Goldman Sachs	25	78.1
3	Union Bank of Switzerland	24	75.0
4	Morgan Guaranty	24	75.0
5	Morgan Stanley	23	71.9
6	Banque Paribas	21	65.6
7	Crédit Suisse First Boston	21	65.6
8	Banque Bruxelles Lambert	20	62.5
9	Nomura Securities	19	59.4
10	Banque Nationale de Paris	19	59.4

Source: Euromoney, October 1986.

Nippon Life stood to gain from possible collaboration with American Express in other areas as well.

Shearson Lehman stood to gain badly needed capital in a period when this factor became a critical competitive factor in the investment banking industry (becoming the most heavily capitalized of all Wall Street firms) as well as access to Japanese clients.

And American Express stood to improve significantly its access to the Japanese market for charge cards and other financial services, and to cross-sell life insurance with its other products in various markets. It agreed not to reduce its holdings in Shearson Lehman Brothers below 40 percent for three years, and to accept two Nippon Life representatives on the Shearson boards as well as appoint a Nippon Life "adviser" to its own board.

Yet another example, from the arena of international retail banking, involves a relationship developed in late 1986 between Citicorp and Dai-Ichi Kangyo Ltd. (DKB) of Japan. Each bank's customers would be able to use the automated teller machines (ATMs) in the other's country, the two banks would act as each other's agents in consumer loans and home mortgages (allowing

Table 3–3. Cooperative Behavior in Underwriting International Equities.

Rank 1986	Bank	Amount $m	1986 Involvement No.	%
	Crédit Suisse First Boston	20,428.10	108	—
1	Banque Nationale de Paris	15,445.10	69	73.98
2	Banque Bruxelles Lambert	14,363.70	58	68.80
3	S.G. Warburg	13,591.60	54	65.10
4	Swiss Bank Corp. International	13,514.20	66	64.73
5	Deutsche Bank	13,096.10	62	62.72
	Nomura Securities	14,321.60	129	
1	Daiwa Securities	8,543.22	72	59.65
2	Nikko Securities Company	8,126.34	63	56.74
3	Yamaichi Securities	7,958.40	62	55.57
4	Union Bank of Switzerland	7,531.28	53	52.59
5	Mitsui Trust & Banking	7,330.39	57	51.18
	Deutsche Bank	12,156.10	92	
1	Union Bank of Switzerland	6,131.70	38	50.02
2	Crédit Suisse First Boston	6,125.69	36	49.97
3	Swiss Bank Corp. International	5,614.78	34	45.81
4	Morgan Stanley International	5,592.45	32	45.62
5	Dresdner Bank	5,423.87	45	44.25
	Banque Paribas	6,779.81	67	
1	Banque Bruxelles Lambert	4,645.54	44	67.35
2	Crédit Suisse First Boston	4,447.34	37	64.48
3	S.G. Warburg	4,310.59	38	62.49
4	Swiss Bank Corp. International	4,267.35	38	61.87
5	Morgan Guaranty	3,657.61	30	53.03
	Merrill Lynch Capital Markets	5,945.45	40	
1	Union Bank of Switzerland	4,293.23	27	72.21
2	Nomura Securities	3,582.22	21	60.25
3	Daiwa Securities	3,582.22	20	60.25
4	Banque Bruxelles Lambert	3,565.45	23	59.97
5	Crédit Lyonnais	3,540.45	22	59.55

Table 3–3.   continued.

Rank 1986	Bank	Amount $m	1986 Involvement No.	%
	Nikko Securities	5,085.18	34	
1	Daiwa Securities	3,102.84	31	61.02
2	Nomura Securities	2,555.97	24	50.26
3	Crédit Suisse First Boston	2,285.52	20	44.94
4	Swiss Bank Corp. International	2,278.43	19	44.81
5	Yamaichi Securities	2,193.43	16	43.13

Source: Euromoney, *Annual Financing Report* (London: Euromoney Publications, Inc., March 1987), pp. 54–55.

customers of each to borrow quickly and easily from the other), with Dai-Ichi "supporting" (distributing and processing charges under) Citicorp's MasterCard in Japan. Each bank would be able to tap into the information base and expertise of the other. The arrangement would help each to establish a full-service presence in the other's country, clearly a case of collaboration as defined in Figure 3–4.

Citicorp's presence in Japan was composed of a consumer finance company, an investment banking presence, loan production offices, and (through Vickers da Costa) a seat on the Tokyo Stock Exchange, but no full-fledged banking affiliate. The link to DKB would provide Citibank with access to Japanese retail customers, who could use the bank's ATMs in the United States and vice versa. Both banks' retail networks are among the broadest in their respective markets. The need for bilingual software and the expense of hardware in the face of small client bases had limited the installation of ATMs by both DKB and Citibank in each other's markets, a problem the collaborative link would eliminate. Under the arrangement, Citibank customers in Japan have full access to all of DKB's 862 ATMs and 621 cash-dispensing machines as well as (for an additional charge) ATMs maintained by other Japanese banks belonging to the DKB network. This permits Citibank to compete in the Japanese retail market, while DKB acquires similar capabilities in those U.S. markets where Citibank operates at the retail level.

Final agreement between Citibank and Dai-Ichi Kangyo was reached in mid-1987, with the blessings of the Ministry of Finance, and the two banks established a joint operations team to work out details and coordinate computer systems to make the link-up possible. Beyond the specifics of the deal itself, the arrangement was expected to defuse criticism of Japan for the failure of Japanese commercial banks to open the ATMs to customers of foreign banks in Japan, and ease the threat of retaliatory action against Japanese banks in the United States.

A somewhat different example of collaboration was the purchase of a share in the Goldman Sachs partnership by Sumitomo Bank of Japan in 1986, presumably with a view toward creating, together, global market power that neither would be able to achieve alone. Yet Sumitomo clearly did not get all it bargained for in the arrangement. Besides stringent Federal Reserve restrictions on what sort of collaboration would be allowed, the insider trading scandals of 1986 and 1987 soon enveloped Goldman Sachs as well, potentially reducing the value of the investment. Sumitomo was limited to its 12.5 percent non-voting share in the Goldman Sachs capitalization, was prohibited from acquiring shares in any Goldman Sachs affiliate or placing members on the board of any such affiliate, could not send trainees to Goldman Sachs without specific Fed approval, and could not increase the amount of business they do with each other—maintaining an arm's length relationship.

But perhaps the best example of a successful cooperative venture in the international financial services industry is Financière Crédit Suisse First Boston (CSFB). Created at a time when both Crédit Suisse and First Boston were having difficulties developing or even maintaining their market positions, the formation of CSFB in 1978 provides an ideal example of a positive-sum game in which both parties had high stakes as well as significant power. Crédit Suisse, recovering from a financial scandal involving its branch in Chiasso (inflicting a loss of SFr

1.22 billion on the bank), brought to the venture its capitalization, ability to bear risk, and ability to place securities in the accounts of institutional and individual investors. It had earlier tried a joint venture in London with White Weld and Company, which in turn was acquired by Merrill Lynch and prompting Crédit Suisse to buy out the Merrill Lynch share and look for a new (less dominant) partner. First Boston, at the time suffering market share losses at the hands of its major U.S. investment banking rivals, brought to the venture its innovative ideas and deal-making prowess, benefiting from Crédit Suisse's financial strength in order to remain a viable independent firm.

Together, the two firms probably did far better in the various markets, especially the Eurobond market, than either could have done on its own. Through CSFB, First Boston appears to have been significantly more successful than other American investment banks in its international operations, contributing about 20 percent of the firm's 1986 net income.

Over time, however, even such a world-class collaboration is likely to show strain. First, international financial markets are changing so quickly that the same mode of collaboration cannot be applied consistently. What was a good approach for doing well in the Eurobond market may not be ideally suited for the Euroequity market. Second, competition has heated up dramatically, with Japanese securities houses and players from the United States, the United Kingdom, and continental Europe bringing about a serious erosion of margins. Third, there is the possibility that each partner may itself acquire some of the same kinds of resources the other initially brought to the venture. If, for example, Crédit Suisse were able to develop its own technical and deal-making capabilities, while First Boston finds it difficult or impossible to acquire the credit standing, capitalization, and placing power of Crédit Suisse, one would expect the arrangement to shift from unequivocal collaboration into a gradual assertion of leverage on the part of Crédit Suisse and perhaps eventually acquisition of the remaining 40 percent share in the venture it does not already own. At the same time, one would expect increasing strains within the firm, and a gradual deterioration in the quality of the relationship. Regulatory changes, such as erosion of the Glass-Steagell Act in the United States, could also exert pressure on the joint venture.

Such dynamics hardly detract, however, from the unprecedented success achieved by the venture. In 1986 it arranged 127 Eurobond and Euroequity issues valued at $21.8 billion, more than any of its rivals in these two markets. Its staff is cosmopolitan, and it has strength in a number of major currencies.

Finally, internationalization has long been an aspect of banking in the United Kingdom, Belgium, the Netherlands, and other relatively open economies with strong links to business activities abroad. This includes Switzerland, where the major banks—Union Bank of Switzerland, Swiss Bank Corporation, and Crédit Suisse—have in recent years made strong strategic moves to become global players from a relatively narrow domestic base. Besides a conventional presence in overseas markets, Crédit Suisse developed the highly creative capital-markets partnership with First Boston Corporation, while Swiss Bank Corporation moved rapidly to become a significant player in the major financial centers through internal growth and carefully targeted acquisitions. Union Bank of Switzerland, the country's largest bank, acquired the London brokerage firm of Philips & Drew in 1985 and rapidly built up its own securities and corporate finance capabilities in London, New York, and Tokyo as well as in Germany, Australia, and other significant markets.

SUMMARY

The Client-Arena-Product model assesses the competitive structure of the international financial services industry. It permits identification of sources of potential supernormal returns as a product of the competitive structure of markets. Strategic groups, contestable markets, and predatory behavior have an important bearing on market structure. Intermarket linkages contribute to global economies of scale and economies of scope. All of these issues are critical to an understanding of protectionism and competitive distortions in this sector.

NOTES

1. Ingo Walter, "Competitive Performance and Market Structure in International Financial Services," New York University, 1987. *Mimeo.*
2. Bank for International Settlements, *Recent Innovations in International Banking* (Basel: BIS, 1986).
3. Michael E. Porter, *Competitive Strategy* (New York: Free Press, 1982).
4. Richard Caves, "Economic Analysis and the Quest for Competitive Advantage," *American Economic Review* (May 1984).
5. Elizabeth E. Bailey and Ann F. Friedlander, "Market Structure and Multiproduct Industries," *Journal of Economic Literature* (September 1982).
6. William Baumol, J. Panzar, and R. Willig, *Contestable Markets and the Theory of Industry Structure* (New York: Harcourt Brace Jovanovich, 1982).
7. BIS, *Recent Innovations in International Banking.*
8. Richard Caves and Michael Porter, "From Entry Barriers to Mobility Barriers: Conjectural Decisions and Contrived Deterrence to New Competition," *Quarterly Journal of Economics* (May 1977).
9. Thomas N. Gladwin and Ingo Walter, *Multinationals under Fire* (New York: John Wiley and Sons, 1980).

4

DIMENSIONS OF COMPETITIVE ADVANTAGE AND INSTITUTIONAL STRATEGY

Clearly, the global market for financial services is open to all players. It is equally clear, however, that the players differ enormously in terms of their success or failure to exploit opportunities available in the client-arena-product matrix, with respect to both individual cells and cell groupings. Individual institutions bring to bear vastly different resources and adopt vastly different organizational strategies.

SOURCES OF INSTITUTIONAL COMPETITIVE ADVANTAGE

A striking aspect of the international financial services industry is the high degree of variation in competitive performance among institutions, as measured by earnings. Financial institutions faced with the identical feasibility set as represented by the Client-Arena-Product model come away with entirely different results. A very limited example of this is depicted in Table 4–1, which gives comparative performance measures for the eleven major U.S. multinational banks during the period 1982–86.

Figure 4–1 illustrates the kinds of differences that exist in banking profitability even among the major industrial countries, all of which have sophisticated financial systems, using both return on equity (ROE) and return on average assets (ROA) as indicators. Besides differences in competitive structure, such variation is also clearly the result of differences between countries in monetary and credit policies, and other governmental measures affecting the banking industry. Variations along these

Table 4–1. Performance Differences among U.S.
Multinational Banks.

Bank Holding Company	5-Year Return on Equity	1986 Net Profit Margin	5-Year Sales Growth	5-Year Earnings per Share
Bankers Trust NY	17.2	8.7	3.3	6.3
J.P. Morgan	16.1	12.6	2.7	13.2
Citicorp	15.5	4.3	7.7	13.0
Chemical Bank NY	15.4	7.2	3.9	7.7
Bank of Boston	15.4	6.1	6.4	9.4
Irving Bank	13.6	6.5	0.6	2.9
Manufacturers Hanover	13.4	5.1	7.6	2.7
Chase Manhattan	12.8	6.0	1.6	2.2
First Chicago	8.7	6.3	3.5	0.9
BankAmerica	5.0	Def.	0.7	Neg.
Continental Illinois	Def.	3.7	−11.3	Neg.

Source: Forbes, January 12, 1987.

Reprinted by permission of Forbes magazine, January 12, 1987. © Forbes Inc., 1987.

Note: Five-year estimates cover the period 1982–86.

lines are presumably much more marked in the case of developing countries and other national financial systems that are less highly integrated into the international capital markets.

Such differences are further elaborated in Table 4–2, a regional breakdown of ROA figures for major U.S. commercial banks during a relatively "normal" period, 1980–82—that is, before the accounting and valuation problems associated with the less developed countries' debt crisis.

All of the six players are subject to U.S. financial deregulation and exposed to the full rigors of the offshore markets. None are protected by the kinds of home-country regulation and barriers to competition that make these numbers look weak by comparison with banks from other countries with relatively sheltered home markets. All were restricted from entering the

Figure 4–1. Bank Rates of Return on Assets and Equity, Various Countries.

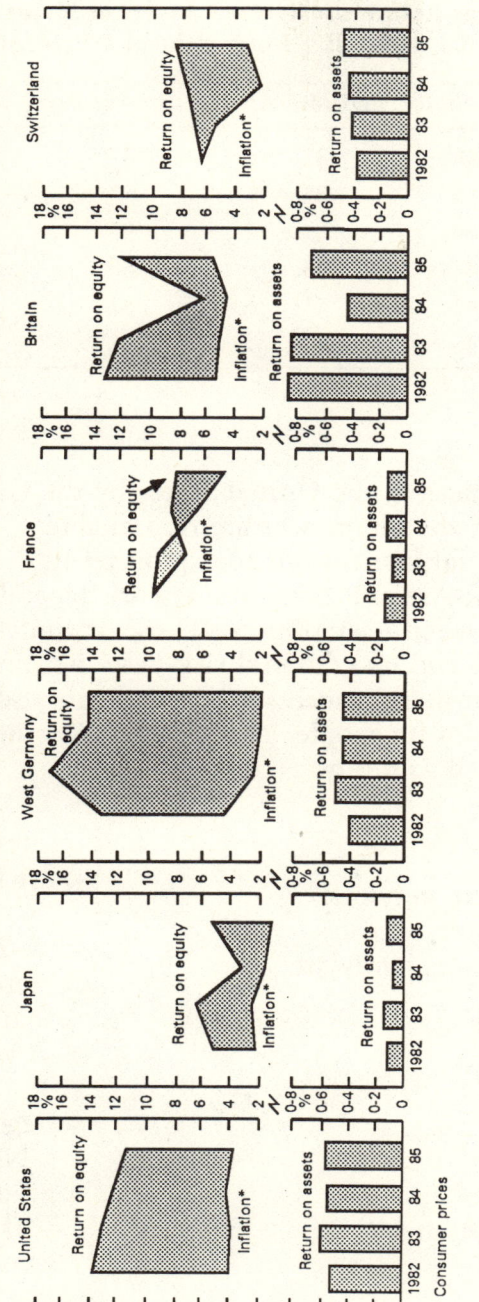

Source: The Economist, March 21, 1987. Copyright 1987, The Economist, distributed by Special Features.

73

Table 4–2. Three-Year Return on Average Assets of Major U.S. International Banks, 1980–82 (Hundredths of 1 Percent).

	Global	EUR/ME/AF	Latin America	Asia
Citicorp	48	32	87	56
Chase Manhattan	46	32	73	55
Morgan Guaranty	69	82	95	73
Manufacturers Hanover	44	43	50	39
Bank of America	42	41	32	70
Continental Illinois	45	52	51	20

Source: Bank of America.

domestic securities business in the United States by the Glass-Steagall Act of 1933. Yet the differences are remarkable.

The ability of financial institutions to exploit profit opportunities within the Client-Arena-Product framework depends on a number of key firm-specific attributes. These include the institution's capital base and its actuarial risk base, its human resources, its information/market access, its technology, and the entrepreneurial qualities of its people. The proximate competitive weapons can be listed as follows:

Fixed resources
   Branch and affiliate network
   Computer hardware
   Telecommunications hardware

Intangible resources
   Franchise
   Knowledge
      Client specific
      Arena specific
      Product specific
   Systems and procedures
   Placing power

Human resources
Professional
Nonprofessional

Financial resources
Capital base
Deposit base

How each of these major sources of competitive power interacts with the C-A-P cell structure will be discussed in turn.

Adequacy of the Capital Base

In recent years, financial institutions and their regulators have started to pay increasing attention to the issue of capital as a source of competitive power as well as prudential control. This has always been true with respect to activities appearing on the balance sheet, such as capital-based lending limits in the case of bank loans, and it is in this area that there has been a perceived deterioration in the general quality of bank assets in various countries, including the United States. With increasing securitization in domestic and international finance, the role of capital has become important as the primary determinant of risk-bearing ability in securities underwriting and dealing, as well as in insurance-related off-balance-sheet activities.

Indeed, innovations in the securities underwriting business and merchant-banking transactions requiring extensive commitments of the firm's own capital have given players with large capital bases a significant competitive advantage. Such innovations as the "bought deal" have meant that only institutions with a large capital base can afford to take entire blocks of securities onto their books. This, and the growing importance of positioning through trading and dealing activities, force institutions to hold larger inventories of securities, giving a key competitive advantage to players with a large capital base. One step removed, a large capital base that allows an institution to be a successful player in securities underwriting and dealing also may enable it

to undertake mergers and acquisitions activities, private placements, and other value-added financial services for its clients.

Capital adequacy thus conveys a decided competitive advantage in bringing specific products to specific international-
markets, in maximizing firepower and reducing costs in funding
operations, and in being able to stick with particular clients in
good times and bad—thus being considered a reliable financial
partner. In addition, regulators in the United States, Japan, West
Germany, and the United Kingdom have imposed required
risk-asset ratios for dealing with off-balance-sheet exposure.
Institutions are therefore only able to increase their asset footings
and insurance-related services by building up their capital bases
(see Chapter 9).

At the same time, of course, there are reasons why institutions are in general reluctant to increase their primary capital.
These have to do with earnings dilution and the importance of
leverage, and some institutions have responded by issuing
subordinated debt, perpetual floating rate notes, and other forms
of debt that can be treated as primary capital.

In June 1987 the U.S. Treasury released a paper putting
forward a plan that would permit the creation of between five and
ten U.S. based "megabanks" capitalized at a level so as to
compete effectively on a global scale with banks of comparable
size based in Japan, France, Germany, and the United Kingdom.
In its position paper, the Treasury thus supported elimination
both of the Glass-Steagall restrictions separating commercial
banking from nonbanking activities and the Bank Holding
Company Act limitations on nationwide branching. Indeed, the
report suggested that large, heavily capitalized industrial companies should be in a position to own banks and use their capital
to support the kinds of mega-institutions envisaged. The report
coincided with evidence that the lending operations of foreign
based banks were almost twice as profitable as those of U.S. based
institutions, and that this limited U.S. banks' ability to become
adequately capitalized in order to compete effectively with the
foreign giants. Additional evidence indicated that the banks'
share of U.S. consumer debt had fallen from 47 to 44 percent, and
that their share of corporate debt had fallen from 36 to 31 percent

over the period 1981 to 1986 as a result of increased securitized lending.

Besides additional capitalization, the Treasury paper pointed to greater earnings stability attributable to geographic and activity based diversification, improved safety and soundness due to a broader funding base and improved capitalization, and greater cost and marketing efficiencies due to economies of scale and scope. At the same time, the reduced costs and greater avail-abilities of banking services were said to lower input costs to manufacturing and services firms exposed to international com-petition, thereby improving their performance in competing for international markets. Implicit was the view that there would be relatively few world-class competitors by the year 2000, and that each of these would have to be based strongly in one national financial system. An absence of deregulation in the United States could result in a complete absence of any U.S. institutions from future lists of world-class players and the progressive "control" of American financial markets by foreign based institutions. This prospect could prove to be a political counterweight to fears about excessive concentration of economic power in the hands of a few very large domestic institutions.[1]

A number of arguments were raised against the notion of creating megabanks along the lines of the Treasury proposal. One view was that most U.S. money center banks, which should already be in the best position to compete with the major foreign based institutions, have in fact been relatively poorly managed and remain thinly capitalized—both in comparison with many of their foreign rivals and in comparison to the emerging domestic "super-regional" banks such as SunTrust, which operates in Florida, Georgia, and Tennessee. In mid-1987 the shares of most U.S. money center banks sold at no more than 120 percent of book value, while the shares of many super-regionals were valued substantially higher. With the growing consolidation of the U.S. banking system to perhaps 5,000 to 8,000 institutions, a signif-icant number of super-regionals having the advantage of major retail deposit networks and solid capitalization could emerge as viable international players and obviate the need for solutions as drastic as megabanks.

The Actuarial Risk Base

Financial institutions fund themselves by creating financial assets held by others. This is obviously the case with respect to customer deposits, interbank dealing, and issuance of certificates of deposit as well as share capital. The assets thus created range from low-return and high-liquidity assets to high-return and low-liquidity assets. Each has a unique risk profile.

In the presence of regulation, banks may be protected from having to pay market rates of return on their deposits. Deregulation of activities in onshore markets usually means that financial institutions are forced to bid for these assets, as they have always had to do in offshore markets. In this context the perceived quality of an institution (its "actuarial risk base") is an important determinant of a bank's ability to sell financial assets to others, and to do so at the lowest possible cost.

The international debt problems of the 1980s, as well as sectoral problems in real estate, energy, agriculture, and other troubled industries have called into question the fundamental soundness of the asset structures of many financial institutions and therefore their credit standing. This in turn has accelerated the pace of disintermediation, with many large corporations and other institutions going straight to the capital markets on the basis of their own credit standing.

Interbank borrowing has been an important source of funding for banks, representing a less secure and higher cost source of funds than customer deposits. At the same time, interbank lending is an important outlet for excess funds on the asset side. The actuarial risk base has become of particular significance in this context, with substantial tiering taking place from time to time in the interbank market. Banks of lesser perceived quality can be caught in a difficult position if they are forced to pay a premium over the other banks in order to fund themselves in the interbank market, yet this premium is taken by other institutions to reflect an impairment of their credit standing.

Table 4–3 shows 1987 Moody and Standard & Poor credit ratings for the major international banks and securities houses.

Table 4–3.   Comparative Credit Ratings of Banks, February 1987.

Bank	Moody's		S&P	
	Short	Long	Short	Long
Citicorp	P-1	A1	A-1+	AA
Chase Manhattan	P-1	Aa2	A-1+	AA
J.P. Morgan	P-1	Aaa	A-1+	AAA
Bankers Trust	P-1	Aa2	A-1+	AA+
Manufacturers Hanover	P-2	A3	A-1	A+
Chemical	P-1	Aa2	A-1+	AA
Continental Illinois	P-3	Baa3	A-2	BBB
First Chicago	P-1	A2	A-1	A+
BankAmerica	P-3	Baa3	A-3	BBB
Barclays	P-1	Aaa	A-1+	AA+
National Westminster	P-1	Aaa	A-1+	AA+
Lloyds	P-1	—	A-1+	—
Midland	P-1	Aa2	A-1	A
Banque Nationale de Paris	P-1	Aaa	A-1+	AA+
Société Générale	—	Aaa	A-1+	AA+
Credit Lyonnais	—	Aaa	A-1+	—
Banque Paribas	—	—	A-1+	AA+
Union Bank of Switzerland	P-1	Aaa	A-1+	AAA
Crédit Suisse	P-1	Aaa	A-1+	AAA
Swiss Bank Corp.	P-1	Aaa	A-1+	AAA
Deutsche Bank	P-1	Aaa	A-1+	AAA
Commerzbank	—	—	A-1	—
Dresdner Bank	P-1	—	A-1+	—
Dai-Ichi Kangyo	P-1	Aaa	A-1+	—
Sumitomo Bank	P-1	Aaa	A-1+	AA+
Mitsubishi	P-1	Aaa	A-1+	—
Bank of Tokyo	—	Aa1	A-1+	AA
Industrial Bank of Japan	P-1	Aaa	A-1+	AAA
Long-Term Credit Bank	P-1	Aaa	A-1+	AA
Salomon Brothers	P-1	Aa3	A-1+	AA–
Merrill-Lynch	P-1	Aa3	A-1+	AA
Daiwa Securities	—	Aa2	—	AA
Nomura Securities	—	—	A-1+	AAA

Source: The Economist, March 15, 1987. Copyright 1987, *The Economist*, distributed by Special Features.

An example of a market recently dominated by foreign based banks on the basis of this competitive variable involves standby letters of credit covering municipal securities in the United States. State and local government entities issue securities backed by standby letters of credit under which the bank, in return for a fee, will unconditionally cover payments due to bondholders if the issuer is unable to do so. This enhances the marketability of the securities and reduces the municipalities' borrowing costs. Foreign banks' advantage in this market is based on their triple-A credit rating, whereas the only U.S. bank remaining in that category is Morgan Guaranty.

Japanese banks moved particularly aggressively into this market. In 1984 Morgan Guaranty provided a standby letter of credit covering a $70 million short-term note for the City of Boston for a fee of seventy-five basis points ($520,000), whereas two years later Sanwa Bank did a similar deal at nine basis points, with the next two lowest bids also coming from Japanese banks. In all, foreign banks captured perhaps 70 percent of this business in 1986. With municipal bond issues of perhaps $60-80 billion annually, the market is very significant indeed.

State and local treasurers were delighted. U.S. banks found returns severely eroded. Foreign banks, in some cases less encumbered by capital requirements, high funding costs, and managerial focus on quarterly earnings growth than their U.S. competitors, considered the returns acceptable, especially in view of the foothold gained in a new market. And U.S. investment banks involved in underwriting municipal general obligation securities were more than happy to have foreign banks involved in the letters-of-credit part of the deals rather than their domestic commercial bank competitors.

Quality of Human Resources

While it has long been recognized that financial services basically constitute a "people business," it is only recently that the importance of having truly superior human resources has become apparent to all of the major players. As Guth notes,[2] in today's evolving competitive environment human capital can be viewed as a financial institution's most important asset, and many of the critical capabilities for exploiting competitive opportunities depend directly upon the quality of human resources captured within the organization.

Judgment based on cumulative experience is a central variable in the production of a broad range of financial services, because many of the decisions that must be taken are so complex. In particular, both credit evaluation and risk evaluation depend upon the intellectual caliber, experience, and training of the decisionmaker. These qualities are no less important in the securities business than they are in the more traditional aspects of banking.

Due to the increase in transactions-driven financial services, individuals are increasingly having to make decisions of a highly complex nature very quickly or lose deals. The need for rapid and accurate decisionmaking is evident in the trading function, where traders have to react almost instantly to exploit arbitrage opportunities and where incorrect decisions can mean substantial and unambiguous losses for the firm. Yet they are no less important in maintaining relationships with clients, to anticipate client financial requirements and respond to them in a way that adds value. This is what in many cases is the root cause of supernormal returns in the financial services industry.

Growing competition and increased complexity has placed a premium on advantages attributable to superior human resources. It is reflected both in severe rivalry to attract top quality managers in the labor markets of various financial centers, with compensation levels bid up at an extraordinary rate, and in ferocious competition for talented young graduates. Indeed some financial institutions are hiring managers from other industries and retraining them, and recent evidence indicates that successful bankers in the future will often have had experience in another industry. Just as financial assets have varying market values so also do people. The international financial services sector attracts some of the brightest individuals, and the emerging reward structure in the industry has caused much comment and may indeed not be sustainable.

Beyond devoting a great deal of time and resources to attracting and retaining superior personnel, firms in the banking industry invest heavily in training at increasingly high levels of sophistication. The training programs of major institutions are renowned for their high standards. This represents nothing more than continuous investment in human capital, as critical in this industry as provision for depreciation and capital investment are in other industries.

Information Asymmetries

If money is "information on the move," then financial services constitute the most information-intensive industry in the international economy. Various financial services (such as financial advisory services) are of a purely informational nature, and the drive by financial institutions to move out of commodity-type activities into higher value-added businesses is augmenting the importance of information-intensive products, both quantitatively and qualitatively. Financial services that are not of a purely informational nature still tend to be highly dependent on quality of information for their value. Moreover, asymmetries of information among the various competitors and their clients contribute a great deal toward explaining differentials in competitive performance.

Beyond information embedded in specific financial services sold in various arenas to various clients, we have noted that one of the most important functions undertaken within financial institutions is risk evaluation, again highly dependent on the quality of information. All forms of lending and credit-related activities depend upon the collection, processing, and evaluation of large amounts of information. Similarly, the assimilation of information about the needs of clients is critical in the development and tailoring of services.

Three special factors are relevant in a consideration of information as a determinant of competitive performance. First, information is the only factor of production that can be used simultaneously in the production of any number of services, and this gives information some unique characteristics. Information generated to build an international cash management system for a multinational corporate client can also be used to develop a long-term financial strategy for the same company, or perhaps to develop a slightly different international cash management system for another multinational firm.

Second, the half-life of information tends to be short and may be decreasing. Because of high degrees of market volatility, vital financial information decays at a rapid rate, and actions that may have been warranted at one moment are no longer appropriate shortly thereafter. It is an environment consisting of many small windows of opportunity. This means that for some financial services constant market surveillance is necessary. For some others immediacy remains somewhat less important.

Third, the growing complexity of the international financial environment and the variety of services on offer has made it increasingly difficult for companies and individuals to plan their financial requirements in a straightforward manner. In effect, clients need a means to evaluate the information that is available, some way of distinguishing relevant information from irrelevant. Financial institutions can provide services that help accomplish this.

Client Insight. A special application of information asymmetries has to do with maximizing client-driven linkage effects. "Client insight" exists when a financial institution has developed a certain base of client-specific knowledge and mutual trust over time, in the course of satisfying that client's financial needs. This is sometimes called "contracting costs" in the economics literature. Potential competitors may face significant contracting costs in trying to generate the client-specific information needed to compete effectively.

This consideration relates to the transition that has taken place from relationship-driven banking to transactions-driven banking, and would imply either (a) that the amount of client insight needed to satisfy its needs is decreasing over time, or (b) that more institutions have the core stock of client-specific information necessary to satisfy clients' requirements. However, client insight remains a key to providing differential value added in financial services, regardless of the importance of transactions-driven banking.

Arena Insight. Positive linkage effects are also attributable to arena-specific information. Just as a financial institution generates over time, a large amount of client-specific knowledge, it also generates an amount of arena-specific information. The nature of this information depends on the level of aggregation of the arena definition. It is at the national level that many arena-specific information characteristics are most relevant, but supranational (regional) and subnational (local) expertise may be important as well. At the national level, important elements will include an understanding of economic institutions, structure, and prospects, formation of economic policies and familiarity with decisionmakers and their objectives, as well as political overlay of economic policies. Information and analytical skills derived from dealing in particular arenas can be transmitted through the organization and used in others.

Placing Information. With the continued securitization in the capital markets the ability of underwriters to place securities with individual and institutional investors has become an increasingly important competitive variable, perhaps most clearly exemplified in the Euronote market. The modern securities industry in essence is *about* distribution, and firms must focus on the number of securities they will be able to allocate to each investor and on the number of investors to whom they can allocate them. In the former case, investors tend to increase their holdings of a given security only if the price is reduced, thus increasing the yield. If the investor base can be increased, however, this placing and distribution power gives an important competitive advantage to certain players. Placing power is equally important in loan selling and syndication, as it is in access to potential clients for other types of financial services.

Financial Technology and Innovation

Financial innovation has obviously dramatically changed the economics of the financial services industry, affecting some parts of the industry more than others via its impact on the use of information incorporated into services that are sold to clients. Those dimensions of the industry that have witnessed the most far-reaching changes are also those that are most highly knowledge-intensive. Information technologies allow bankers to have ever increasing amounts of information at their disposal, as well as decreasing drastically the time necessary to transfer information across arenas, client segments, and product applications. With increasing amounts of information hitting institutions at an increasing pace, internal systems have come under pressure from information overload, and new systems have had to be built, including ways of accelerating the decision process. Back-office operations have likewise been revolutionized by technological change, as have transaction-based systems at both the wholesale and retail levels.

Although innovative capabilities—the continuous application of new product and process technologies—are very much a function of the quality of embodied human capital, they are also highly sensitive to the "culture" of an organization, its management, and its incentive structure. Innovation could therefore be treated separately as a determinant of competitive performance in the international financial services industry. Still, it is difficult to pinpoint the actual source of innovation, especially since institutions compete in the same labor markets for employees and personnel move from one institution to another with increasing frequency. And yet some institutions are consistently more innovative than others.

As noted, innovation in financial services tends to be rather cell specific: client, product, and arena-specific. It can be looked upon as the introduction of a new financial process or technique, new in terms of a particular cell, that provides durable returns and adds value to the investor/lender/issuer/borrower. The spread of an innovation through the matrix allows the firm to take advantage of its inherent profit potential across the cells. Innovation is particularly important for those players with a substantial presence in the offshore markets, where there are few barriers to competitive behavior. Their unregulated nature allows each of the players far more freedom to innovate than is true in many onshore markets.

Since the interval before imitations appear is short for most innovations and may be decreasing, it is important for an institution to maintain a continuous stream of innovations. In this sense an institution's most important innovation is its *next* one. There seems to be a positive relation between the complexity of the innovation and the imitation lag. At the same time, there would also seem to be a negative relation between product complexity and the success of the innovation, many innovations being too complex to be put to effective use and therefore ultimately failing.

It thus appears that innovation is a composite of embodied human capital and technology, market information, and the corporate culture of the organization. The natural intelligence and creativity of the individual can be enhanced or reduced as a result of his or her level of product expertise and training, management's attitude to financial and process technologies, the incentives to innovate successfully versus the penalties of unsuccessful innovation, and the amount of horizontal communication and information transfer that take place within the organization.

Franchise

An institution's "franchise" may be its most important asset, as well as its most intangible asset, one that clearly distinguishes *ex post* the most successful competitors in the international financial services industry from the rest. It is the product of an institution's cumulative track record. A franchise can arise from any number of different sources but generally derives from a specific type of competence and expertise that the market values and that the institution has developed over time.

The franchise concept has been used to explain a variety of competitive phenomena and appears to be related to an institution's standing in the market as a result of a synergistic combination of all the above attributes, the whole being greater than the sum of the parts. The franchise, or "goodwill", embedded in an institution is thus a product of its past performance projected into the future.

MARKET PERFORMANCE

Tables 4–4 through 4–10 provide examples of how different institutions fared in lead-managing international loans, arranging note issuance facilities and Euro-commercial paper; managing international bond issues, Euroequity issues, and swaps; and putting together international merger and acquisition deals during 1986. Note the degree of concentration of American, British, Swiss, and Japanese firms among the top players in each league.

The determinants of a multinational financial institution's performance fit well with the location-specific (cell) characteristics and ownership-specific (resource) factors identified by Dunning in his electric theory of the multinational firm.[3] Each of the institution's resources will tend to have differing degrees of cell specificity, ranging from arena-specific fixed assets to generic knowledge that is not cell specific.

An initial attempt to match the principal competitive resources of international financial institutions with the principal product groups identified in Chapter 3 is presented in Table 4–11.

As described in Chapter 3, a firm in the financial services industry faces a given C-A-P cell configuration and a set of intercell linkages at a given point in time, alongside a particular institutional capability profile composed of the elements just discussed. Some of the cells have already been accessed, and some form a feasibility-set for possible further development. The firm's expansion path and the desired cell configuration of its business depend on the level of perceived risk-adjusted economic rents

Table 4–4. Lead-Manager Rankings in the International Syndicated Loan Market.

Rank 1986		Amount ($m)	No. of Transactions
1	Citicorp Investment Bank	32,728.63	92
2	Chase Investment Bank	17,462.68	174
3	Morgan Guaranty	16,777.06	65
4	Manufacturers Hanover	8,831.26	49
5	Bankers Trust	5,807.61	58
6	Standard Oil Finance	5,500.00	2
7	RBC/Orion Royal Bank	5,490.21	35
8	Mitsubishi Bank	5,268.50	99
9	BankAmerica Capital Markets Group	4,734.09	54
10	Crédit Suisse First Boston	3,603.79	31
11	Chemical Bank	3,589.21	37
12	Midland Bank Group	3,382.52	58
13	S.G. Warburg	3,120.29	34
14	First Chicago	2,901.12	46
15	Bank of Tokyo	2,836.32	92
16	Westpac Banking Corp.	2,805.87	18
17	National Westminster Bank Group	2,685.45	53
18	Crédit Suisse	2,569.72	20
19	Bank of Nova Scotia	2,473.76	29
20	Toronto Dominion International	2,471.98	13
21	Banque Nationale de Paris	2,424.33	33
22	Standard Chartered Bank	2,377.95	31
23	Barclays Bank Group	2,358.85	38
24	Lloyds Merchant Bank	2,200.19	40
25	Industrial Bank of Japan	1,933.47	71
26	Morgan Grenfell	1,802.30	25
27	Société Générale	1,736.35	23
28	Banque Paribas	1,633.63	49
29	Swiss Bank Corp. International	1,403.94	14
30	Fuji Bank	1,128.25	48
31	Arab Banking Corp.	1,104.33	31
32	Mitsui Bank	1,053.60	50
33	HongkongBank Group	1,004.55	29
34	Bank of Montreal	963.38	13
35	Sumitomo Bank	952.74	33
36	ANZ Banking Group	936.33	13
37	Long-Term Credit Bank	929.81	46
38	Bank of New York	919.66	3

Table 4–4.   continued.

Rank 1986		Amount ($m)	No. of Transactions
39	Nippon Life Insurance	913.24	23
40	Ford Europe	900.00	2
41	CIBC	891.87	11
42	Dai-ichi Kangyo Bank	887.07	53
43	Guinness Mahon	881.59	17
44	Salomon Brothers International	832.27	5
45	Crédit Lyonnais	764.22	30
46	Deutsche Bank	748.49	20
47	Union Bank of Switzerland	735.84	11
48	Kleinwort Benson	718.54	8
49	Sanwa Bank	689.29	41
50	Nippon Credit Bank	646.21	31

Source: Euromoney, *Annual Financing Report* (London: Euromoney Publications, Inc., March 1987), p. 61.

associated with the feasibility-set of cells, resistance lines impeding access to those cells, and the assessed value of intercell linkages. That financial institutions do not always perform better abroad than at home is illustrated in Figure 4–2 (for British clearing banks only), although this ignores potentially favorable linkage effects from their international business to their domestic performance.

Successful players in the international financial services industry must excel at identifying (1) the specific sources of their own competitive advantage; (2) those cells where this competitive advantage can most profitably be applied, adds value to specific clients, and is sustainable; and (3) the competitive potential inherent in the cell linkages. They must also correctly assess other important dimensions in the organization's delivery system. These include formal and informal responsibility and accountability structures, as well as the availability and use of state-of-the-art decision support systems. Application of a competitive-structure framework, such as the one presented in Chapter 3, will help point out the cells and cell clusters where significant returns based on market power are likely to exist, and

Table 4–5. Rankings of Arrangers of Note Issuance Facilities.

Rank			1986	
			Amount	No. of
1986	1985	Arranger	$m	Issues
1	2	Citicorp Investment Bank	6,792	21
2	5	Chase Investment Bank	4,397	9
3	4	Morgan Guaranty	4,275	9
4	9	Bank of Tokyo	3,260	6
5	7	Merrill Lynch Capital Markets	2,040	17
6	50	Svenska Handelsbanken	2,000	1
7	8	Bankers Trust International	1,488	13
8	42	Barclays Bank Group	1,420	10
9	45	Shearson Lehman Brothers International	1,360	3
10	14	Chemical Bank	1,235	4
11	6	Salomon Brothers	1,100	5
12	1	Bank Of America International	1,085	7
13	15	Goldman Sachs	1,020	4
14	13	Lloyds Merchant Bank	1,004	7
15	10	Société Générale	975	4
16	11	S.G. Warburg	897	7
17	64	N.M. Rothschild	860	4
18	12	Crédit Lyonnais	810	2
19	65	Mitsubishi	800	2
20	34	Morgan Stanley	620	2

Source: Euromoney, Annual Financing Report (London: Euromoney Publications, Inc., March 1987), p. 64.

(equally important) where they are likely to be durable, as well as the power of the horizontal, vertical, and lateral linkages.

BOUNDED RATIONALITY

Given the size of the matrix presented in Figure 3–1, and the complexity of the linkages that exist among the individual cells, it is clear how wide is the range of strategic options that faces a financial institution in the global environment. Consequently, it is not surprising that individual organizations' international structures and their development through time often appear

Table 4–6. Ranking of Arrangers of Euro-commercial Paper Issues.

Rank 1986	Bank	1986 Amount ($m)	No. of Issues	Share %
1	Citicorp Investment Bank	17,189.80	78	18.79
2	Merrill Lynch Capital Markets	19,084.50	64	20.86
3	S.G. Warburg	13,368.40	58	14.61
4 =	Swiss Bank Corp. International	17,031.00	56	18.62
4 =	Crédit Suisse First Boston	13,114.10	56	14.34
6	Morgan Guaranty	12,103.60	52	13.23
7	Morgan Stanley International	19,377.00	49	21.18
8	Shearson Lehman Brothers International	17,053.10	42	18.64
9 =	Salomon Brothers International	15,196.20	30	16.61
9 =	Chase Investment Bank	6,255.05	30	6.84
9 =	County Natwest	5,997.23	30	6.56
12 =	Bankers Trust International	6,978.06	25	7.63
12 =	Enskilda Securities	2,530.00	25	2.77
14 =	Union Bank of Switzerland (securities)	4,853.00	23	5.31
14 =	Midland Bank Group	3,728.86	23	4.08
16	Bank Of America International	4,580.00	18	5.01
17	First Chicago	3,735.00	17	4.08
18	Barclays Bank Group	2,909.12	16	3.18
19	Lloyds Merchant Bank	3,930.46	15	4.30
20	Morgan Grenfell	2,113.81	13	2.31
21	CIBC	2,581.52	12	2.82
22	Chemical Bank International	3,350.33	11	3.66
23	Goldman Sachs	2,394.50	10	2.62
24	First Interstate Capital Markets	2,060.00	9	2.25
25 =	Paine Webber International	4,600.00	8	5.03
25 =	Banque Indosuez	1,208.33	8	1.32
25 =	Manufacturers Hanover	1,085.00	8	1.19
25 =	Nomura Securities	1,010.00	8	1.10
29 =	Algemene Bank Nederland	1,111.16	7	1.21
29 =	Kansallis Banking Group	1,015.00	7	1.11
31 =	Deutsche Bank	975.00	6	1.07
31 =	Schroders	783.85	6	0.86
33 =	Saudi International Bank	2,194.00	5	2.40
33 =	Orion Royal Bank	1,369.00	5	1.50
33 =	Kleinwort Benson	679.30	5	0.74
33 =	Bank Of Tokyo	628.21	5	0.69
37 =	Dai-Ichi Kangyo Bank	855.00	4	0.93

Table 4–6. continued.

Rank 1986	Bank	1986		
		Amount ($m)	No. of Issues	Share %
37 =	Hong Kong Bank Group	780.00	4	0.85
37 =	Westpac Banking Corp.	775.00	4	0.85
37 =	Amsterdam Rotterdam Bank	595.81	4	0.65

Source: Euromoney, *Annual Financing Report* (London: Euromoney Publications, Inc., March 1987), p. 62.

somewhat haphazard, lacking in consistency or coherence. This haphazardness is the product of management actions under conditions of bounded rationality when faced with the *ex ante* task of determining expansion paths.

In effect, management confronts an enormous opportunity set, of which it is usually familiar only with a small part. Hence management appears to operate much of the time by a process of trial and error—trying various options under best available information, assessing results to the extent this is possible, and trying again. It is therefore not surprising that many institutions appear *ex post* to have a relatively incoherent and ambiguous strategic positioning in the global market for financial services.

STRATEGIC PROCESS

In order to maximize performance in the international financial services industry, a firm clearly has to go through some sort of strategic process to seek an optimal expansion path within the client-arena-product matrix that may involve either deepening penetration of individual cells or incursions into new cells. Decisions in this regard obviously depend upon the perceived cost and risk versus benefits of opportunities that present themselves or that are sought out. The process itself will look something like this:

Table 4–7. Rankings of Bookrunners in the Eurobond Market.

Rank			1986		
1986	1985	Bank	Amount $m	No. of Issues	Share %
1	1	Crédit Suisse First Boston	20,428.10	108	11.20
2	8	Nomura Securities	14,321.60	129	7.85
3	5	Deutsche Bank	12,156.10	92	6.66
4	3	Morgan Guaranty	9,821.74	64	5.38
5	12	Daiwa Securities	8,779.09	87	4.81
6	6	Morgan Stanley International	8,764.36	73	4.80
7	4	Salomon Brothers	8,362.25	55	4.58
8	10	Banque Paribas	6,779.81	67	3.72
9	2	Merrill Lynch Capital Markets	5,945.45	40	3.26
10	25	Nikko Securities	5,085.18	54	2.79
11	9	Union Bank of Switzerland	4,811.71	46	2.64
12	20	Yamaichi Securities	4,358.39	59	2.39
13	15	Shearson Lehman Bros. International	4,122.48	23	2.25
14	7	Goldman Sachs International	3,654.68	23	2.00
15	21	Société Générale	3,090.89	27	1.69
16	35	Long Term Credit Bank of Japan	2,941.90	26	1.63
17	14	SBC International	2,877.99	24	1.60
18	36	Industrial Bank of Japan	2,771.99	25	1.54
19	13	S.G. Warburg	2,734.39	24	1.52
20	17	Commerzbank	2,695.37	39	1.50
21	16	Bankers Trust	2,546.33	20	1.41
22	24	Samuel Montagu	2,459.36	10	1.37
23	30	Chase Manhattan	2,124.29	15	1.18
24	37	West LB	2,109.56	21	1.17
25	26	Banque Nationale de Paris	2,080.96	25	1.16
26	23	Crédit Commercial de France	1,859.53	24	1.03
27	11	Orion Royal Bank	1,823.90	35	1.01
28	45	Baring Brothers	1,742.51	11	0.97
29	32	Morgan Grenfell	1,734.52	15	0.96
30	28	Dresdner Bank	1,678.73	16	0.93
31	46	Amsterdam-Rotterdam Bank	1,600.28	21	0.89
32	38	Wood Gundy	1,319.27	20	0.73
33	34	Bank of Tokyo	1,300.64	15	0.72
34	49	Algemene Bank Nederland	1,253.86	14	0.70
35	19	Lloyds Merchant Bank	1,095.95	7	0.61
36	31	Crédit Lyonnais	995.42	9	0.55
37	43	Kidder Peabody International	827.50	11	0.46
38	29	Barclays Bank Group	824.31	2	0.46

Table 4–7.   continued.

Rank			1986		
1986	1985	Bank	Amount $m	No. of Issues	Share %
39	—	EIBC Limited	758.64	16	0.42
40	—	Chemical Bank	734.46	7	0.41
41	22	Bank of America	700.03	11	0.39
42	27	Citicorp Group	697.43	7	0.39
43	40	Mitsubishi Finance International	603.82	7	0.34
44	47	Kleinwort Benson	566.91	7	0.31
45	33	Hambros Bank	522.26	10	0.29
46	50	D.G. Bank	519.12	8	0.29
47	—	Prudential Bache Securities International	498.50	4	0.28
48	44	Berliner Handels-und Frankfurter Bank	487.23	8	0.27
49	39	Henry Schroder Wagg	484.32	7	0.27
50	—	Privatbanken A/S	462.00	9	0.26

Source: Euromoney, *Annual Financing Report* (London: Euromoney Publications, Inc., March 1987), pp. 10, 14.

1. Development of a consensus on the future macroenvironment (interest-rate and exchange-rate stability, disequilibria, real-sector shocks, and so on), which could affect markets and products globally or represent sources of covariance in returns and hence systematic risk

2. Surveying of existing cell-based activities in terms of market structure, risk and return, linkage effects, and impact on overall competitive performance, and identification of the product, client, or arena characteristics of each

3. Assessment of the feasibility-set of additional cell-based activities in terms of market structure, risk and return, linkage effects, and prospective impact on overall competitive performance, as well as product, client, or arena characteristics

Table 4–8. Top Twenty Lead and Co-Lead Managers in International Equity Issues.

Rank 1986		Lead Managed			Co-Lead Managed			Total Lead and Co-Lead		
		Amount $m	No. of Issues	Share %	Amount $m	No. of Issues	Share %	Amount $m	No. of Issues	Share %
1	Deutsche Bank	4,002.17	7	34.04	1,321.66	9	11.24	5,323.83	16	45.28
2	Crédit Suisse First Boston	1,603.26	22	13.64	3,649.83	19	31.04	5,253.09	41	44.68
3	Swiss Bank Corp. International	665.15	13	5.66	3,367.91	14	28.65	4,033.06	27	34.30
4	Banque Paribas	135.52	3	1.15	3,069.29	9	26.11	3,204.81	12	27.26
5	Shearson Lehman Bros. International	387.17	9	3.29	2,590.53	9	22.03	2,977.70	18	25.33
6	Salomon Brothers	340.56	6	2.90	2,547.92	8	21.67	2,888.48	14	24.57
7	Dresdner Bank	293.63	1	2.50	2,511.92	6	21.37	2,805.53	7	23.86
8	Mediobanca Banco di Credito Finanziario	0.00	0	0.00	2,427.82	4	20.65	2,427.82	4	20.65
9	Commerzbank AG	0.00	0	0.00	2,425.64	6	20.63	2,425.64	6	20.63
10	Daiwa Securities Co.	0.00	0	0.00	2,212.01	4	18.81	2,212.01	4	19.81
11	ABC Investment & Services	0.00	0	0.00	2,121.61	3	18.05	2,121.61	3	18.05
12	Merrill Lynch Capital Markets	705.22	12	6.00	580.67	6	4.94	1,285.89	18	10.94
13	Morgan Stanley International	552.48	12	4.70	417.90	7	3.55	970.38	19	8.25
14	Nomura Securities	180.58	1	1.54	726.40	6	6.18	906.97	7	7.71
15	Banque Nationale de Paris	566.79	4	4.82	183.48	2	1.56	750.27	6	6.38
16	Enskilda Securities	381.59	2	3.25	352.02	4	2.99	733.61	6	6.24
17	Union Bank of Switzerland	179.90	2	1.53	534.35	6	4.54	714.24	8	6.08
18	Amsterdam Rotterdam Bank (AMRO)	87.02	1	0.74	567.02	3	4.82	654.04	4	5.56
19	Creditanstalt Bankverein	0.00	0	0.00	538.16	3	4.58	538.16	3	4.58
20	Wood Gundy	206.15	2	1.75	327.84	3	2.79	533.98	5	4.54

Source: Euromoney, *Annual Financing Report* (London: Euromoney Publications, Inc., March 1987) p. 60.

Note: The table includes all equity issues placed abroad using a separate international syndicate. Hybrid equity instruments such as stock plus warrant issues and exchangeable preference shares are included. Also included are equity issues targeted at foreign investors but where some equity is placed domestically. In these instances, at least 50 percent of the equity must go abroad. Lead managers receive credit for the amount of equity placed internationally.

Table 4–9. Estimated Swap Transactions (volume, 1986).

	$ Billion
Citibank	
Bankers Trust	
Salomon Brothers[a]	30–45
Morgan Guaranty	
Chase Manhattan	
Chemical Bank	
First Chicago	
Prudential Bache	15–25
First Boston[a]	
BankAmerica	
Security Pacific	
Kleinwort Benson	13–15
Manufacturers Hanover	
Merrill Lynch[a]	
Banque Paribas[a]	
Union Bank of Switzerland	
Nomura[a]	10–12
Swiss Bank Corp. International	
Lloyds	
First Interstate	
Morgan Stanley	
DKB	
Morgan Grenfell	
Drexel Burnham Lambert	4–10

Source: Euromoney, *Annual Financing Report* (London: Euromoney Publications, Inc., March 1987), p. 72.

Note: This table shows Euromoney's educated guess of the volume of swap contracts undertaken by banks as principal for 12 months ending June 30, 1986. It was compiled from information received by canvassing International Swap Dealers Association members and other participants in the swap market. Banks marked with a superscript [a] confirmed their volumes to Euromoney. The figures for banks that would not disclose were estimated after extensive consultations with market sources. Newcomers to watch are Prudential-Bache and Paribas. Among houses that do not act as principals but arrange deals, Goldman Sachs is considered to be the most active. Other leading arrangers include Morgan Stanley and Shearson Lehman. The Japanese houses are catching up in the game after a slow start. Nomura is in the lead but others, including Dai-Ichi Kangyo, are close behind, with Daiwa active in arranging.

Table 4–10. Merger and Acquisition Advisers Ranked by Number of Deals.

Rank by Number of Deals	Company	Total Number of Deals	Number of Deals Cross-Border	Domestic
1 =	First Boston/Crédit Suisse First Boston	145	34	111
1 =	Goldman Sachs[a]	145	26	119
3	Shearson Lehman Brothers	122	22	100
4	Schroder Group	106	39	67
5	Hill Samuel	100	45	55
6	Merrill Lynch	92	22	70
7	Morgan Stanley	91	17	60
8	Kidder Peabody	90	11	79
9	Salomon Brothers	85	12	73
10	Lazard Group[b]	77	17	60
11	Morgan Grenfell & Co.[c]	74	—	74
12	Drexel Burnham Lambert	65	9	56
13	Samuel Montagu	50	18	32
14	S.G. Warburg & Co.	47	17	30
15	Henry Ansbacher	41	6	35
16	Smith Barney, Harris Upham	40	4	36
17 =	Dillon Read & Co.	33	6	27
17 =	Paine Webber	33	2	31
19	N.M. Rothschild & Sons	30	8	22
20	Baring Brothers Halkerston	24	15	9
21 =	Baring Brothers[d]	22	9	13
21 =	Charterhouse Japhet	22	None	22
21 =	Donaldson Lufkin[a]	22	None	22
24	Barclays Merchant Bank	21	None	21
25 =	Hambros Bank	19	None	19
25 =	Kleinwort Benson	19	None	19

Source: Euromoney, February 1987, p. 135.

a. No value of transactions available.

b. Data do not include Lazard Freres, Paris. Undisclosed transactions refer to United Kingdom only.

c. Domestic transactions only. International transactions were not available at the time of publication.

d. Data are for the period January–September 1985.

Table 4–11. Alignment of Competitive and Product Dimensions in International Financial Services.

Financial Services	Competitive Resources						
	A	B	C	D	E	F	G
Funding	1					3	1
Lending	3	3	2				
Financing	3	3	2				2
Credit activities	1	2	2		2	2	
Trading	3	3	3		2		
Brokering	2	2	3	2		1	
Advisory services		3	3		1	2	3
Asset management services		3	3		1	3	1
Underwriting	3	2	2		2	3	3
Distribution			1	3			
Payments activities			3		3		
Insurance services	3	2	2				
International trade services		2	2		2	1	

Key:

A. Adequacy of capital base.
B. Quality of human capital.
C. Information.
D. Placing power.

E. Technology.
F. Innovative capability.
G. Franchise.

3. Principal factor.
2. Important factor.
1. Contributing factor.

4. Breakdown of the relevant product, client, and arena variables into components that identify key competitive factors

5. Development of an inventory of organizational resources and prospective access to incremental resources

6. Identification of strategic options involving possible deepening or broadening of cell activities, acquisitions or divestitures, and their impact on economies of scale and scope, as well as actuarial risk base

7. Identification of resistance lines, cost and risk dimensions associated with each strategic option

Figure 4–2. Performance of British Clearing Banks at Home and Abroad (Pretax Profit or Loss as a Percentage of Average Assets).

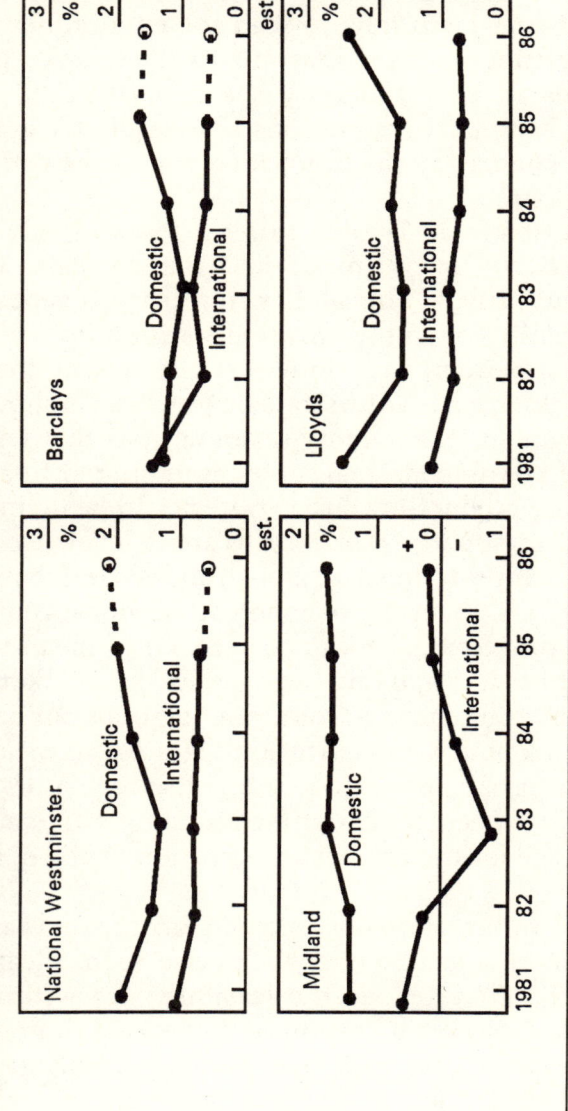

Source: The Economist, March 19, 1987. Copyright 1987, *The Economist,* distributed by Special Features.

8. Selection of optimum strategic path consistent with prospective returns/cost/risk profiles and institutional resource constraints

In order to perform well in developing the strategic process, institutions must first learn how to scan the environment and anticipate competitive changes that are likely to take place, including changes in the regulatory setting. While all such forecasting is probabilistic, institutions that explicitly analyze the possibility of changes in the principal competitive variables will tend to dominate.

Some institutions will be able to react more rapidly than others to competitive opportunities and thereby gain a key advantage over their rivals. This ability to react will depend on the inherent flexibility of an organization's structure.

Finally, it is important that some sort of coherent competitive positioning emerge from the strategic process. As shown in Figure 4–3, there are at least twenty-seven options that fall out of a taxonomy of possible strategies for international financial institutions. At the product level the strategy can be defined as niche, diversified or supermarket; at the arena level it can be defined as national, international, or global; and at the client level it can be defined as focused, segmented, or nonsegmented. Segmentation in this context does not necessarily mean that a financial institution has actively segmented the market, but rather that it supplies products to some client groups but not all.

Across this taxonomy, an institution's strategic positioning and clarity is invariably projected to clients, regulators, and competitors alike. It becomes a significant competitive advantage or disadvantage for the financial institution in the marketplace.

The strategic implications of market distortions and barriers to competition in financial services likewise seem clear (see Chapters 6 and 7). They reduce the feasibility-set within the C-A-P matrix. They place a premium on "windows of opportunity." They increase the importance of horizontal linkages that remain available. And they raise the importance of lobbying

Figure 4–3. Strategic Positioning Options in International Financial Services.

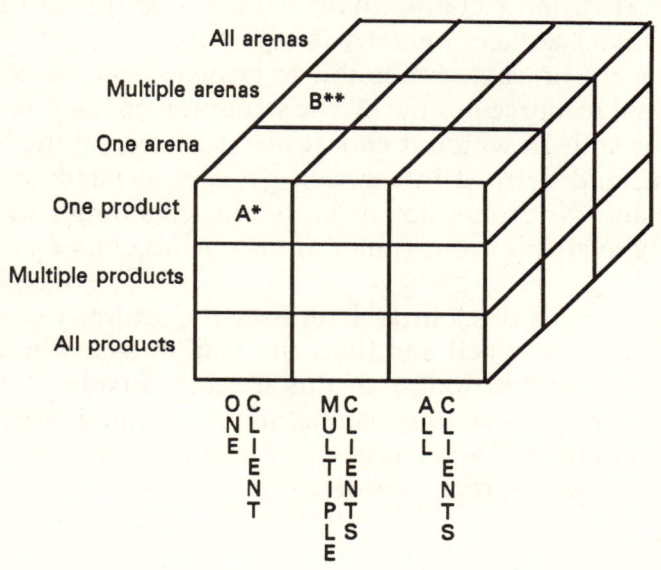

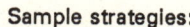

Sample strategies:

Single product
Single arena   } A. Focused national product niche(*)
Single client

Single product
Multiple arenas   } B. Focused international product niche (**)
Single client

Multiple products
Multiple arenas   } C. Segmented international diversified
Multiple clients

All products
Single arena   } D. Segmented national supermarket
Multiple clients

All products
All arenas   } E. Global supermarket
All clients

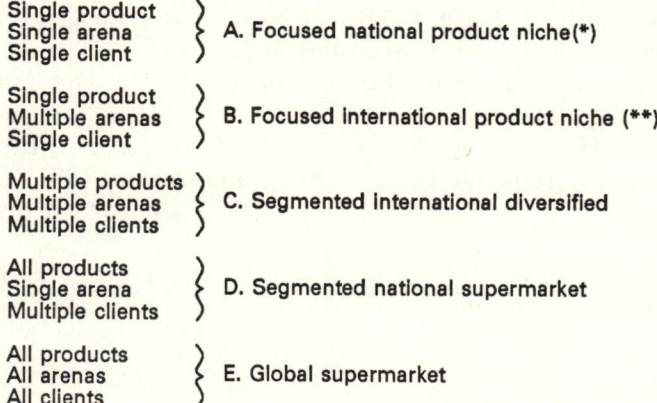

activity to open up markets where cells having potentially attractive returns are blocked or restricted, and to keep them that way when barriers to competition are the *source* of such returns.

101

SUMMARY

An institution's competitive performance in the international financial services industry is a function of (1) the competitive power the organization is able to bring to bear, based on its institutional resource profile, (2) the structural characteristics of the various cells in which it chooses to compete, (3) the lateral, horizontal, and vertical integration gains associated with cell linkages, and (4) economies of scale and economies of scope potentially available from transactions within cells and across cells.

These dimensions jointly determine the returns that can be extracted from each cell and from the market as a whole. The goals of strategic positioning in this industry involve correctly assessing each of these dimensions, including the institution's relative strengths and weaknesses, and to then create and project an unambiguous strategic profile.

NOTES

1. Nathaniel C. Nash, "Treasury Now Favors the Creation of Huge Banks," *The New York Times*, June 7, 1987.
2. Wilfried Guth, "Bank Strategy in the 1980s," *The Banker*, April 1986.
3. John H. Dunning, *International Production and the Multinational Enterprise*, (London: Allen and Unwin, 1981).

5

INTERNATIONAL TRADE IN FINANCIAL SERVICES

Having surveyed the nature of financial services as a global industry in terms of market characteristics, sources of institutional competitive power, and strategic imperatives, we can now turn the discussion to the level of the countries in which the various players are home-based or in which they operate outside their home environments.

We have defined trade in financial services in terms of *value added* created using the factors of production of one country and then sold to residents of another country. By this definition, trade in the financial services industry is extraordinarily difficult to measure. International lending activity, for example, is a very poor proxy for value added, even more so as international capital flows have become heavily securitized. Moreover, most types of internationally traded financial services have nothing whatsoever to do with cross-border lending—for example, mergers and acquisitions deals done in Europe by U.S. investment banks, structuring international cash management systems by U.S. commercial banks for foreign based multinational corporate clients, or developing a local-currency lending business in the United States by a major British bank.

CHARACTERISTICS OF TRADE IN FINANCIAL SERVICES

International trade in services differs from international trade in goods in terms of the linkages that exist between the producer and the consumer, or user, of the product. In merchandise trade, goods are manufactured in one country and marketed in another, either through independent, arm's length business relationships or through local agents or affiliates of the manufacturer. In trade in services, either the consumer has to be physically transported to the product (as in tourism) or the service has to be taken to the consumer via direct contact, which often entails the supplier's establishing its presence in the importing country. To a lesser degree this also occurs in trade in manufactures through foreign direct investment, especially where product, process, management and marketing know-how, as well as after-sales service, are important characteristics of the product that is being bought and sold. But the direct connection remains much more important in the case of services. In the absence of foreign direct investment and the establishment abroad of branches or other types of affiliates, widespread international trade in financial services, would be virtually unthinkable.

It has been argued that trade in services and trade in goods are not nearly as distinct as is usually assumed.[1] Instead, a great deal of trade in goods involves the simultaneous international delivery of postproduction services: marketing and distribution, warehousing, repair, and maintenance, for example. Difficulties in supplying these services increase with physical, economic and cultural distance (interaction costs) and may well impair trade in the associated goods as well. Barriers to access to national markets for postproduction services may therefore act to inhibit trade in goods as well wherever there are elements of simultaneity.

A loan by a London-based bank to a private borrower in Malaysia clearly fits the definition of a financial service produced by residents of one country and sold to residents of another. But without some physical presence in the importing country to provide contact with the customer and facilitate credit evaluation, such a transaction—while not impossible—would be extraordinarily difficult or would have to be handled through participation in a loan syndication. Even then the lead manager(s) would have to have close contact with the borrower. Similarly, confirmation of an export letter of credit by a New York bank requires little more than a correspondent relationship with a bank in the importing country.

Arm's length transactions among institutions in the provision of financial services are certainly not the most profitable. Much more common are transactions that require some form of foreign direct investment in order to work, ranging from a low-level presence, such as a representative office, through successively higher levels of involvement in the form of agencies, subsidiaries, consortiums, joint ventures, and full branches in the host country. The more complex and sophisticated the financial product, the greater tends to be the importance of such investment. (See Table 2–6.)

APPLICATION OF TRADE THEORY

Most of the theoretical underpinnings of international trade find application in the financial services sector. In particular, the technical attributes of the industry and the determinants of competitive performance discussed in Chapter 4 can be more or less readily linked to most of the traditional (as well as nontraditional) theories of international trade.

The classical concepts of trade attributed to Adam Smith, John Stuart Mill, and David Ricardo, for example, emphasize international differences in production functions (the linkage between productive inputs and outputs), and this certainly applies in the case of financial services. The fact is that production technology in the financial services sector is not uniform worldwide, and this gives institutions in some countries a competitive edge over those home-based in others in the Ricardian view of what drives international trade.

Eli Heckscher, Bertil Ohlin, and Paul Samuelson later emphasized the differences between countries in the availability and cost of productive factors, clearly an important determinant of trade in financial services as well, particularly with respect to (correctly defined) physical and human capital.

Both in the Ricardian and Heckscher-Ohlin-Samuelson views, traditional theory of international trade, as applied to goods, starts from the supposition that there exist human or physical resources or characteristics at the national level that are not themselves mobile between countries. This is what gives countries a comparative advantage in the production of certain goods and a comparative disadvantage in others. In the case of financial services what is really exported consists principally of embodied knowledge and skilled labor.

This is true whether these services are provided directly from the institution's home country or indirectly through an affiliate or other presence abroad. The home country's resources go into the development of the knowledge and skilled labor upon which the provision of these services is based, and which in turn are embodied in the "firm-specific" advantages that form the basis of their competitiveness in national as well as international markets.[2] So Britain and the United States would be expected to be home base for powerful competitors in world markets for financial services, but Bangladesh and Paraguay would not.

Beyond the applicability of the traditional ideas of what determines international trade, there are also the "technology gap" and "product cycle" schools of thought. Both trace international competitiveness at the industry and product level to long-term and short-term leads and lags among countries in the development of new processes and (more particularly) products. Both views are again applicable to the financial services industry. The underlying (often temporary) technology gaps may be the result of differences in domestic market characteristics and size, as well as national patterns of investment in human resources and research.

Even some of the less orthodox views of international trade, such as that of the Swedish economist Staffan Burenstam Linder, who focuses on intercountry demand similarities, can be helpful in explaining the worldwide competitive thrust of major contestants in financial services. It is certainly clear that there is substantial intraindustry trade in financial services (for example, U.K. banks active in the United States and American Banks banks active in the United Kingdom), which points to the importance of qualitative product or service differentiation and the significance of demand-related factors that must be taken into consideration alongside the traditional supply-related determinants of international trade.

Some countries have certainly carved out profitable niches in the international financial services business based on some rather unusual sources of sectoral competitive advantage. One such example is Luxembourg. Traditionally a banking center for tax and regulatory reasons (especially for the large German universal banks), Luxembourg has increasingly positioned itself as a secrecy haven at a time when intensified pressure emanating from insider trading cases and political scandals has called into question the durability of Swiss banking confidentiality.[3] Laws passed by the Luxembourg parliament in 1981 and 1984 strengthened already rigorous secrecy provisions. As was traditionally the case in Switzerland, confidentiality cannot be cracked unless a crime is alleged that is also a crime in Luxembourg. Self-enforcement of banking standards is the rule, with limited external regulation. There is no tax on interest, capital gains, or dividends.

As of the end of 1986, banks in Luxembourg (population 360,000) had booked a total of $160 billion in assets, with over 120 foreign banks present. The nonmultinational character of domestic banks positioned them to resist pressure on confidentiality from foreign authorities, unlike the Swiss banking system, which is dominated by three large and global players. Tight financial secrecy is explicitly viewed as an export product, creating income and jobs (about 10 percent of the labor force) in a small country that has few alternatives and providing the basis for diversification into a broad range of other financial services. As one observer noted, "the 1000 year old Grand Duchy has become a thriving free enterprise zone on a continent that, so often, seems to be sinking into a morass of taxation and regulation that stifles enterprise."[4]

More generally, in the first systematic attempt to apply modern trade theory to the financial services sector, Sagari[5] tested the Heckscher-Ohlin model on international patterns of bank lending, and found that skilled labor is indeed a statistically signficant determinant of competitive advantage, while endowments of arable land appear to be significantly associated with competitive disadvantage in this sector.

X-EFFICIENCY AND DYNAMIC GAINS

The classic argument for liberal international trade, derived from traditional trade theories, is that it will promote maximum allocative efficiency in the global output of goods and services by shifting production among countries according to comparative cost advantage. The conventional argument, however, is limited by the assumptions inherent in the static models on which it is usually based, and which may understate the damage that can be caused by the imposition of trade-distorting measures.

International trade also tends to benefit global production by inducing industries continually to minimize the use of inputs in production—that is, to maximize the attainment of "X-efficiency." It forces producers constantly to minimize the costs of inputs (labor, capital, and intermediate goods and services) in order to stay in business, and it limits the ability of players in the market to obtain excess profit margins over long periods.

It also stimulates the introduction of new products and processes. It may result in "positive externalities" in the pattern of the allocation of resources and of efficiency outside the financial services industry itself. And, in a world characterized by rapid changes in technologies and patterns of demand, it prevents locking resources into existing economic structures and thus accelerates a country's economic growth. Such aspects may be especially important in an industry as rapidly evolving and dependent on sensitive and timely adjustment to changing circumstances as the financial services sector.[6]

TRADE VERSUS INTERNATIONAL
FACTOR MOVEMENTS

International trade in the classic sense thus promotes global efficiency because inputs into the production process are available in different countries at different opportunity costs. By comparison with manufacturing, these inputs in financial services are more likely to be proprietary in nature and to consist, moreover, of product-related and process-related technologies and industry-specific human capital (see Chapter 4).

In fact, a country can obtain gains from improved allocation of the factors of production *either* through trade *or* through international movements of the factors themselves. Thus, international factor mobility and transfers of technology are to a significant extent substitutes for trade.

Grubel[7] has argued that international trade in services cannot be compared with international trade in goods. Instead, what is commonly termed trade in services is really international movements of labor and capital on the part of suppliers of the services, or movement of people to the services-production sites in another country (tourism). However, services can be embodied in goods, which then enter directly into the channels of international trade. Grubel concludes that traditional efforts to liberalize goods trade are sufficient to bring about an optimal pattern of international resource allocation along the lines of comparative advantage, and that there is no need whatsoever to negotiate about trade liberalization in services. Instead, he argues, it is the right of establishment and the ability to move factors of production internationally that is the focus of discussions about "trade" in services.

To the extent that establishment of a commercial presence is necessary in order for a foreign based firm to supply residents with a service, Grubel has a point. Returns to the home country come in the form of returns to labor and capital. Liberalization is thus broadly equivalent to achieving the right to a commercial presence equivalent to that afforded local firms. But some financial services (such as securities underwriting and advice on mergers and acquisitions) may be supplied by a foreign based firm even in the absence of a commercial presence in the country of the client. There are a number of examples in this category that do not fit either the factor-transfer view or the embodiment-in-goods view.

It is well established in the literature that proprietary inputs tend to be most efficiently introduced into a foreign country by multinational enterprises, which can be viewed as having proprietary control over factors of production that are internationally mobile.[8] The establishment by a multinational enterprise of a production affiliate abroad is responsive to the internal availability of such mobile factors, as well as to access to a global information network and client contacts, because it must overcome the costs of being foreign in competition with indigenous firms in an alien business environment. Multinational enterprises achieve a maximum contribution to the global private allocation of resources when their mobile proprietary assets are located among countries and combined with local factors of production in such a way that the firms maximize the present value of their shareholders' equity.

If international trade and foreign direct investment serve similar purposes in improving efficiency in the allocation of resources globally, as well as generating dynamic economic gains, then measures that inhibit the establishment and operation of affiliates of multinational enterprises in other countries must work in the opposite direction.

Consider a situation in which the advantages of serving a foreign market through foreign direct investment or exports are identical. The multinational enterprise will choose the least restricted approach to serving that market and, hence, impediments to investment and impediments to trade are seen as close substitutes. For any given advantage of exporting from the home country over serving foreign markets through direct investment under conditions of free trade, there exists some barrier to trade (not necessarily a prohibitive one) that will persuade the firm to choose the direct investment option instead. Rival host-country firms will be made more efficient, however, by their exposure to foreign competition and the foreign availability of proprietary inputs, no matter which way the multinational enterprise chooses to compete in the market in question.

We have emphasized that there is a natural predisposition in the financial services industry to serve foreign markets by foreign direct investment rather than by seeking to provide services from the firm's home base. Thus, the parallel between conventional barriers to trade and controls over the establishment and operation of local banking offices on the part of host-country authorities must be explicitly recognized. The presumption is that international trade in financial services, involving the creation of value by productive factors home-based in one country and its utilization by a client in another, is unusually hindered by difficulties involving establishment and operation of foreign affiliates.

THE ROLE OF COMPETITIVE DISTORTIONS

In banking and other financial services, it is the presence of controls over the establishment and operation of foreign affiliates that will, in large measure, determine the degree to which effective access to a national market is open to foreign competition, and the resulting static and dynamic benefits to the national economies of both the home and host countries. And, because financial institutions provide a broad range of services (particularly in an advanced economy), it is possible that such controls can have quite selective effects, protecting certain domestic financial institutions at the expense of other players in the national economy by distorting market conditions.

With respect to national regulatory and supervisory measures, some form of "national treatment" is broadly equivalent to free trade in financial services, and discriminatory controls over the establishment and operation of foreign affiliates are broadly equivalent to protection. In this context, it is important to recall that most-favored-nation (MFN) treatment still governs much of international trade as a cornerstone of the General Agreement on Tariffs and Trade (GATT), but there is no comparable acceptance of nondiscrimination in foreign direct investment and the right of establishment among foreign firms by country of origin.

SUMMARY

It would appear that the theory of international production and trade can be directly applied to the financial services sector. Most of the major trade theories, ranging from the Ricardian

111

model and the Heckscher-Ohlin view to the more modern theories related to the multinational firm and product cycles, find application in this industry. Product differentiation will tend to produce intraindustry trade, with individual countries both importing and exporting financial services. It is largely the need for a direct presence in the target market that distinguishes trade in the financial services sector from trade in most other industries—although even here the difference is more a matter of degree than a matter of kind. The difference is important, nonetheless, because trade distortions in financial services do not take the form of border charges or qualitative trade controls, but rather restrictions in the ability of firms to operate on the ground in the target market itself.

NOTES

1. Seev Hirsch, "Services and Service Intensity in International Trade." Trade Policy Research Centre, London; 1987 Mimeo.
2. John H. Dunning, "Explaining Changing Patterns of International Production: In Defense of the Eclectic Theory," *Oxford Bulletin of Economics and Statistics* 41 (November 1979): 269–95.
3. Ingo Walter, ed., *Deregulating Wall Street* (New York: John Wiley & Sons, 1985).
4. Edwin A. Finn, Jr., and Tatiana Pouchine, "Luxembourg: Color It Green," *Forbes*, April 20, 1987, p. 49.
5. Sylvia B. Sagari, *The Financial Services Industry: An International Perspective.* Doctoral dissertation, Graduate School of Business Administration, New York University, New York, 1986.
6. J.M. Letiche, "Dependent Monetary Systems and Economic Development," in W. Sellekaerts (ed.), *Economic Development and Planning* (London: MacMillan, 1974).
7. Herbert G. Grubel, "There Is No Direct International Trade in Services," *American Economic Review*, Papers and Proceedings, (March 1987).
8. Peter Buckley and Mark Casson, *The Future of the Multinational Enterprise* (New York: Holmes & Meier, 1984).

6

THE POLITICAL ECONOMY OF PROTECTION IN FINANCIAL SERVICES

Applying the principles of international commercial policy involves two sets of questions. First, what is the nature of the political economy of protection in the financial services sector? Second, what kinds of competitive distortions are applied, and how do they influence sectoral patterns of trade, production, competitive structure, and the strategies of financial institutions? The first issue will be taken up here, the second in Chapter 7.

POLICYMAKING AND PERCEPTIONS OF THE NATIONAL INTEREST

Based on patterns of international comparative advantage bearing on the financial services industry, perceptions of national interest should be reflected in trade policy debates as they relate to the financial services sector. First, it would be expected that countries with an international comparative advantage in banking and other financial services would generally tend to apply the principle of "national treatment" of foreign firms in their domestic financial markets and, at the same time, press for the opening of foreign markets to their own firms (possibly using leverage through reciprocity provisions). The same firms would be expected to lobby hard for such a policy stance. For them, it is simply a matter of broadly defined reciprocity in international trade relations—to insist on market access for an export in which they have a comparative advantage in return for domestic market access for goods or services in which they have a comparative disadvantage.

Conversely, it would be expected that countries with a comparative *disadvantage* in this sector may be disposed to take a highly protectionist view, particularly if successfully influenced by protection-seeking lobbying pressures from import-competing firms. Many developing countries would be expected to be in the latter category, even though the national interest (as opposed to sectional interest) might argue for a different policy stance.

As countries develop, and as their international comparative advantage profiles change, a corresponding evolution would be expected in their attitudes toward liberal trade versus protection in banking and financial services. They should increasingly perceive the real economic costs of competitive distortions in this particular sector, costs in the allocation of resources and in terms of economic growth.

Terms-of-trade arguments for protection raised as a matter of national interest say that restrictions on competition in financial services may improve the terms under which those services can be purchased from abroad. As Chapter 7 shows, the evidence seems to be that this argument backfires (because of the quota-like nature of many of the distortions in this sector) and that protection in the financial services industry can actually worsen a country's terms of trade.

The economic policy rationale for protection in the national interest is that prudential and regulatory objectives may be undermined by the presence of financial institutions based abroad.[1] Besides the problems of monetary control, they may be thought to impede the effectiveness of government policies aimed at economic development by virtue of their size, their externally developed business goals and the possibly dominant role they may play in a country's international transactions.

Strategies and policies of foreign based institutions may be thought to reflect conditions at the firm's head office (or the dictates of the home government) rather than those of the host country. There may indeed be a certain element of realism in this line of reasoning, but the costs of protectionist responses, in terms of static and dynamic efficiency, are very high indeed.

114

However valid such national-interest arguments for control over foreign banks and other financial services firms may be for a developing country, their applicability in developed countries is markedly less. Foreign based financial institutions are unlikely to represent a serious challenge to national economic policy-making because, even in the absence of discriminatory measures, they are not likely to control a dominant share of national financial markets. Local financial institutions in developed countries should be much better able to compete with foreign firms even in the face of imported innovations. And techniques of central banking, supervision and control, as well as antitrust policy, are likely to be much more effective. Hence, in developed countries, the losses in efficiency associated with restrictions on competition from foreign based financial institutions are far more difficult to justify in terms of any compensating gains.

RENT-SEEKING BEHAVIOR

The political economy of protection has been extensively developed in the literature.[2] Several models have been suggested, most of which involve rent-seeking behavior on the part of market participants. Firms, labor unions, and other groups find that it makes more sense to devote substantial resources to lobbying for government protection than it does to devote comparable resources to adapting to changes in the marketplace.[3] In essence, the expected risk-adjusted net present value of returns from lobbying, at the margin, is deemed to be higher than comparable returns from affirmative adjustment and redeployment of productive resources.

Lobbying takes the case out of the economic marketplace and into the political marketplace, where those seeking protection are exposed to counterarguments by other groups (such as consumers and exporters fearing foreign retaliation) under established political rules of the game. In the financial services industry, the typical argument is that the country is already "overbanked," and needs no additional players.

115

ARGUMENTS FOR PROTECTION

Protectionist interests seek to bolster their argumentation in several ways.

First, they can argue that the activities to be protected have significant external benefits for the national economy or society. The national defense argument is typical of this reasoning, basically designed to keep up uneconomic levels of output as insurance against a future political or military eventuality. High-technology industries, agriculture, and import-sensitive industries employing large numbers of low-skilled, disadvantaged labor are among those interests frequently making use of this argument.

Protectionists can use the adjustment-equity argument. Few people can challenge the notion that economic adjustment creates costs that, barring government intervention, those directly affected are forced to pay. At the same time, society as a whole obtains significant static and dynamic gains from economic adjustment. This asymmetry in costs and benefits can be related to political norms of equity, or fairness, to make the case that some of the gains should be siphoned-off through taxation and allocated to support those who are injured. Many find considerable social justice in this argument. Its problems lie in the difficulty of implementing temporary protection or subsidization in such a way as to promote rather than retard structural adjustment, and to avoid robbing people of the incentive to adjust to new competitive realities (the "moral hazard" argument in this context).

Third, protectionists can use the "infant industry" argument that free trade will, by exposing it to world-class competition prematurely, prevent an industry that is fully capable of eventually competing internationally without government help from ever reaching that stage of development.

Fourth, the argument may be raised that the real world is far from the perfectly competitive market—that there are economies of scale and economies of scope involved that require a certain firm size in order to attain their full potential.[4] This, it is argued, can be achieved only through government assistance and perhaps some form of "industrial targeting" to maximize the gains from international trade and production obtained by the nation.

All of these arguments in support of basic rent-seeking interests at the sectoral level must then be marshaled and transformed into political influence. Economic interests, in other words, must be translated into political power. This depends on the ability of an industry to claim that it is in some way "critical," and it depends on the level of employment and the availability of alternative opportunities for those employed at present, the degree of regional concentration of the industry, and the ability to form political coalitions with other interest-groups.

Finally, if protectionist interests seem unlikely to survive such argumentation and political counterpressures in open "high road" debate, they may have access to "low road" protection through administrative measures such as discriminatory health and safety requirements, government procurement, licensing and other forms of quantitative controls, and similar nontariff barriers to market access.[5]

PROTECTIONIST PRESSURE IN FINANCIAL SERVICES

How do these political arguments relate to protectionism in the financial services industry? It is clear that the normal rent-seeking drive for protectionism applies here. Financial services firms are highly sensitive to competition in various dimensions of their activities where natural entry barriers are limited. This is probably truer in the wholesale and capital markets end of the business than it is on the retail side (dependent on a large number of outlets), although even here there is ample scope for entry by foreign players. Market penetration by foreign based competitors thus threatens to erode indigenous players' returns and raises the classic set of rent-seeking motivations.

Given the economic interests involved, it can be argued that banks and other financial institutions are in an excellent position to convert them into political power. They are often exceedingly well connected politically, and their lobbying power can be awesome on critical issues. In some cases the financial institutions themselves are government-owned and may thus have direct access to the levers of protection. They can form powerful coalitions by engaging their clients at both the wholesale and retail levels on their behalf.

Moreover, protection in financial services is likely to come through the regulatory process, and to the extent that financial institutions have co-opted the regulators to their mutual benefit, access to the vehicles of protection is facilitated.

Besides applying entry and operating restrictions to foreign based players, regulators may tolerate a certain amount of anticompetitive, cartel-like behavior on the part of domestic institutions. Foreign players that become troublesome may be stepped on by concerted action on the part of domestic institutions, and the competitive consequences conveniently overlooked by the authorities.

Strength of access to the political process on the part of banks and other firms engaged in the financial services industry can be seen in the United States. Legislation affecting banking and finance is rarely very interesting politically, so that institutions directly governed by legislation have often been able to achieve extraordinary influence. This helps to account for the slowness with which barriers to interstate banking have come down (resisted by regional and local banks, which have often formed into politically powerful state bankers' associations) as well as the reassessment of the division between commercial and investment banking created by the Glass-Steagall provisions of the Banking Act of 1933 (resisted by the investment banks, in part through politically astute lobbying by the Securities Industry Association).

In 1984, when the U.S. Treasury attempted to institute a partial withholding tax on savings deposit interest, the banks mounted a fierce letter-writing campaign—sometimes misrepresenting the action as an *increase* in taxation—and got the move repealed in record time. Such access is of substantial value in protectionist actions, of course. In 1987, Rep. Charles Schumer of New York, who has usually reflected the views of the

Securities Industry Association and has led the battle to retain the Glass-Steagall legislation, sponsored a bill in the House of Representatives that would have denied primary U.S. government bond dealer status to firms from countries that do not accord U.S. securities firms equal access. Similar bills sponsored by Sen. William Proxmire and Rep. Don Riegle would give the president sweeping powers to apply strong reciprocity sanctions against foreign based institutions' access to U.S. financial markets.

It is also important to note that a substantial share of financial services is sold to *producers* of goods and services in the national economy, rather than to ultimate *consumers*. Shielding from import competition, therefore, has a high "effective protection" content. That is, protection of financial institutions raises costs to large numbers of firms in other industries that are themselves exposed to international competition and therefore erodes their competitive performance. Interests indirectly affected in this manner can be expected to resist protectionism in the financial services sector, alongside consumers whose welfare is directly affected through high credit costs, low deposit rates, and the excessive cost and inferior quality of other financial services.

In their efforts to marshal these various arguments and appeals to the national interest, protectionist financial institutions would seem to be on very much weaker grounds than many manufacturing firms. First, they cannot argue convincingly that there will be significant job losses and adjustment costs as a result of market penetration by foreign financial institutions, since these will tend to absorb roughly the same number of employees with roughly the same skill content. Indeed, it is possible (even likely) that participation by foreign firms could lead to a significant expansion of activity and employment *gains* in the domestic financial services sector.

Financial institutions may be able to use the externalities and infant-industry arguments in support of their cause. As an integral part of the national payments system, the banking and financial services industry is a source of significant external benefits for society at large. The same is true of its safekeeping function, its role in financial intermediation, and its role as a "transmission belt" for monetary policy. It is therefore often argued that financial services represent a public good whose private costs and returns do not accurately reflect the social costs and returns. How would people in small villages have access to such services without bank branches, which are inherently unprofitable?

Whether financial institutions are domestically owned or foreign owned, economists would argue, has nothing to do with any of these issues. Nondiscriminatory regulation can assure that financial institutions continue to generate the full range of external benefits in most cases. In problem cases, such as rural bank branches, targeted government subsidies can take care of maintaining external benefits, perhaps better than cross-subsidization by protected domestic financial institutions. In short, the public-good characteristics of the industry can be maintained, while at the same time achieving the static and dynamic gains associated with increased competition.

The infant-industry argument may be more difficult to deal with in a political context. On the one hand, domestic financial institutions are never really "infants" in the classic sense, since all countries have had them for decades. (In many developing countries they have arisen from colonial institutions.) On the other hand, since many dimensions of the financial services industry are today knowledge-intensive and technology-intensive, with economies of scale and economies of scope also giving a competitive edge in certain areas, it is possible, even likely, that domestic financial institutions in many countries are economically "retarded" rather than infantile and would indeed have a difficult time competing with outsiders capable of importing know-how at very low marginal cost.

Yet retarded financial sectors can have a severely adverse impact on the process of economic development by supplying substandard channels of savings into investment, inefficient payments mechanisms, and high transactions costs, thus discouraging economic activity and possibly encouraging capital flight. Competition from foreign based financial institutions, perhaps in partnership with local interests and using primarily local human resources, can invigorate such institutions and promote large potential allocational and dynamic gains for the economy as a whole.

Such argumentation notwithstanding, the infant-industry case remains a powerful force in the political context, especially when combined with the assertion that inroads by foreign based institutions would somehow lead to an erosion of national sovereignty. Countries like Singapore, which now has some of the most sophisticated banks in Asia, continue to restrict the onshore business of foreign banks in order to shield 25-year-old "infants."

SUMMARY

The underlying factors determining international competitive advantage or disadvantage in the financial services sector, described in Chapter 5, are one basis for revealed protectionist behavior in the form of nationally imposed competitive distortions bearing on foreign based institutions. A second is prudential and regulatory considerations, and a third is political definitions of sovereignty. The final basis, which stems directly from the model developed in Chapter 2, is rent-seeking behavior on the part of financial institutions themselves, seeking to bolster the excess returns derived from cells in the client-arena-product matrix through political or administrative action.

It should also be clear that domestic protectionist interests will tend to be joined by foreign financial institutions that have previously secured the ability to compete locally and now want to shield the excess returns obtained in this way from incursions by new foreign based entrants. And it should be apparent that domestic financial institutions based in a protected domestic environment will tend to have serious difficulties in performing well in highly competitive environments in other countries or in the offshore markets.

NOTES

1. Anthony Saunders and Ingo Walter, "International Trade in Financial Services: Are Bank Services Special?" paper presented at a Symposium on New Institutional Arrangements for the World Economy, University of Konstanz, July 1-3, 1987. Mimeo.
2. Robert E. Baldwin, *The Political Economy of Postwar U.S. Trade Policy* (New York: Salomon Brothers Center for the Study of Financial Institutions, New York University, 1976).
3. W.A. Brock and S.P. Magee, "The Economics of Special Interest Politics: The Case of the Tariff," *The American Economic Review* 68 (April 1978); 246–49.
4. Thomas N. Pugel and Ingo Walter, "U.S. Corporate Interests and the Political Economy of Trade Policy," *Review of Economics and Statistics* 67 (August 1985); 465–73.
5. J.M. Finger, H.K. Hall, and D.R. Nelson, "The Political Economy of Administered Protection," *The American Economic Review* 72 (June 1982); 452–66.

7

DISTORTIONS OF INTERNATIONAL COMPETITION

Controls over the operations of foreign firms in financial services affect either their entry into the national market or their freedom of operation. Both are of concern only if the treatment discriminates according to the home base of the parent organization.

Previous studies by the U.S. Treasury, OECD, and Walter have undertaken extensive surveys of the restrictions that are imposed on foreign based banks and other firms in the financial services industry,[1] and data on specific barriers have been updated periodically by the office of the U.S. Special Trade Representative and its counterparts in other governments as part of a program of submissions to the secretariat of the General Agreement on Tariffs and Trade. Unlike tariffs and other barriers that impede trade in merchandise, those affecting the international delivery of financial services tend to change continually, making inventories of such barriers obsolete very quickly. This, combined with extraordinary difficulties in measuring the restrictive effects of barriers on value added in financial services, has made empirical research in this area virtually nonexistent.

There are basically two types of barriers to market penetration in the financial services sector: entry barriers and operating barriers. Both types operate to a large extent as *paraquantitative* restrictions to markets by limiting access to all or certain segments of the market, although some act as *paratariffs* by making market access more costly than it would otherwise be. The following sections briefly describe the impact of the two types of barriers to international trade in financial services and then link them to the client-arena-product matrix introduced in Chapter 3.

BARRIERS TO ENTRY

Entry barriers act to inhibit foreign based firms in the financial services industry from servicing the needs of domestic clients. They range from complete embargo (including denial of visas to foreign bankers) and limiting foreign presence to representative offices only (with no banking powers), to restrictions on the forms a foreign presence can take and limits on foreign equity positions in local financial institutions.

Global Versus Selective Entry Barriers

As with other quantitative restrictions of international trade, entry barriers can be either *global* or *selective*. Global measures apply equally to all foreign based institutions, while selective measures apply differently depending on the specific foreign institution involved or its home country. Global entry barriers may prohibit a foreign presence entirely (embargo), or limit foreign presence to certain forms of involvement in the domestic financial system *ab initio*.

Selective measures may permit differential entry for institutions from different home countries, based on considerations of banking reciprocity or general reciprocity in bilateral trade relations. They may also allow entry by institutions singled out on the basis of desirability, with criteria such as past or potential future contributions to the development of the national financial system.

It is sometimes difficult to determine whether the administration of entry barriers is indeed global or selective. A case in point is Australia's decision in 1985 to permit for the first time liberal foreign bank entry. A total of sixteen banks were selected from an extensive list of applicants, based on composite criteria combining reciprocity considerations and assessed potential contributions on the part of individual applicants. While nominally discriminatory, the selection process appears to have been carried out in a substantially open manner, giving it some of the characteristics of a global quota.

As things developed, however, the Australian market at least initially did not quite live up to the hopes of the foreign bankers. First, the Australian economy and its currency went into a serious decline, limiting profitable banking opportunities. Second, the competition emanating from the Australian banks was considerably more vigorous than expected, narrowing margins and market opportunities. Third, the number of foreign banks admitted was much larger than many of the sixteen successful applicants had expected, further increasing competitive pressure. Fourth, deregulation stiffened competition for corporate clients from the 150-odd merchant banks operating in Australia, about 60 of which had entered the business since deregulation. The result was wholesale scaling down of growth objectives and retargeting of business strategies under tight cost controls, although few showed any inclination to disengage. At the end of 1986, foreign banks had captured about 10 percent of the total assets of the Australian banking system.

The new banks were restricted more heavily than domestic banks in terms of the overall size of their loan assets—to fifteen times capital—and banking regulations required high reserves to be maintained at the central bank earning low interest.

Of the sixteen foreign banks offered licenses, all except J.P. Morgan began operations in 1985. Morgan continued to operate as a merchant bank, which involves far fewer restrictions but does not provide funding recourse to the Reserve Bank of Australia. As of 1987, Bankers Trust was the most profitable entrant, having avoided the highly competitive retail sector and limited itself to the merchant banking business. Citicorp was likewise profitable, yet undertook some retrenchment of its retail presence. National Westminster and the Royal Bank of Canada chalked up significant losses. Most of the others were marginally profitable or made small losses. Many engaged in cost-cutting or closed unprofitable facilities. BankAmerica's joint venture with Australia's largest retailer appeared to be coming apart, as did Chase Manhattan's joint venture with the largest life insurance company.

New Zealand followed Australia's lead in liberalizing foreign participation in its financial system. In 1986 eight new foreign banks were registered by the Reserve Bank of New Zealand, including Barclays, Citibank, the Hong Kong and Shanghai Banking Corporation, Indosuez, and several Australian banks, bringing the total of foreign based players to twelve. The intent was to increase competition in the New Zealand banking system in both the wholesale and the retail markets. No limit was set on the number of foreign based institutions that would be permitted to operate. Uniform requirements included a minimum capitalization level, banking expertise, and deposit-taking ability. Deregulation also applied to nonbanks, which could undertake most banking functions except check issuance, and trust banks as well as building societies were also expected to be allowed into the banking business.

Selectivity in entry into domestic financial services markets is heavily based on reciprocity considerations. Domestic financial institutions, in developed countries as well as developing countries, usually find it necessary or desirable to establish a presence abroad. This may involve foreign countries with intensive trade, investment, or migration links, locations of major significance for foreign-currency funding requirements, or a representation in the important financial centers of the world. Domestic institutions thus face an inherent conflict between their interest in accessing foreign markets for financial services and their desire to keep foreign based players out of domestic markets. This assessment, and the domestic lobbying activity that results, obviously depends on the stakes involved in each case, as well as the probability that the foreign government will demand reciprocity (and that its own institutitons will lobby for it).

Some cases in point are the more or less explicit linkage of foreign banking entry into Brazil with the interests of Brazilian institutions in expanding abroad, and the highly selective linkages between the opening of various parts of Japan's financial system to outside competitors and the growing activities of Japanese financial institutions in Europe and the United States.

In the past, British regulators generally opposed the acquisition of U.K. financial institutions by foreign interests. This was exemplified by the Bank of England's rejection of the Hong Kong and Shanghai Bank's bid to acquire the Royal Bank of Scotland in 1981 and, after it acquired Anthony Gibbs (a small British merchant bank), forcing that institution to resign from the Accepting Houses Committee, the regulatory and trade association for merchant banks. The Bank of England's "fit and proper" standards for evaluating institutions permitted to operate in British financial markets thus served as a vehicle for keeping undesirable foreigners out.

That a restrictive posture of this type was inconsistent with the role of London as the premier financial center in Europe became apparent during the 1980s and coincided with the Thatcher government's favorable attitude toward market-driven development of the financial services sector in Britain. Deregulation culminating in the "Big Bang" of 1986 brought acquisitions of British merchant banks and brokers by outsiders such as Citicorp (Vickers da Costa), and National Australia Bank (Clydesdale Bank). Other foreign institutions making acquisitions included Chase Manhattan, Crédit Suisse, Swiss Bank Corporation, Hong Kong and Shanghai Bank, and Security Pacific. Significant foreign holdings developed in firms such as Hambros, Guinness Peat, Morgan Grenfell, Standard Chartered, Midland Bank, S.G. Warburg Group, and Henry Ansbacher Holdings.

Besides the need to maintain a relatively open competitive environment, there was the question of where traditional U.K. firms would fit in an emerging world of very large and global financial institutions—where Morgan Grenfell's 1986 asset total of $9.73 billion compared with Nomura's $237 billion.[2]

Japan has been perhaps the most attractive among the various banking arenas from the perspective of foreign based players. Driven by an extraordinarily high savings rate, Japanese investments in foreign securities rose from $4.1 billion in 1966 to $145.7 billion at the end of 1986 (in addition to $435 billion in foreign real estate and direct investments), and projections were that they could reach $1 trillion by 1995.

As of early 1987 there were seventy-nine foreign banks and thirty-six investment firms established in Tokyo, with six foreign firms admitted to the Tokyo Stock Exchange at the end of 1985. Goldman Sachs, Jardine Fleming, Merrill Lynch, Morgan

127

Stanley, S. G. Warburg, and Vickers da Costa (the British subsidiary of Citicorp) were the foreign based players among the ninety-three Tokyo Exchange members in 1987. British negotiators applied substantial pressure to the Japanese in 1987 to admit British firms such as Kleinwort Grievson Securities Ltd., Schroder Securities Ltd., and Baring Brothers & Co. Ltd. to the Tokyo Stock Exchange, with reciprocity considerations on the part of Japanese securities firms in London clearly in the background.

In 1987, some thirty-six foreign based firms had been licensed as securities dealers. In March 1987 the Ministry of Finance announced its decision to permit U.S. commercial banks to operate securities affiliates in Japan—powers not allowed these same banks at home under the Glass-Steagall Act or their Japanese commercial bank competitors under Article 65. The U.S. banks are permitted to trade in all kinds of securities, with no limits on allowable business volume. This gives major U.S. commercial banks powers in Japan that have been accorded their European universal bank competitors since 1985.

In order to paper over the Article 65 restrictions, any firm that already has a banking unit in Japan can apply to enter the Japanese securities business only through a non-Japanese subsidiary that is not majority-owned by a financial institution. Bankers Trust, for example, teamed up with the Exxon Corporation to establish a securities operation in Japan in mid-1987. This involved Exxon's purchase of a 50 percent interest in the Bankers Trust Hong Kong affiliate, BT Asia Securities Ltd., which in turn applied to the Japanese Ministry of Finance for permission to engage in underwriting, trading, and brokering of debt and equity securities through a Tokyo branch. Similar hookups were established between Manufacturers Hanover and Chrysler Corporation, between J.P. Morgan and Bechtel Investments, Inc., and between Chemical Bank and Lord Howard DeWalden, a British real estate investor.

Such arrangements supplied additional arguments for deregulation in both Japan and the United States. Japanese commercial banks and securities firms could argue that foreigners were able to circumvent Article 65 and obtain a presence in both commercial and investment banking businesses, access that is denied them at home. Under existing regulations, Japanese banks cannot increase their holdings of securities firms to more than 5 percent. U.S. commercial banks could argue that Japanese deregulation was well ahead of American deregulation, which, when combined with the grandfathering of various foreign banks under the International Banking Act of 1978, hardly serves the interests of a level playing field at home.

In June 1987 six additional European financial institutions were permitted to open securities subsidiaries in Japan: Lloyds Asia Securities Ltd., Barclays de Zoete Wedd Japan Ltd., Alexanders Laing & Cruikshank (Japan) Ltd., B.V. Capital Markets (Asia) Ltd. (Bayerische Vereinsbank), B.H.F. Securities (Asia) Ltd. (Bank fuer Handel und Industrie-Frankfurter Bank), and Crédit Lyonnais Finanz A.G., Zurich.[3] Together with the European universal banks' permission to have securities units in Japan since December 1985, and changes in the way certain government securities are auctioned to improve access by foreign dealers, the new entrants promised to broaden and deepen Japan's securities markets substantially—and to make them considerably more competitive. Expectations were that about fifty foreign based firms would have securities licenses in Japan by 1988.

Foreign players are permitted to trade in some kinds of securities but are limited to dealing with the 120 largest Japanese financial institutions and prohibited from securities dealing with corporate or retail clients, as well as being restricted to a minuscule share of government bond underwriting. They also must execute stock trades through members of the Tokyo stock exchange, which have been subject to a fixed commission and limited price competition.

Controls on deposit interest rates, fixed commissions on stock transactions, the absence of stock index futures and commercial paper markets, as well as separation of commercial and investment banking, for a number of years continued to impede full integration of Tokyo into the global financial markets. In April 1987 the Japanese Ministry of Finance announced that financial institutions based in Japan could henceforth use foreign futures and options markets to hedge their investment portfolios. This represented a major step in further integrating Japan into the international financial market and increasing the scope for Japanese financial houses to expand in global markets. Given the assets of Japanese trust banks, investment trusts, and insurance companies, as well as securities firms and other financial houses, the impact promised to be very significant indeed.

Gradual deregulation in Japan thus has proceeded in each of the salient regulatory dimensions, but always with an eye to maintaining the preeminence of Japanese players in the home market. Besides the slow pace of market liberalization, foreign firms faced the "Buy Japan" mentality so familiar in the industrial sector on the part of Japanese consumers, corporations, and investors.

It should be emphasized once again in this context that foreign based institutions that are already in a particular market, either because they were grandfathered in when entry barriers were imposed or because they have achieved entry in some other manner, will have an unambiguous incentive to resist further opening of the market to foreign players. They have no reciprocity incentive with respect to their home countries or third countries, and unless they perceive significant external benefits from additional entrants they have every reason to resist additional, potentially powerful competition.

Patterns of Barriers to Entry

Appendix 7-A presents an inventory of entry restrictions that confronted foreign based financial institutions in various national markets in 1986.[4] Competitors from individual home countries confront broadly comparable restrictions, although they may vary in detail partly as a result of "grandfathering" provisions and partly as a result of the astute use of reciprocity by the home countries of certain financial institutions in intergovernmental bargaining.

Of 141 countries surveyed by the U.S. Department of the Treasury in 1984 (including 24 former colonies of European powers), 13 had no explicit entry restrictions to foreign banks and 3 others prohibited only the acquisition of a major interest in an existing indigenous bank.[5] Eighteen others prohibited additional foreign presence, or allowed none at all, and 23 limited foreign banks to representative offices, the most passive form of foreign banking presence. Representative offices may not take deposits or make loans and are useful mainly for developing new business contacts, conveying local market information to the head office, maintaining a relay service with correspondents and providing a visible presence of the parent bank to clients.

From such surveys, it is quite clear that barriers to the entry of foreign financial institutions vary greatly among countries. At one extreme is exclusion: the complete prohibition of all foreign presence, extending even to representative offices. Frequently such an embargo coincides with the existence of a nationalized domestic banking industry in which all private banking (domestic or foreign) is prohibited. More common is some form of conditional restriction on the entry of foreign banks, which usually relates to the type of presence that is permissible and to the nature of the associated banking powers. Even conditional restrictions are not entirely unambiguous. Within a set of domestic regulations and laws there often exists substantial discretion. In the same vein, policies may mean different things in different situations and precedent is certainly not an infallible guide to future policy responses.

In general, entry restrictions can be described as essentially quota-like. They specify whether or not a foreign financial institution may operate in the domestic market and, if so, how. The form of participation may specify only a representative office, a separately capitalized and locally incorporated subsidiary, a nonbank such as a finance company which cannot take deposits but can make certain types of loans, a minority foreign-equity participation, mandatory partnership with the government, and the like. Occasionally, new foreign financial institutions are limited to certain home countries, based on past colonial relationships or existing regional economic arrangements such as the European Community. Most-favored-nation treatment is certainly not characteristic of the rules imposed by countries on entry of foreign financial institutions. Often a complete moratorium is placed on new entrants because there are "already enough banks," or because of the "frailty of the domestic banking structure," and the infant-industry argument. Red tape in processing new applications is a perennial problem.

Sometimes an explicit price may be exacted for entry, for example, a U.S. $10 million foreign-currency deposit with the country's central bank for each branch to be established, with the same deposit also forming the basis for the legal lending limit in local currency. Exceedingly high capital requirements for new subsidiaries may be used as an entry barrier as well. So may a mandatory volume of foreign-currency loans to the government or to specified domestic institutions, a commitment to set up a national branch network or to rescue failing local institutions, or a commitment to render certain types of financial services that are not yet domestically well developed.

Bargaining leverage may extract a certain benefit perceived to be of value by the host government, a benefit that might not materialize as quickly under open-market access. But, once safely in, foreign financial institutions can exact a heavy price in terms of high profits from the continued monopolistic climate of the domestic financial industry. Indeed, these same institutions are sometimes in the forefront of the ranks lobbying for continued policies of exclusion, once their own entry has been achieved. Restrictive entry policies, selectively applied, may thus provide leverage to help a country achieve certain developmental goals, but at a substantial potential cost in adverse shifts in its effective terms of trade.

DISTORTIONS OF OPERATING CONDITIONS

Similar to entry restrictions, operating controls can seriously influence competition in domestic banking and financial markets, so that even if liberal entry is possible it is by no means certain that foreign competitors will be permitted to meet rival firms on equal terms.

Incidence of Domestic Regulation

Once having gained entry to a particular market, foreign based financial institutions generally become fully subject to domestic monetary policy, supervisory, and regulatory controls. At this point there are three possibilities:

1. Domestic controls, in law or in administrative practice, fall *less seriously* on foreign players than on their domestic competitors.

2. The nominal incidence of regulation is *identical* for both.

3. Foreign players are subjected to *more restrictive* regulation than their local competitors.

Domestic Disadvantage. The case where controls fall more heavily on domestic than foreign players seems to be a relatively rare occurrence. Probably the most important example involved foreign banks in the United States prior to the passage of the International Banking Act of 1978 (IBA). Foreign based institutions were exempt from membership in the Federal Reserve System, from the Bank Holding Company Act and the McFadden Act restrictions on branching across state lines, and from the Glass-Steagall prohibitions against an institution's involvement in both commercial and investment banking. The IBA eliminated this discrimination in favor of foreign players, except that institutions already involved in both commercial and investment banking, and those already having branches in multiple states, were grandfathered. This created a degree of tension that has become more important with the continued securitization of financial flows in the United States.

Given the continued restrictive effect of Glass-Steagall in the U.S. domestic market on their American competitors, the fifteen foreign banks that were grandfathered under the International Banking Act of 1978 (and could thus maintain both a commercial and investment banking presence in the U.S. market) as well as foreign based securities houses that are principal competitors to U.S. commercial and investment banks generally tended to tread softly in exercising their full potential power in the U.S. capital market. In 1986, however, they began to flex their muscles. Nomura Securities and Daiwa Securities led significant issues in the U.S. market for prime names. Sumitomo Bank and Trust Company purchased a 12.5 percent share in Goldman Sachs, in the face of Article 65, Japan's version of Glass-Steagall, albeit under tight restrictions on the part of the Federal Reserve. Securities affiliates of Swiss Bank Corporation, Union Bank of Switzerland, and Deutsche Bank led fifteen debt issues amounting to over $2.5 billion during 1986. American commercial banks that were attempting to be major players in global finance saw some of their principal rivals do deals in their own market that were prohibited to them. This was a rare case of foreign firms being treated significantly more favorably than domestic firms and being able to exploit that treatment to good effect in developing their worldwide competitive positioning.

In April 1987 the Senate Banking Committee approved a bill that would prevent regulators from granting new powers to U.S. commercial banks for roughly one year, as well as inhibiting foreign banks with grandfathered securities firms in the U.S. from "expanding" their activities. Such a moratorium was an important objective of the Securities Industry Association, with the aim of limiting further commercial bank incursions into mortgage-backed securities, municipal revenue bonds, commercial paper and mutual funds, and eventually corporate debt and equity securities.

In a similar vein, we have already noted that foreign based commercial banks in Japan were allowed to enter the domestic securities business despite Article 65 barriers that continued to restrict local banks in this critical area. Certain developing countries, such as India, have required that local banks become actively involved in providing financial services to clients in rural agriculture, a requirement that does not bear on foreign based institutions. Except for a few such anomalies, usually based on historical reciprocity considerations, preferential treatment of foreign institutions is not likely to be encountered.

Equal Incidence Regulation. The case in which regulation affects domestic and foreign players equally applies in many OECD countries and a number of developing countries. Foreign institutions here are subject to precisely the same nominal operating constraints as are domestic institutions. This applies to reserve requirements, asset ratios, lending limits, exposure constraints, capital adequacy, banking powers, access to funding sources and central bank lending, and more. Despite nondiscrimination *de jure*, the incidence of such measures may in fact fall more heavily on newcomers, or on foreign players that are forced to enter the market through affiliates that do not have the capital base enjoyed by branches. In some cases these are unintentional operating barriers and can either directly limit market access or raise the cost of doing business.

Disadvantage to Foreign Competitors. Operating barriers are used by some countries to restrict the competitive positioning of foreign based institutions after they have achieved access. The measures range from restrictions on expatriate employment, number and location of offices, client groups that may be served, types of business that may be handled (including trust business, lead-management in securities underwriting, and retail deposit-taking), mandatory linkage of allowable business to international transactions, and the like. Most are paraquantitative restrictions in that they place positive limits on the nature and scope of activities. Some, however, may be paratariffs, as in the case of funding restrictions that raise the cost of funds in the local market relative to domestic competitors.

Four basic types of operating restrictions can be identified:

1. Market delineation acts to restrict market access directly by identifying groups of clients that may or may not be served (or that *must* be served) and how they are to be served.

2. Growth limits set a maximum on the size of a foreign financial institution's presence in the local market, either in absolute terms or by market share.

3. Funding limits increase the cost of debt and equity capital (including bank deposits) taken up in the local financial markets, either to restrict market share or to adversely affect profitability.

4. Nuisance measures may raise the cost of doing business in the local market or compromise the quality of products.[6] Appendix 7-B surveys operating restrictions found to apply in OECD and other countries in 1986.

Market Delineation

Some operating restrictions are quota-like in that they limit the markets that foreign based financial institutions are allowed to serve. A "permitting" procedure, for example, may subject all loans beyond a certain size to the scrutiny of the central bank. The institution's presence may be limited to a few cities (usually the capital and major ports), to a single city, or even to a single office. Additional offices may be permitted only after five to ten years of satisfactory operations.

In 1983, for example, the Brazilian authorities told foreign banks that they could open two offices in provincial cities for each one they closed in Rio de Janeiro and São Paulo, an opportunity promptly grasped by some in anticipation of a resumption of Brazil's resource-based economic growth later in the 1980s.

Various types of profitable business may be reserved for state-owned banks, and foreign banks may be prevented from letter-of-credit business involving the government. No liens on real property may be permitted to be taken by foreign institutions (effectively banning asset-based financing); or they may be prevented from entering the trust and investment-management field or holding the proceeds of equity sales. They may be forced to divest themselves of finance companies or other "nonbank" affiliates in order to prevent their use as banking outlets.

The host government may direct domestic public and private enterprises not to do business with foreign institutions or to limit any such business to areas not adequately served by local institutions. Foreign banks may be excluded from participation in the government's export-credit guarantee program, and subsidized export financing may have to be done only through domestic banks. Foreign institutions may be restricted to export/import financing, foreign exchange, and foreign-currency lending only. A certain proportion of total assets may have to be placed in government bonds. Some types of large financings may have to be lead managed by local banks, precluding foreigners from lucrative income from fees. Advertising may be limited in various ways and mandatory financing of certain economic sectors or nationalized enterprises may be imposed. The list goes on.

Under a rule promulgated in 1984, for example, advertising for new deposits in the United Kingdom by banks based outside the European Community was restricted by the necessity of including a warning about the absence of deposit insurance, possible transfer risks and exchange risks and detailed information on financial condition. While this action was clearly a matter of prudential control, the discriminatory competitive side effects represented a potential threat.

As noted earlier, foreign banks in Japan have long felt systematically discriminated against in an opaque structure of financial control that delivered much the same sort of protection that has traditionally shielded favored manufacturing and agricultural interests. The foreign banks, for example, have been discouraged from taking aggressive leadership roles in yen-denominated syndicated loans for foreign borrowers. Although foreign banks had been present in Japan for over three decades, they still accounted for only 3 percent of total lending and 2 percent of total deposits in 1982. Whereas the foreign banks were long protected through a monopoly on so-called impact loans, aimed at financing Japan's foreign trade, removal of this protection in 1981 was not matched by liberalization in other areas, particularly funding.

Nevertheless, various foreign banks entered into the trust-banking business in Japan through joint ventures with local security houses, but these ventures were rendered far less attractive when in late 1984, under strong pressure from the Reagan administration, the government decided to permit five American and three European (British, German, and French) banks to enter the trust business in Japan directly. Swiss banks apparently were initially excluded because of secrecy laws, which were said to prevent the Japanese authorities from adequately judging bank performance. Japanese trust banks professed to be "shocked" at the prospects for increased competition and American negotiators thought they had an agreement to open the Japanese market to all qualified institutions. Nevertheless, the highly controlled market opening suggested continued protectionism.

How difficult it is to separate discrimination against foreign financial institutions from the legitimate exercise of national economic and financial policy prerogatives came to light in Korea during 1986. The forty-seven foreign banks operating in the country had survived in large part on swap facilities made available to them by the central bank, which encouraged foreign-currency lending to the country, as well as government guarantees covering lending to the major Korean industrial groups. Concern over the size of the country's foreign debt led the Ministry of Finance in 1986 to freeze dollar loans by all banks operating in the country, seriously discourage local-currency financing of business by issuing Bank of Korea "monetary stabilization bonds" at extremely attractive interest rates, and curtail swap facilities. Also included was a requirement that 35 percent of all new lending go to small and medium-sized local businesses, an increase from a previous requirement of 25 percent.

On the funding side, foreign banks in 1986 obtained the right to sell certificates of deposit, but only up to 7 percent of a bank's capital and with the requirement that the issuing bank give up swap facilities equal in amount to its issued certificates of deposit. Meanwhile, the interest rate they could pay on local-currency deposits was linked to a range set by a cartel of domestic banks. They were also required to give up swap facilities in the amount of one-half of any discount-window borrowings. The authorities indicated that these were simply steps on the way to phasing-out swap facilities entirely.

All of this is was taken by the foreign banks as partial revocation of a 1984 agreement, reached with considerable U.S. trade pressure, to (1) reduce barriers to competition particularly in local-currency lending, (2) provide partial access to discount-window facilities, and (3) partially lift legal lending limits. A variety of other government interferences in the operation of foreign banks, however, were not in fact liberalized by Korea as agreed, or were made ineffective by other discriminatory rules and regulations. Korean officials, on the other hand, viewed the measures simply as elimination of "special privileges" that afforded unusually favorable treatment of foreign banks during a time when Korea was in serious need of foreign-currency financing for its industrialization, a need that had come to an end.

Asset Growth and Size Limits

Besides telling foreign based financial institutions where they may not (or must) do business, governments have shown great ingenuity in limiting the share of the overall market that foreign competitors may obtain. Leverage (gearing) ratios, reserve requirements, and capitalization limits may be set at different levels for domestic and for foreign institutions, all in order to constrain their overall market share. Foreign currencies may have to be placed with the central bank in some proportion to the volume of domestic lending, or explicit quotas may actually be placed individually, or collectively, on foreign institutions to limit their share of the overall market. Such limits may be either static or dynamic, thereby permitting a gradual and controlled expansion of growth in their share of the market and in their portfolio loans. Restrictions on growth have both quota-like and tariff-like effects, depending on whether they physically limit the overall value of business or raise its cost. In some cases, they increase costs progressively as the volume of business grows and thus they are somewhat akin to tariff quotas in commercial policy.

The Canadian Banking Act of 1980 limited all foreign banks to an 8 percent share of total domestic Canadian assets, or about C$11 billion in 1981. At the same time, several dozen additional foreign banks applied for charters as full branches, further dividing the asset ceiling imposed on them. In effect, the ceiling excluded foreign banks from funding a major part of Canadian financing needs, particularly in resource-based industries, at the very time Canadian banks were moving aggressively to expand their market share in the United States and other countries. This obvious lack of reciprocity generated a great deal of criticism at the time.

Funding Limits

Besides restricting overall growth and restricting the markets to be served, which generally affects the asset side of the balance sheet, governments also place restrictions on the liability side. In addition to capital-related restrictions, foreign financial institutions may be prevented from accepting deposits altogether, or from accepting certain types of deposits (for example, time, savings, or demand deposits), or deposits from certain types of customers (for example, individuals in the retail banking market). They may have no access whatsoever to deposits from the government, which may direct its own business (and that of firms over which it has some influence) to domestic banks or only to those banks in which it has an equity interest.

All such restrictions force foreign institutions to fund themselves in the local interbank market, certainly resulting in higher costs and, given the limited depth and breadth of that market, in the periodically restricted availability of funds as well. If the interbank market is dominated by a few large and powerful domestic institutions, those domestic institutions can easily have the foreigners over the proverbial barrel if they become nettlesome. Indeed, a few governments actually *require* foreign based financial institutions to borrow significantly from domestic banks.

Additionally, foreign based financial institutions may not be eligible for interest subsidies made available by the government, thus effectively narrowing loan spreads, and foreign institutions' bankers acceptances arising from trade financing may not be acceptable for discount in the domestic money market. Foreign banks may be prevented from having access to the discount services of the local central bank, thereby forcing suboptimal asset and liability management. All such measures increase the difficulty in arranging local sources and uses of funds in such a way as to erode the profitability of foreign based institutions.

The role of operating distortions on the funding side can be illustrated by the experience of foreign banks in Japan. Given the practical impossibility of matching their Japanese competitors' extensive branch offices and retail client penetration, foreign banks were almost entirely reliant on the domestic money market for funding. This created three competitive disadvantages.

First, money market rates were significantly higher than the cost of retail deposits, which were controlled by the Bank of Japan, permitting Japanese banks actually to lend to clients at rates below the funding costs of foreign banks.

Second, there was no free interbank market in yen: the MOF set the interest rate payable by banks, thereby impeding foreign banks' access to that alternative source of funding.

Third, low-cost short-term funding required collateral in the form of promissory notes covering debt to the bank, against which a bank could borrow up to a level of 70 percent — in effect, over 100 percent collateralization — obviously a major competitive constraint for foreign banks.

Despite the fact that regulations covering this situation were fully consistent with a national treatment criterion, it was clear that the results did not in any sense represent equality of competitive opportunity. Indeed, the foreign banks' share of the yen loan market declined from about 3.5 percent in 1982 to under 2.5 percent in 1986, and their share of bank profits declined to under 1 percent of the total, a factor partly responsible for foreign banks' growing emphasis on the securities business and the

141

interest on the part of some in acquiring Japanese banks with significant branch networks.

Another example of discriminatory capital requirements applied to foreign banks occurred in Portugal in 1986. In order to protect overstaffed and inefficient but heavily capitalized domestic institutions, the government increased capital requirements by 64 percent for "new banking institutions," mainly foreign, which had been operating profitably. Maximum leverage for foreign banks was set to four times capital, compared to forty-four to sixty times capital for the nationalized Portuguese banks. Combined with other regulatory measures favoring indigenous banks and severe branching restrictions applied through refusal to act on applications, Portuguese policy was seen as a clear protectionist thrust, in conflict with a 1984 law that was basically aimed at nondiscrimination as well as in conflict with Portugal's obligations as a new member of the EEC with respect to the right of establishment.

Nuisance Measures

Besides acting on the core element in the business of financial services (the size and shape of the balance sheet), governments have found other ways to restrain foreign competition. Access to telecommunications facilities, to electric power, to transportation, to postal services, and to building permits may be subject to restrictions. Transborder data flows, which have been identified as the competitive lifeblood of multinational financial networks, may be impeded or taxed.[7] Foreign financial institutions may be saddled with discriminatory rates of profit tax, stamp duties, or transfer fees; or they may be forced to do all their foreign-exchange business through local banks, sometimes at government-prescribed rates.

Not least important, there are frequent staffing and managerial restrictions. Job quotas for local people may be imposed either in the aggregate or by the level of employment. All managers and directors may have to be local residents or nationals and senior expatriate personnel may have to be vetted on an individual basis by the authorities. Sometimes work and residence permits are employed in this connection and even the issue of visas may be used to restrict visits of home-office or third-country personnel. If, indeed, banking and financial services is a "people business," then such measures can have extraordinarily harmful effects by raising costs, reducing the quality of products, and constraining the ability to expand. Throughout, red tape raises transactions costs and heightens uncertainty surrounding the business.

There is in various countries an impressive range of operating restrictions on banking and the provision by foreign based institutions of other financial services. It should be noted, however, that not all the restrictions are intended solely to discriminate against them. Nevertheless, even under such circumstances, a handicap may still exist.

An unintentional differential impact can occur because of specific variations that may exist between the character of domestic and foreign operations. Some countries, for example, set maximum permissible limits on the size of bank loans to individual borrowers. These limits are usually specified in terms of the size of the bank's capital. If a bank's local office is treated as a separately capitalized entity, instead of on a consolidated basis with its parent, its ability to extend loans to large corporate borrowers can be severely constrained although direct loans from the parent may be a way of circumventing this problem. Moreover, if local requirements include minimum capital-asset ratios, treatment of foreign banks as separate entities may deprive them of a significant advantage, if not impose a severe handicap.

General constraints on bank growth and on certain types of lending, as well as limits on the profitability of banks, may represent *de facto* discrimination against foreign banks because (1) they tend to be among the later market entrants, except perhaps in former colonies; (2) they tend to have a heavier concentration of their business in the wholesale end of the market, and (3) they often have the potential to attain a faster rate of growth than indigenous banks. Another unintended discrimination exists when limits are placed for balance-of-payments reasons on the repatriation of bank profits.

A good example of such a problem arose in Argentina during 1986. The country had over 200 banks with over 5,000 branches and 150,000 employees at the end of 1985, and was generally regarded as freewheeling, bloated, and poorly supervised. The system's fragility was demonstrated after revelations of bank fraud, unsound banking practices, and negligence caused a number of private institutions to fail, and resulted in a rush to deposit in state banks. Their share of deposits rose from 38 percent to 60 percent in 1986, while their share of banking assets rose from 34 percent to 66 percent. To cope with the problem, the authorities significantly increased reserve requirements, thereby causing an increase in lending rates and stimulating the rapid growth of a parallel market of intercompany and other loans totally outside the banking system—which in turn threatened a loss of government control of the domestic credit system.

In response, the authorities encouraged twenty-three mergers between weaker and stronger banks. They also sharply cut reserve requirements and proposed a law to increase the central bank's supervisory authority and effectiveness, restrict banks to activities specified in the law and spell out which institutions are in fact banks, and define banking as a public service. Foreign based banks in Argentina, which had largely stayed clear of the problems, vigorously objected to some of the proposed restrictions as well as the public-service definition of banking. In particular, they objected to the imposition of capital requirements double those applied to local banks, as well as to a provision tying their deposit-taking ability to their volume of international trade credits.

An example of how the existence of a direct presence in a foreign market exposes operations to the threat of external political pressure from local government occurred in the Philippines in early 1987. During the renegotiations of the Philippine debt, Citibank took a relatively hard line and refused to go along with other banks in accepting a relatively low interest margin on the $8.6 billion of restructured debt. This prompted the local authorities to consider action against Citibank's Philippine business, including closing offices and limiting the permissible range of business. Brazil had previously closed Mellon Bank's representative office in Rio de Janeiro for its refusal to renew about $150 million in trade credits to that country. Citibank had a presence in the Philippines for 85 years and operated three bank branches; a subsidiary, CityTrust, was one of the major Filippino banks. However, most observers viewed this threat as posturing by the government during tense negotiations in which the role of Citibank was considered critical.

On the other hand, "foreignness" can be beneficial if liabilities denominated in other currencies are excluded from the base used to compute required reserves. Similarly, exclusion of foreign financial institutions from the requirement to make (possibly unprofitable) priority-sector loans or to support government debt issues may have a favorable effect on their position in the market.

Besides operating barriers affecting conventional banking services, impediments may also hinder foreign based firms offering such financial services as charge cards.

One type of operating barrier facing foreign based charge card issuers is lack of access to the domestic bank clearing system. In order for their cards to be usable in automated teller machines, charge card issuers usually must have access to that system. In some countries where payments clearing is controlled by the government or by a cartel of local banks, access to the system may be denied to foreign based issuers. Canada and Malaysia have been cited by American Express Company as examples of two countries imposing operating restrictions of this type.

In addition, foreign based firms may be prohibited entirely from offering charge cards. In Taiwan, for example, only debit cards are allowed (charges are debited from the cardholder's bank account), thus limiting issuance of charge cards to a cartel of local banks, most of which are controlled by the Taiwanese government. Without access to domestic bank accounts foreign based firms cannot issue debit cards, and all are therefore excluded from the card business in Taiwan.

Another impediment (in Norway and Denmark, for example) involves controls on the pricing of charge card services. Merchants and other clients accepting the card for charge purchases must pay fees. Some countries prohibit such fees entirely and require any fees to be imposed solely on the card user. This can put the issuers of charge cards at a severe disadvantage against the issuers of credit cards, where returns are largely derived from interest charges on purchases. If these are predominantly issues by local banks, such policies may represent discrimination against foreign based suppliers of charge-card services.

Occasionally the government or government-owned entities may supply financial services in competition with the private sector and hence foreign based card issuers. Air Canada, for example, issues a charge card that is given preference in bidding for the government's card and related travel services contracts.

On balance, then, foreign based financial institutions can probably expect to operate at a disadvantage with respect to indigenous competitors in most countries because of intentional or accidental discrimination against them, although these disadvantages tend to wane with time.

Foreign based financial institutions generally seek entry into national markets at the wholesale end of the business and pursue activities that have some trace of internationality, such as foreign-currency loans, trade financing, or loans to multinational enterprises. Local retail and middle-market business tends to become more important only after the enterprise has been more or less fully integrated into the national financial environment. This may give pioneer international financial institutions a competitive edge over new entrants into the international banking arena and over new banking competitors in general. Yet, even when foreign banks have been long established as retail competitors, local banks often resist innovations involving new technologies or ones that promise radical alterations of banking practices, such as automated teller machines and credit cards.

INTERNATIONAL DISTORTIONS AND COMPETITIVE PERFORMANCE

Returning to the basic Client-Arena-Product model, reproduced in Figure 7–1, how do competitive distortions affect the

Figure 7–1. Trade Barriers in the International Financial Services Activity Matrix.

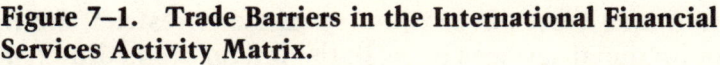

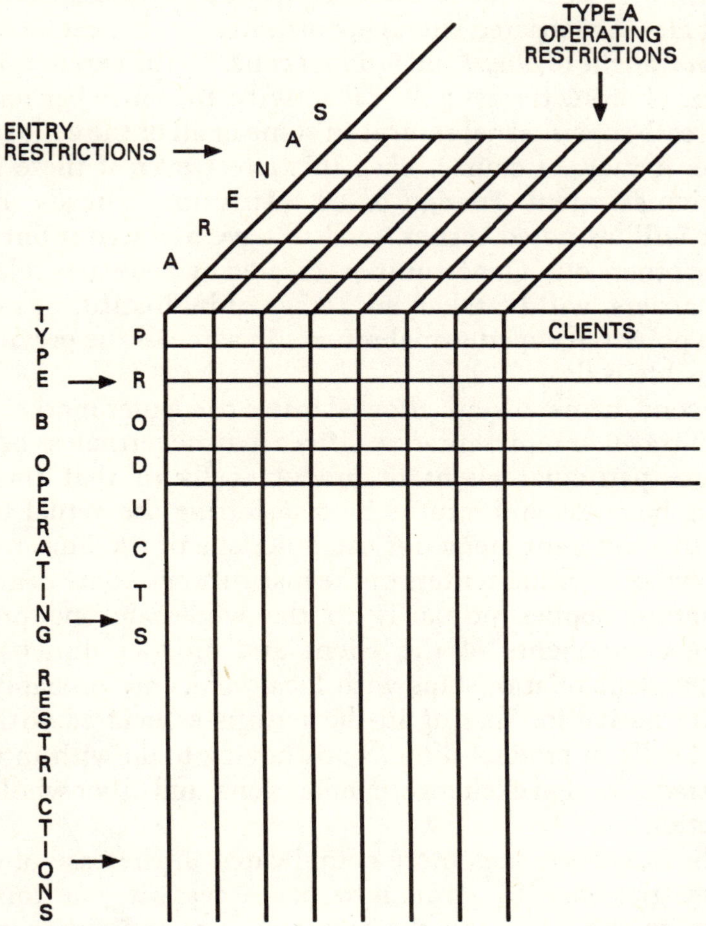

individual cells in the matrix and, therefore, the formulation and execution of institutional strategies? This can be discussed in terms of entry barriers, operating restrictions that affect access to client groups (Type A), and operating restrictions affecting the ability to supply the market with specific products (Type B).

First, and most obvious, entry barriers, restrict the movement of financial services firms in the lateral *arena* dimension of the matrix. A firm that is excluded from a particular national market faces a restricted lateral opportunity set that excludes the relevant tranche of *client* and *product* cells. To the extent it is the outcome of protectionist political activity, the entry barrier will itself create supernormal returns in some or all of the cells in the tranche. It may, of course, have this effect even if there is no protectionist intent. Foreign based institutions already in the market will, as noted earlier, tend to have a vested interest in keeping others out. Opportunities, created by countries relaxing entry barriers, will be taken advantage of by institutions envisioning potential supernormal returns in some of the previously inaccessible cells.

Second, firms that are allowed into a particular market only through travel or representative offices may nevertheless be able to access particular client or product cells in that tranche, securing business and returns by transferring the actual transaction to a different arena (for example, one of the Euromarket functional or booking centers or the institution's home country). This option applies primarily to the wholesale and private banking components of the client and product dimensions. Correspondent relationships with local banks are probably the only alternative for sharing in the returns associated with the blocked cells in product dimensions having to do with international trade, foreign exchange, syndications, and other wholesale transactions.

The story becomes more complicated in the case of operating restrictions. The firm now has access, in one form or another, to the arena tranche but is constrained either in the depth of service it can supply to a particular cell (lending limits, staffing limits, restrictions on physical location, for example) or in the feasible set of cells within the tranche (limits on services foreign banks are allowed to supply and the client groups they are allowed to serve). These limits may severely reduce profitability associated with the arena concerned.

To the extent that horizontal integration is important in the international financial services industry, despite the presence of barriers and other competitive distortions affecting a given arena tranche, supernormal returns may still be obtained in unaffected cells. Even a limited scope for transactions with the local affiliate of a multinational enterprise may generate business with that company elsewhere in the world, for example. The value of a physical presence of any sort in an otherwise restricted market may thus support competitive positioning elsewhere in the institution's international structure. Obviously, the value of these linkages is very difficult to assess.

A good example of attempted arena penetration has involved the Peoples Republic of China. With the economic reforms of the early 1980s, the presumption was that China would require substantial financial services from foreign institutions and that their customers elsewhere could benefit from a presence in China. It would facilitate trade finance, promote joint ventures, and engage in correspondent banking activities. The presumption also was that financial deregulation, permitting a range of activities in China, would follow as a natural consequence of liberalization in other sectors. As of early 1986, a total of ninety-three foreign banks were represented in China, thirty-seven of them with more than one location in the country. Most of these took the form of representative offices in Beijing, although eighteen foreign banks had one or more branches (significantly in the Special Economic Zones, such as Shenzhen and Xiamen).

Given the high costs of even maintaining a representative office, it was uncertain how many banks could actually report a profit on their activities in China. Full branches are permitted to do foreign-currency financing, foreign-currency deposit-taking (only from foreigners and overseas Chinese), local-currency deposit-taking (only as commission agent for the government Industrial and Commercial Bank), trade financing, and letters of credit, with the focus of their business essentially entirely on nonlocal enterprises and individuals. Even in the Special Economic Zones foreign banks are strictly controlled in order to protect local institutions from competition. On the other hand, the absence of conventional supervisory constraints could lead to difficulties down the road. A $12.5 million capital requirement and limits on business that may be done with Chinese enterprises, when coupled to the high cost of maintaining even a representative office in China, caused a number of institutions to have second thoughts about the near-term prospects in that country. Whereas none of the U.S. representative offices in China had banking powers, Chinese banks in the United States are full branches capable of doing the complete range of commercial banking business.

Another interesting nontraditional case of market penetration occurred in early 1987, when Banque de l'Union Européenne established a joint venture in the Soviet Union along with two Soviet banks under a new law designed to promote East-West business partnerships. Up to 49 percent foreign equity holdings are now allowed, although management control must rest with the Soviet interests. Over thirty applications for joint ventures were received within the first month. The State Bank and the Bank for Foreign Trade are involved on the Soviet side, as is the Banque Commerciale pour l'Europe du Nord in Paris, which in turn is owned by Soviet trading organizations and banks.

The intent of the Banque de l'Union Européenne arrangement was for the bank initially to provide consultancy services to the joint venture, using a working group of French and Soviet financial experts in Moscow, aimed mainly at facilitating industrial projects involving cooperation between Soviet state enterprises and French firms. This initial phase would be followed by financings through a joint financial holding company, to begin about a year later. The rapid signing of the joint venture agreement, in spite of the absence of a capitalization arrangement or settlement of other operating details, appeared to indicate strong interest on the part of the Soviet Union in increasing links to international capital markets and in the transfer of financial technology. The new arrangement was deemed likely to set a pattern for at least some of the forty other foreign based banks maintaining representative offices in Moscow.

The strategic implications of barriers to trade in financial services thus seem clear. They reduce the feasibility-set within the client-arena-product matrix. They place a premium on opportunity. They increase the importance of horizontal linkages and the assessment of their value. And they raise the importance of lobbying activity to open up markets where cells having potentially supernormal returns are blocked or restricted, and to keep them that way when barriers to competition are the source of such excess returns.

THE ISSUE OF RECIPROCITY

The Oxford English Dictionary defines reciprocity as "mutual or correspondent concession of advantages or privileges, as forming the basis for the commercial relations between countries." The principle of reciprocity as it is conventionally applied to trade in financial services implies that a country discriminates in its treatment of foreign firms by affording each of them exactly the same treatment the country's own firms receive in its home country. Reciprocity is therefore analogous to retaliation in trade policy. By treating foreign based firms the same as the foreign government treats home-country firms there, a country may hope to improve the mutual investment climate. One of the arguments in favor of reciprocity in the provision of financial services is that it will maintain overall barriers at a lower level than would passive acceptance of unilaterally imposed impediments to open competition.

In the case of trade in goods, reciprocity is certainly easier to define than in services. Swaps of tariff concessions on particular volumes of trade have formed the basis for reciprocity in past trade negotiations. But there is no comparable standard for measuring reciprocity in financial services. Access to one market for one set of firms may carry entirely different significance from access to another market for another set of players. Understanding reciprocity in this context clearly requires an intimate knowledge of markets, products, and competitors.

Nor is it always clear that reciprocity is in the interest of firms seeking access to foreign markets, in whose interests it is ostensibly being applied. Strict reciprocity, for example, would require foreign countries to apply geographic branching limitations and restrictions of the Glass-Steagall type to U.S. financial institutions doing business there, which even Japan does not do.

On the other hand, reciprocity is often espoused as the most equitable standard for a foreign presence in the domestic provision of financial services. In practice, however, full reciprocity encounters a number of pitfalls that make it virtually impossible to administer in its narrowest form and very few countries appear to adhere strictly to such a policy, although many include reciprocity in their consideration of other factors related to the entry of foreign banks.

In drafting the International Banking Act of 1978, for example, the U.S. Congress in effect rejected reciprocity in favor of "national treatment," putting foreign based financial institutions on the same competitive footing as domestic institutions. To apply the concept of reciprocity in its strictest sense would conceivably have required thirty-three different policies covering foreign banks from the thirty-three different countries represented in the United States at the time. Such a policy would necessarily have been largely reactive in nature and would have resulted in an incoherent amalgam of petty regulations entirely inconsistent with the objectives of equity and efficiency of the American financial system. According to C. Stuart Goddin, then of the U.S. Department of the Treasury:

> A nation applying reciprocity restricts a party of another nation to conducting only those activities which the government of the second nation allows foreigners to conduct in its own territory. When two nations apply this principle bilaterally, restrictions are imposed from both sides, leaving the least common denominator of activities allowable in each.
>
> During hearings on the [International Banking Act], it was recognized that a policy based on reciprocity could create an administrative nightmare, requiring enforcement of different sets of rules for banks from different countries. Since a policy of reciprocity entails reacting to regulations or restrictions imposed by other governments, it also implies a critical loss of control by the domestic authority over the

regulatory rules and structures applicable to banks operating within its own territory.[8]

While reciprocity may be impractical as a policy for large and internationally oriented financial sysems, it is nevertheless frequently used as justification for various national policy actions concerning the entry of foreign banks. Brazil, for instance, applies the concept to U.S. banks on a one-to-one basis, permitting one American bank in Brazil for every Brazilian bank in the United States. And, if existing American or British banks in France or Mexico were nationalized, it would be very surprising if their governments failed to retaliate against French or Mexican banks in their own countries.

In mid-1987 the Peruvian government decided to seize thirty-three private financial institutions, including ten banks, six finance companies, and seventeen insurance companies, pending action by the Congress to nationalize them. The purpose was to halt capital flight and to channel savings toward domestic investments. The government initially indicated that this would include foreign banks, primarily BankAmerica, Citicorp, Chase Manhattan, Lloyds Bank, and Banco Central of Spain. But this impression was reversed shortly thereafter, and it was made clear that foreign banks would be left in private hands but more closely supervised.

Reciprocity has perhaps been most widely used in recent years with respect to Japan, perhaps in part a reaction to the perceived lack of Japanese reciprocity over the years with respect to trade in industrial goods, and in part a response to the attractiveness of the Japanese capital market as the second largest in the world. It is doubtful that thirty-six foreign firms would have obtained securities licenses, or that the Tokyo Stock Exchange would have accepted six foreign members in December 1985 without threats of retaliation from the United States, the United Kingdom, and Switzerland. Foreign players have used this opening to good advantage. Salomon Brothers, for example, had become one of the top-tier security traders in Tokyo by 1986. At the same time, foreign banks have been permitted to enter the trust business, bond futures trading, and bankers' acceptance

153

business in Japan, while the authorities have eased debt-to-equity limits.

In December 1986 the Federal Reserve Bank of New York awarded licenses as primary securities dealers to only two Japanese securities houses, Nomura and Daiwa (instead of all four that applied) and made it clear that even these licenses could be revoked in the absence of significant further progress in opening Japan's securities industry to U.S. firms. A third Japanese firm, the Industrial Bank of Japan, had already gained access to this market by acquiring a U.S. dealer, Aubrey Lanston and Company through its subsidiary, J. Henry Schroder. In 1986 foreign investors accounted for $2,065 billion of gross trading volume in U.S. Treasury securities and added a net total of $24.3 billion of them to their portfolios. They represented $277.3 billion in gross equity trading in 1986, and added $43.5 billion to their portfolios.

A certain amount of irritation was also displayed by the German authorities at the slow pace of liberalization of Japanese capital markets. Liberalization measures by the Bundesbank allowing foreign banks to lead manage new securities for foreign issuers in the German bond market specifically excluded Japanese firms—although they were permitted to participate in issues lead-managed by others—as a display of reciprocity in the attempt to accelerate action in Japan.

In response, change was sought, for example, in the prevailing system of government bond allotments to an underwriting syndicate of 775 firms (including 42 foreign firms). Even as outsiders, Japanese securities firms purchased at least half of all U.S. government securities, while an American firms' allotments in Tokyo amounted to only 0.07 percent. Complete liberalization of membership in the Tokyo Stock Exchange was also sought, as was liberalization of commercial banking. As noted earlier, in 1986 a total of seventy-six foreign banks held only 5 percent of Japanese banking assets.

The issue of reciprocity came up once again in the context of Japanese direct participation in Wall Street financial houses during 1987, when Nippon Life Insurance bought a 13 percent share of Shearson Lehman Brothers from the American Express Company for $538 million, following the 1986 acquistion of shares in Goldman Sachs by Sumitomo Bank. Together with other foreign participations and joint ventures such as Crédit Suisse First Boston, the Japanese purchase of Aubrey Lanston and Company, European holdings in Drexel Burnham Lambert, South African holdings in Salomon Brothers, and Arab investments in Smith Barney (prior to its sale to Primerica Corp.), the political profile of a strong foreign presence in the U.S. securities industry has grown significantly. The specter was raised of a repeat in the financial services industry of foreign "domination" of the American markets for steel, garments, consumer electronics, and automobiles as foreign players (especially the Japanese) developed a strong foothold in U.S. capital markets and acquired world-class training and financial technologies.

This became a fertile ground for raising the issue of reciprocity, and an amendment to a U.S. House of Representatives international trade bill would require strict reciprocity in the financial services sector. The focus appeared to be on specific lines of activity. For example, while three Japanese securities houses had primary dealer status for government bonds in the United States, no U.S. firms had comparable status in Japan at the time.

Like Glass-Steagall in the United States, Japan's Article 65 has constrained competition between banks and securities firms. Differences on how to deregulate developed between the Banking Bureau, the Securities Bureau, and the International Financial Bureau, all within the Ministry of Finance and each attempting to be responsive to the conflicting interests of its respective constituency—domestic banks, domestic securities firms, and foreign based players intent on entering the Japanese market. In particular, Japanese banks reacted in a hostile manner when the Ministry of Finance licensed not only the securities affiliates of European banks, but subsequently those of U.S. commercial banks as well. This was in response to the licensing of Nomura Securities and Daiwa Securities as primary government bond dealers in the United States, in addition to the Industrial Bank of Japan through its Aubrey Lanston affiliate in New York. Bankers Trust, Chemical Bank, Manufacturers Hanover, and Morgan

Guaranty were awarded securities branch licenses, thereby heading off a threat to revoke the Japanese firms' U.S. licenses.[9]

The number of seats on the Tokyo Stock Exchange held directly or indirectly by U.S. firms was another matter of contention, challenging the Japanese assertion that physical space and efforts to computerize the trading floor precluded increasing the number from the existing six firms in the near term. The Japanese authorities argued that the auction system of stock trading used in Tokyo requires a physical presence on the floor of the exchange, so that each firm must occupy a booth, and that only ninety-three could be squeezed in. The top Japanese securities firm (Nomura) in 1986 accounted for 20 percent of the volume of trading on the Tokyo exchange and the top three firms accounted for over 50 percent of all trading volume under a system of fixed commissions underlying high levels of profitability.

On December 16, 1987 the Tokyo Stock Exchange granted 22 new memberships, 16 of which were to foreign-based firms. This raised the number of foreign-owned seats from 6 out of 93 to 22 out of 115. The new members, paying about $8.6 million per seat, included Prudential-Bache, Smith Barney, Salomon Brothers, Kidder Peabody, First Boston and Shearson Lehman from the United States, Kleinwort Benson, Schroders, Barings and County NatWest from Britain, W.I. Carr and Sogen Securities from France, securities affiliates of Deutsche Bank and Dresdner Bank from Germany, and the securities affiliates of Union Bank of Switzerland and Swiss Bank Corporation.

However, despite Japanese liberalization moves, including permission for foreign banks to establish 50 percent owned securities firms in the face of prohibitions against local banks' ability to do likewise, allegations of market distortions persist. Alleged distortions include the allocation system for government bonds that relegates foreign players to a minor role in primary markets and the massive role played by the postal savings system in the allocation of individual savings in Japan.

The fact that only the Japanese securities houses had relatively free access to each of the three major world financial centers—London, New York, and Tokyo—was viewed as an unacceptable state of affairs in an increasingly globalized financial market.

The reciprocity issue also arose during a dispute between the United Kingdom and Japan in March-April 1987, extending the concept beyond the financial services sector itself. Like the United States, the United Kingdom had long pressed Japan for increased access for U.K. securities firms to its capital markets, in view of the virtually unrestricted access of Japanese banks and securities houses to London markets. At the end of 1986, twenty-nine Japanese banks, nine insurance companies, and fifty-eight securities firms operated in the United Kingdom. All four of the largest securities firms were members of the London Stock Exchange. At the same time, five British banks and fourteen securities firms (including some taken over by foreign interests as part of London's "Big Bang") were operating in Japan. Of the six foreign members of the Tokyo stock exchange in 1986, one (S. G. Warburg) was British and another (Vickers da Costa) was a wholly owned British subsidiary of Citicorp.

In addition, British authorities were upset about the apparent exclusion of Cable and Wireless PLC (C&W), a telecommunications company, from significant access to the Japanese market for long-distance communications. The Japanese government proposed merging two rival consortia into a single new international telecommunications carrier, limiting the 13 interested foreign companies (most of them not international carriers) to a 20 percent stake and denying Cable and Wireless "meaningful" participation. This stance was justified by the Ministry for Post and Telecommunication as a matter of national security, but appeared clearly aimed at limiting competition from C&W's strong global network.

Hampered by EC membership in retaliating through the telecommunications sector (for example, by reducing the 28 percent share of Japan in the U.K. market for imported equipment) and the limited role of Japanese firms in British telecommunications services, the Department of Trade and Industry, backed by the Treasury and many members of Parliament, sought a broader retaliatory approach that focused the powerful position being established by Japanese banks and securities firms in

157

London. The U.K. authorities threatened to revoke the licenses of some of the fifty-eight Japanese firms in London and proceeded to secure the necessary punitive powers under the U.K. Financial Services Act to do so. The government also made it clear that Japanese applications for new bank licenses would be refused, an action evidently intended to pressure Yamaichi and Nikko Securities, whose main competitors, Nomura and Daiwa, already had banking licenses in the United Kingdom. Under the Act, the retaliation could only be triggered by restricted access to the Japanese market for financial services, so that the C&W case was only a proximate cause of the British threats.

Concern about the use of retaliation in financial services came mainly from the Bank of England, given the possible erosion of London as a world financial center at a time of growing importance of Japanese players. The prospects of Japanese firms moving to Frankfurt, Amsterdam, or Paris were raised, given the fact that, unlike Tokyo and New York, London is the only global financial center not founded on a massive base of domestic capital. Equity-market capitalization at the end of 1986 in New York, Tokyo, and London was $2.2 trillion, $1.75 trillion, and $440 billion, respectively, with even Osaka surpassing London in 1987. This ignores, of course, London's role as the center of the Eurocurrency, Eurobond, and Euroequity markets and as a pivotal arena for foreign exchange trading.

On the other hand, the growing importance in international finance of the principal Japanese houses is clear, and they employed over 5,000 people in London in 1986. The debate proved to be lively, with popular sentiment appearing to be lined up against the central bank's cautious view and the bankers lined up behind it in a "forest of pinstripes" accused of ignoring the fact that financial services should properly be viewed as part of the broader system of international trade.

In some countries, the principle of reciprocity is applied at the subnational level as well, as is true in several American states. A number of states restrict the entry or operations of foreign banks, sometimes citing considerations of reciprocity as their motive, despite the consistent approach oriented toward national treatment at the federal level. Japan, for example, denied

Texas-based banks permission to establish branches in Tokyo because Texas did not allow foreign bank branches, although there were a number of Japanese representative offices there.

But many developed and some developing countries seem to favor some form of national treatment of foreign financial institutions after they have overcome whatever entry barriers exist (see Appendix 7-C for reciprocity requirements in OECD countries and elsewhere). Thus the principles of reciprocity and national treatment in fact co-exist and are often complementary. As noted earlier, the former is sometimes negative and often punitive, while the latter is generally positive and constructive.

THE EUROMARKET BENCHMARK

The existence of a substantially free offshore market (at least in the wholesale commercial and investment-banking segments of the industry) provides policymakers with a better tool with which to assess the implications of domestic distortions in the financial services industry than is, perhaps, available in any other sector of the international economy.

To a significant extent, the Eurobond and Eurocurrency markets remain subject to limited taxation, regulation, and control, with protection essentially unknown and keen competition being continuously waged among countries that have decided to establish Eurofacilities in the form of offshore banking centers.

Briefly, these centers permit banks to accept deposits and make loans in various currencies on a separate set of books entirely divorced from similar activities within the domestic monetary system. For banks, there are no reserve requirements, asset ratios, or other restrictions that form key elements of safety and soundness in domestic banking systems. Supervision of offshore branches is supposed to be exercised by the bank's home authorities, while other forms of offshore banking (subsidiaries and consortiums) are under the jurisdiction of the country in which the center is located. In principle, no offshore banking center is supposed to be able to escape prudential safety and soundness constraints. This is anchored in the work of the Group of Offshore Banking Supervisors. But there appears to be a good deal of discrepancy between theory and practice, in part fostered by fierce competition among the centers themselves.

While offshore banking is conducted in many countries around the world, the major centers are the Bahamas, Bahrain, the Cayman Islands, Hong Kong, London, Luxembourg, New York, Panama, and Singapore. There are several factors which make a given locale attractive as an offshore banking center. The most important are permissive local regulation of administrative operations, foreign borrowing and lending, and foreign-exchange operations, in addition to favorable tax treatment. Many centers permit business that is booked in their jurisdictions to be administered in another country, which allows substantial economies in staffing and other expenses. Additional factors important to the development of a center are the receptiveness and stability of the host government, time-zone positioning and, in the case of functional centers, the local supply of skilled labor as well as the sophistication of their transport and telecommunications network.

Transactions and earnings in offshore banking centers are largely free of tax and even minimal levels of taxation can quickly price a center out of the market. Eurodeposits and redeposits within and among these centers serve to fund loans in various maturities, including major syndicated credits often involving dozens of banks. Sharing the long end of the market in several centers are Eurobonds, debt instruments of private and public issuers sold to nonresidents in bearer form and, hence, generally free of tax and free from the kinds of tight regulatory and disclosure requirements usually found in domestic bond markets. Euroloans and Eurobonds have been joined by short-term Euronotes, which are underwritten and distributed in the offshore markets and supported by note-issuance facilities (NIFs) revolving underwriting facilities (RUFs), or other variants on these backstops provided by financial institutions. Euro-commercial paper has increasingly supplemented Euronote issues of late. Euroequity is an emerging part of the market whereby equity shares may be issued and distributed offshore as well.

The major area of the offshore activities of banking centers are thus the funding, syndication, booking and administration of loans, underwriting, dealing in and clearing of securities, and the management of tax-sheltered investments for nonresidents. The importance of these centers stems from the number of commercial banks, affiliates of these banks, and investment banks that operate in them, the volume of transactions they handle and the significant earnings derived from them. Artificial barriers to entry and exit are minimal, competition is intense, and limited regulatory controls mean that spreads between deposit and lending rates are thinner than in most onshore financial markets.

Table 7–1 indicates the relative sizes of offshore markets in various financial centers. In New York, Tokyo, and Singapore, they involve accounts of nonresidents that are separate from domestic accounts and benefit from reduced regulatory constraints. In London and Hong Kong, regulatory constraints are in any case minimal, so that transactions of residents and nonresidents need not be separated and "offshore" transactions really represent onshore transactions between nonresidents of the United Kingdom and Hong Kong, respectively. To this are added tax-haven incentives for nonresidents in countries like the Bahamas and the Cayman Islands, which represent "booking" rather than "functional" centers (the actual transactions are done elsewhere).

The Tokyo International Banking Facility (IBF) was officially begun in December 1986, and by the end of January 1987 had booked assets of $110 billion, but still only one-tenth of the size of the onshore Japanese market for foreign currency lending. Initially, eighteen banks applied for offshore licenses. Many of the banks operated through their overseas branches, thus limiting the benefits of the Tokyo IBF, and were inhibited through tight governmental tax and regulatory measures. Foreign banks had similar access and appear to have applied for IBF status simply to establish a presence. Of the $55 billion initially

161

Table 7–1. Characteristics of Selected Offshore Markets.

	New York IBF Type[a]		London Type[b]			Tax Haven Type
	Tokyo	New York	Singapore	London	Hong Kong	Bahamas
Established	Dec. 1986	Dec. 1981	Nov. 1968	End 1950s	1957–58	Late 1960s
Assets ($ billions)[c]	97[d]	261	155	751	143	126[e]
Taxation						
Corporate	48.3%	Max. 46%	40% + 10% of overseas profits	40%	18.5%	No
Other	Local (12.3%) and stamp duty	—	—	—	—	Registration and licensing fees
Securities business allowed?	No	No	Yes	Yes	Yes	No

Source: Bank of Tokyo, as reported in *The Economist*, February 21, 1987, p. 83.

a. Domestic and foreign transactions separated.

b. Domestic and foreign transactions integrated.

c. December 1985.

d. December 1986.

e. December 1984.

deposited in IBF accounts, $53 billion represented deposits of Japanese banks.

The Euromarkets are basically efficient, in both a static and dynamic sense, and exist as useful benchmarks for comparing the losses in efficiency associated with protection, as well as general prudential and regulatory controls that exist in domestic financial systems. They also serve in part to limit the damage that protection imposes on international financial institutions, since there is often the possibility to transfer transactions for clients out of the national environment and into the Euromarkets. Indeed, this option and the fear of competitive erosion of national financial centers has triggered a spate of deregulation in many countries.

SUMMARY

Foreign based financial institutions of necessity operate in one of the more highly regulated environments in international trade. Restrictions are often justified by the need for effective domestic prudential or monetary control. They can also reflect strong protectionist pressure emanating from indigenous financial institutions and political pressure relating to national control of the "commanding heights" of the economy. When the financial systems of countries are opened to foreign involvement, it is sometimes only for a brief period in order to accept new entrants and these "windows of opportunity" can lead to a mad scramble among international financial institutions to establish themselves before the windows are closed again. Once in, operating restrictions can also severly limit the activities of foreign based financial institutions.

Barriers to entry as well as operations, whether imposed for reasons of financial control or protection, may constrain financial efficiency and the prospects of economic growth for the host country. Yet the restricted competition itself can be highly profitable to those foreigners who have managed to find a niche in the market. This helps explain the ambiguity that even the

163

most international of financial institutions have exhibited toward the prospects of aggressive liberalization of international trade in banking and other financial services.

Unlike international trade in goods, trade in services generally and financial services in particular tends to be directed toward taking the product directly to the customer and this usually requires a supplier's presence in the host country. Because the rules of the game for foreign direct investment are ill defined and not covered by internationally accepted principles of conduct, GATT-type rules of nondiscrimination do not apply.

Given the structure of entry barriers and distortions of operating conditions, it would appear that "national treatment" is the substantive equivalent of free trade in a highly regulated industry such as financial services, an industry whose sensitivity to systemic problems will assure that it will continue to be subject to regulatory controls. This is not necessarily the case, however. As we have noted, even nominal national treatment can have differential effects on domestic and foreign based institutions because of their different starting positions and operating characteristics. What is really required is "equality of competitive opportunity," in the sense of a level playing field. This is extraordinarily difficult concept to define, much less to deliver, in the case of an industry as complex as financial services. But as a goal, it is the equivalent of free international trade as applied to this sector.

Discriminatory barriers imposed on foreign competitors in national financial markets are analogous to protection in merchandise trade and, as we have seen, include tariff-like and quota-like distortions. Finally, reciprocity in rules governing financial services is similar to reciprocity found in regulation conventional merchandise trade, except that the principle tends to be far more narrowly defined at the subsector and even the individual enterprise level.

APPENDIX 7-A.

BARRIERS TO THE ESTABLISHMENT OF A COMMERCIAL PRESENCE, 1986

1. Prohibition by law of foreign bank presence in any form

Countries. Afghanistan, Bulgaria, Cuba, Czechoslovakia, Ethiopia, Guinea, Iraq, Laos, Libya, Madagascar, Somalia.

Country Specifics. All of these countries have wholly nationalized banking systems and thus prohibit both domestic and foreign privately owned banking operations. For recent changes in USSR, see text.

2. Prohibitions by current policies of licensing practices of foreign bank entry in any form

Countries. Benin, Kuwait, Netherlands Antilles, Surinam, Tanzania, United Arab Emirates, Guyana.

Country Specifics. The governments of UAE and Guyana previously permitted foreign banks. They have decided that the number of foreign banks already present is sufficient for the size of their respective banking markets.

Implications/Comments. The absence of banking presence may inhibit the development of the normal contacts through which foreign countries become familiar with another country's markets and business procedures as a first step in establishing and enhancing trading relationships.

3. Prohibition by law of all forms of banking entry except representative offices

---

Source: Letter to author from the Office of the United States Trade Representative, Executive Office of the President, USTR Computer Group, 1986.

Countries. Algeria, Burma, Colombia, Portugal, Syria, USSR (see text), Yugoslavia, Venezuela.

Country Specifics. Some of these countries allow previously admitted foreign banks to continue operations (grandfather clauses).

Implications/Comments. Representative offices cannot, by definition, engage in any type of banking business and are frequently constrained from advertising the services of the parent bank. Although they cannot take deposits or make loans for the parent, they can establish banking relationships with local firms.

4. Prohibition by current administrative practices of all forms of banking entry except representative offices

Countries. Peoples Republic of China, El Salvador, German Democratic Republic, Guatemala, India, Indonesia, Poland, Saudi Arabia, Trinidad and Tobago, Mexico.

Country Specifics. Some of these countries allow previously admitted foreign banks to continue operations (grandfather clauses).

Implications/Comments. Representative offices cannot, by definition, engage in any type of banking business and are frequently constrained from advertising the services of their parent bank. Although they cannot take deposits or make loans for the parent, they can establish banking relationships with local firms.

5. Prohibitions by law of foreign banks entering via branches

Countries. Bermuda, Cameroon, Peoples Republic of the Congo, Costa Rica, Finland, Gambia, Ghana, Hungary, Iceland, Ireland (with the exception of EC member country banks), Niger, Peru, Philippines, South Africa (permits bank subsidiaries), Uruguay, Canada (permits nonbank subsidiaries in the financial services sector). Several of these countries permit affiliates.

Implications/Comments. Most of the worldwide expansion of banking over the past two decades has taken place through branches. Elimination of the branch choice may completely deter any entry by some banks that find other forms either inadequate, such as representative offices, or too expensive and unwieldy, such as subsidiaries and affiliates.

6. Prohibition of foreign banks from purchasing any interest in indigenous banks

Countries. Bangladesh, Costa Rica, Pakistan, Papua New Guinea, Surinam.

7. Prohibition of foreign banks from acquiring controlling interest in indigenous banks

Countries. Australia (10%), Bermuda (40%), Canada (10%; permits an individual foreign party to own up to 10% of a bank, and up to 25% of any bank may be foreign-owned), the Congo (49%), Denmark (30%; requires a merger if any party, foreign or domestic, acquires 30% or more of a bank), Ecuador (20%; for non-Andean pact nations), Finland (20%), Gambia (20%), Japan (5%), Nigeria (40%), Philippines (30%; 40% with presidential approval), Republic of Korea (10%), Upper Volta (49%), Bahrain (49%), Dominican Republic (30%), Greece (49%), Iceland (49%), Morocco (50%), Oman (49%), Qatar (49%), Singapore (20%), South Africa (50%; once a foreign-owned bank reaches U.S. $24 million in share capital, it must open its shareholdings to local participation, with the goal of eventually reaching 50% local ownership), United Kingdom (14%). Maximum foreign participation allowed.

Central African Republic, Cyprus, Egypt, Iceland, Malaysia, Malawi, Malta, Netherlands, Oman, Trinidad and Tobago, Tunisia: no majority control; no specific maximum.

APPENDIX 7-B.

OPERATING BARRIERS FACING
FOREIGN-BASED BANKS, 1986

1. Prohibition or limitation on expansion on branch network

Countries

Brazil: Since 1964, Brazil has allowed only one new branch facility [1977]. Branch operations are, however, free to relocate.

Greece: Foreign bank branching is basically limited to Athens, Piraeus, and Thessal. Without formally disallowing branching beyond these cities, the currency committee has in the past discouraged foreign banks from establishing branches in other locations.

Indonesia: Foreign banks established prior to the exclusionary policy are limited to one branch and one sub-branch office in Jakarata.

Ireland: Foreign banks may open a second office only after seven years of operations.

Korea: Moratorium on foreign branch expansion in Seoul.

Lebanon: Very limited.

Malaysia: Existing foreign banks are not permitted to expand their branch operations.

Mexico: Since 1930, Mexico has limited foreign bank entry to representative offices. One foreign bank, established in Mexico prior to 1930, continues to be allowed to operate in branch form under a grandfather clause. This bank has five branches in Mexico

Source: Letter to author from the Office of the United States Trade Representative, Executive Office of the President, USTR Computer Group, 1986.

City and has been prohibited from establishing additional branches.

Pakistan: It is more difficult for foreign banks to obtain approval to expand their branch networks than for domestic banks.

Philippines: Existing foreign branch banks are not permitted to expand their networks.

Singapore: Very limited.

Thailand: Limits existing foreign bank branching to the capital city.

Turkey: Approval to expand is difficult to obtain.

Some countries prohibit any additional branching by both foreign and domestic banks. Foreign banks are usually more adversely affected. However, since they typically have fewer established branches than domestic banks. Where foreign branches are subject to constraints both on accepting certain types of deposits and on expanding their branch networks, the combination severely restricts their access to inexpensive local sources of funds.

2. Prohibition or limitation on foreign banks' solicitation of certain kinds of deposits

Countries

Costa Rica: Only state-owned commercial banks are permitted to accept demand and time deposits. Deposits are usually one of the bank's lowest cost sources of funds. To the extent that deposit-taking limitations force foreign banks to use more expensive sources of funds, they constitute a significant competitive disadvantage to foreign banks.

Egypt: Only banks at least 52 percent owned by Egyptians are permitted to accept local currency deposits.

169

El Salvador: The one foreign bank branch operating in El Salvador is not permitted to accept savings deposits.

Federal Republic of Germany: Branches of foreign banks are not allowed to become banks of deposit for mutual funds.

Indonesia: Prohibits soliciting demand deposits.

Japan: Prohibits soliciting local deposits. Deposits are usually one of the bank's lowest cost sources of funds. To the extent that deposit-taking limitations force foreign banks to use more expensive sources of funds, they constitute a signficant competitive disadvantage to foreign banks.

Philippines: Foreign banks are not permitted to solicit retail deposits.

Spain: Limitation on amount of deposits a foreign bank may obtain from Spanish customers to 40 percent of its portfolio of investments and loans to Spanish entities, public and private.

Sudan: Foreign banks are excluded from taking individual deposits from Sudanese residing in Sudan.

Taiwan: Foreign banks are not permitted to solicit demand and time deposits.

3. Restriction on access to government deposits

Countries

Brazil: Banco de Brasil is the sole banker for the large and growing public sector.

India: Almost all government agencies and publicly owned enterprises bank with Indian banks.

Jamaica: No access.

Liberia: Government corporations are obliged to keep their funds on deposit with the National Bank of Liberia.

Nigeria

Paraguay: No access.

Philippines: No access.

United Kingdom: Foreign banks are denied access to government and thrift institution deposits.

4. No access to subsidized funds for export financing

Countries

Austria: Subsidized export financing placed only with Austrian banks.

Japan: The Japanese Export-Import Bank and the Bank of Japan have programs and facilities to help finance imports and exports. Foreign banks are not able to participate.

South Korea

Nigeria

Peru: Foreign banks in Peru are required to contribute to a fund that subsidizes financing of some exports, but only domestic banks are eligible to write these loans.

Taiwan

United Kingdom: Foreign banks excluded from some phases of the export credit guarantee programs.

5. Limitation or denial of foreign bank access to Central Bank discount facilities

Countries

Dominican Republic: Rediscount facilities with the Central Bank permit the rediscounting of 100 percent of local banks' capital and reserves, but only 90 percent of foreign banks. This places foreign banks at a disadvantage in meeting liquidity needs in a timely and inexpensive manner, forcing them to hold a larger portion of their assets in lower yielding secondary reserves.

Egypt: No access.

El Salvador: The one foreign branch operating in El Salvador is not permitted to rediscount most paper with the Central Bank.

Germany: Rediscount quotas limited to branch capital.

Indonesia: No access.

South Korea: No access.

Taiwan: No access.

United Kingdom: No access. Foreign banks are forced to pay a premium to place their paper in the discount market.

6. Policies that limit the services foreign banks can offer

Countries

Bangladesh: Government policy is to restrict foreign banking to import/export financing, foreign-exchange projects, and local currency loans for which the government banks lack sufficient liquidity.

Guyana: State corporations and government employees are required to do as much of the their banking as possible with the government-owned banks.

Indonesia

Japan: Foreign banks may not engage in retail banking. Approval is required of yen loans to non-Japanese borrowers.

South Korea: Prohibits foreign banks' access to new customers. Korean companies are required to designate a "prime" bank to manage certain aspects of the company financing. The use of foreign banks for this purpose is discouraged.

Malaysia: Prohibits foreign banks' access to new customers. Local borrowers must deal with domestic banks. Foreign-controlled corporations operating in Malaysia must give at least half of their loan business to domestic banks.

Philippines: Prohibits foreign banks from providing trust services.

Switzerland: Swiss insurance companies were prohibited by law from depositing funds in or investing in obligations of foreign banks; foreign banks were excluded from the security management and underwriting business; foreign banks were not permitted to manage municipal or domestic bond issues.

Taiwan: Prohibits foreign banks from lending to individuals.

Trinidad and Tobago: Government corporations are discouraged from doing business with foreign banks.

7. Foreign banks' loan capacity limited vis-à-vis domestic banks as a result of the method of calculating bank assets

Countries

Denmark (1), (2); Italy (1); South Korea (1); Switzerland (1), (2). Under certain conditions the bank commission tolerates branch liabilities of up to double the limits.

Implications/Comments. Banking regulations in virtually all countries require banks to maintain a certain ratio of net capital to total liabilities. This percentage is usually the same for both domestic and foreign banks. Yet this regulation differentially restrains foreign branch operations in those countries (1) which base net capital for domestic banks on the capital and reserves of the whole bank, while for branches of foreign banks it is based on only the bank's assets within the country.

Similarly, in some countries (2) branches of foreign owned banks must reduce their net capital by the amount of branch claims on their head office or any of their subsidiaries or branches outside the country.

8. Specified loan portfolio structure

Countries

Bolivia: Foreign banks required to allocate 25 percent of total loans to industrial and manufacturing credits. Percentage for domestic banks is less.

Ecuador: Foreign branches must invest 25 percent of their portfolios in low yielding government bonds. The requirement for local banks is only 20 percent.

Peru: Foreign banks are required to extend two lines of credit to the government, one equal to twice the foreign bank's local capital and the other equal to the amount of domestic currency deposits held.

9. Policies that place constraints on foreign banks' investment portfolios

Countries

Bolivia: Reinvestment of earnings may not exceed 5 percent of capital annually.

Brazil: Foreign banks are permitted to hold only up to 50 percent of capital stock and up to 33 percent of voting shares in Brazilian financial institutions. Precludes foreign banks from matching, the major domestic banks' diversification into banking-related activities.

Spain: Prohibition of foreign bank equity participation in Spanish business in contrast to Spanish banks, which already control close to 48 percent of private industry. Limits the investment portfolios of foreign banks to holdings of government securities and fixed interest obligations.

10. Discriminatory or excessive capital requirements

Countries

Bolivia: Initial capital required for foreign branches is twice that required on domestic banks.

South Korea: Foreign banks are required to capitalize each branch separately.

Spain: Branches of foreign banks must have capital of $10.7 million, and subsidiaries twice that amount (as of 1978). These capitalization requirements have been criticized by foreign banks as too high. It should be noted, however, that the capital requirement for Spanish banks is even higher.

11. Discriminatory or excessive reserve requirements

Countries

Ecuador: Foreign banks must deposit a larger proportion of their foreign exchange with the Central Bank.

Egypt: Foreign banks operating in Egypt required to deposit 15 percent of their currency with Central Bank.

Greece: Foreign banks must deposit U.S. $10 million in foreign exchange with the Central Bank for each branch office established.

12. Limitations on foreign exchange transactions

Country Australia

Country Specifics. All foreign exchange transactions must be done through Australian banks and at rates of exchange fixed or authorized by the Central Bank. This gives Australian banks a monopoly on foreign exchange transactions to the competitive disadvantage of foreign bank subsidiary operations.

Implications/Comments. Limitations on foreign-exchange transactions are often the product of general economic and balance-of-payments policy measures. In such instances, limitations apply evenly to all banks, foreign and domestic, yet they tend to have a harsher impact on foreign banks because of the international orientation of their business.

13. Restrictions on repatriation profits or funds

Countries

Brazil: Up to 12 percent of existing capital and reinvestment funds may be remitted, excessive amounts subject to progressive tax of 65–85 percent.

Bolivia: Profit repatriation may not exceed 20 percent of capital annually.

Ghana: Difficult to obtain approval for remittance of profits.

Kenya: Difficult to obtain approval for remittance of profits.

South Korea: Retained earning requirements.

Lebanon: Retained earning requirements.

Netherlands: Retained earning requirements.

Pakistan: Retained earning requirements.

Philippines: Retained earning requirements.

Singapore: Retained earning requirements.

Tanzania: Retained earning requirements.

Zambia: Repatriation of profits prohibited. Up to 30 percent of equity capital may be transferred abroad provided that the amount is less than 50 percent of net profits.

Appendix 7–C.   Reciprocity Provisions for Banks in OECD and Selected Countries.

Reciprocity Tests[a]	Yes	No	Not Applicable[b]
Australia	X		
Austria		X	
Belgium		X	
Canada	X		
Denmark	X[c]		
Finland	X		
France	X		
West Germany		X	
Greece		X	
Iceland			X
Ireland	X[c]		
Italy	X		
Japan	X		
Luxembourg		X	
Netherlands	X[c,d]		
New Zealand	X		
Norway			X
Portugal			X[e]
Spain	X		
Sweden		X	
Switzerland	X		
Turkey	X		
United Kingdom		X	
United States	X[f]		

Source: Organization for Economic Cooperation and Development, *Trade in Services in Banking* (Paris: OECD, 1983), p. 21. Updated.

a. Apply with regard to entry of foreign banks.

b. Foreign bank entry *not* permitted.

c. Applies only to banks from non-European Community countries.

d. Directives necessary for the application of reciprocity tests have not been issued.

Appendix 7–C. (continued).

e. No reciprocity clause is explicitly embodied in the banking law.

f. Some states apply reciprocity provisions with regard to the entry of foreign bank agencies and branches.

Notes: A random sample of national reciprocity provisions follows:

Canada: The Minister of Finance must be satisifed that treatment as favorable for Canadian banks exists, or will be arranged, in the home jurisdiction of a foreign bank wishing to establish operations in Canada.Denmark: There are no specific legal provisions on reciprocity; circumstances are taken into account when banks from outside the countries of the European Community apply for entry.

Finland: No legal provisions, but according to the Government Propositions to Parliament concerning legislation on foreign banks, the principle of reciprocity is applicable to foreign banks' presence in Finland.

France: When considering an application for a license by a foreign bank, the Conseil National du Credit takes into consideration the conditions applied to entry of foreign banks in the applicant's home country.

Federal Republic of Germany: At present there are no reciprocity provisions; it is, however, being considered that such provisions be introduced with regard to branches of foreign banks.

Republic of Ireland: In considering an application by an overseas bank for a license, the Central Bank would have regard to the attitude of the authorities of that bank's country of origin to possible applications by Irish banks to be established there. This, however, would not be a determining factor.

Italy: Authorization for the establishment of branches of banks outside the European Community is subject to the proviso that the principle of reciprocity be respected.

Japan: Under specific circumstances, application of the reciprocity principle is required.

Netherlands: Section 7 of the Act on the Supervision of the Credit System empowers the Crown to determine grounds and directives, on the basis of which the bank shall refuse to grant a license, revoke a license granted or grant a license subject to conditions in cases where institutions are involved which have their registered office outside the European Community. This section permits a policy of reciprocity to be conducted vis-à-vis countries where Netherlands banks meet with difficulties in setting up operations. So far, however, no such directives have been issued.

Spain: The authorization for the establishment of foreign banks' branches or subsidiaries is granted according to criteria that take account of the principle of reciprocity.

Switzerland: The reciprocity principle is enshrined as a specific criterion in the Swiss banking law for granting authorization to the establishment of foreign banking organizations.

Turkey: Reciprocity could be applied in terms of conditions required by the Council of Ministers at the stage of granting the authorization for entry.

United States: There are no federal reciprocity provisions, but such provisions are applied to branches and agencies of foreign banks by some states.

NOTES

1. U.S. Department of the Treasury, *Report to the Congress on Foreign Government Treatment of U.S. Banking Organizations* (Washington, D.C. Department of the Treasury, 1979; updated 1984). Organization for Economic Cooperation and Development, *Trade in Services in Banking* (Paris OECD, 1983); Ingo Walter *Barriers to Trade in Banking and Financial Services* (London Trade Policy Research Centre, 1985).
2. Craig Forman and John Marcom, Jr., "Britain's Bank Regulators Opening the Door Wider to Foreigners," *The Wall Street Journal*, July 17, 1987.
3. *International Herald Tribune*, June 4, 1987; *Business Week*, June 22, 1987.
4. Letter to the author from the Office of The United States Trade Representative, Executive Office of the President, USTR Computer Group, 1986.
5. U.S. Department of the Treasury, *Report to the Congress on Foreign Government Treatment of U.S. Banking Organizations*.
6. Walter, *Barriers to Trade in Banking and Financial Services*.
7. H. Peter Gray, and Jean M. Gray, "The Multinational Bank A Financial MNC?", *Journal of Banking and Finance* (March 1982).
8. C. Stuart Goddin, "Memorandum on National Treatment and Reciprocity." Office of the Comptroller of the Currency, United States Department of the Treasury, Washington, D.C., September 12, 1983. Mimeo.
9. "Banks, Brokers Split on Liberalization Plan," *International Herald Tribune*, June 6, 1987.

8

TRADE LIBERALIZATION
IN FINANCIAL SERVICES

In a very real sense, the growth of international trade in financial services has already progressed very far indeed. Beginning with the removal of exchange controls by many industrial countries in the 1960s and the simultaneous overseas expansion by American commercial banks as they followed their multinational corporate clients into Europe—and continuing into today's intense market and product interpenetration on the part of financial and nonfinancial institutions of all types—the expansion of international trade in financial services appears to have been rapid. One can thus argue with some justice that international trade in financial services has in fact been one of the few really bright spots on the trade-policy scene—all without formal negotitations or the pro-active involvement of the GATT, the OECD, the EEC, or any other official body.

This would seriously overstate the case, however, since such a conclusion would be largely (though not entirely) limited to the industrial countries. In much of the rest of the world, the ability of foreign based players to supply financial services remains severely restricted. Even in the OECD countries there continue to be significant restrictions with respect to specific forms of involvement, client groups, and products that bear differentially on foreign based institutions. Nevertheless, the direction of change has definitely been toward liberalization of capital markets and globalization of finance, and the pace of change has been impressive.

THE STARTING POINT

Banking and financial services within national markets existand often prosper in a highly controlled environment. Because banks are financial intermediaries with fiduciary responsibilities, and because negative externalities are always associated with financial failures and crises, freedom from prudential regulation and control in this industry is out of the question. The same holds true of restrictions bearing on financial institutions as instruments of national monetary and economic policy. There may well be losses in efficiency by comparison with the largely unregulated offshore financial markets, but there are compensating gains in safety. Some sort of balance has to be struck. Whether a given country's financial supervisory and regulatory policies are themselves efficient is a matter for debate. Often they clearly are not, and reform in many cases seems long overdue. But this is a matter of national prerogative.

Protectionism in financial services refers mainly to discriminatory barriers against foreign based institutions competing in the national financial environment. Such barriers are departures from the principle of "national treatment," and have the effect of either raising costs or limiting the access of foreign competitors to markets or to funds and do not also apply identically to competing indigenous financial institutions. Protection by this definition is widespread and the very complexity of financial services offers an extraordinarily broad range of tariff-like and quota-like competitive distortions. Moreover, since there are no internationally agreed rules governing services generally, and services supplied through foreign direct investment specifically, governments have essentially free rein in applying protectionist measures, limited only by the inevitable losses in efficiency and possible constraints imposed by reciprocity.

Trade distortions in financial services broadly follow the outlines of sectoral competitive advantage (see Chapter 7). Countries that are home bases to highly competitive players in the financial services industry tend to be characterized by relatively liberal policies toward domestic activities of foreign based banking and financial institutions, while countries that are not tend to be protectionist. Some try to have it both ways by combining a highly restricted onshore environment with the creation of an offshore banking center. As countries develop, especially under outward-oriented strategies for growth, the static and dynamic costs of protection become ever more apparent and movement toward liberalization can often be expected. In many ways, therefore, protectionism in financial services parallels the state and evolution of national trade policies generally.

Several additional points deserve restatement:

1. The offshore Euromarkets (arguably) provide a permanent standard of efficiency with respect to an internationally competitive financial services environment, at least at the wholesale end of the market. Countries can thus compare relatively easily the financial environment in domestic competitive conditions with the projected environment if offshore competitive conditions were to prevail at home. The opportunity costs of protection, therefore, are perhaps more clearly apparent in financial services than in other industries. They expose to countries how debilitating distortions can be for the national economy, and how lagging liberalization and deregulation can impair both a country's chances of maintaining a role as a financial center *and* its institutions' chances of becoming world-class competitors. Financial institutions which do well at home but cannot keep up with the competition in offshore markets are living examples that such opportunity costs do exist. For those promoting the very real benefits of trade liberalization in financial services, the Eurobenchmark is thus an unusual asset in their argumentation.

2. Unlike the manufacturing sector, in financial services even the most highly competitive of firms are not always unambiguously in favor of free trade. Since onshore markets tend to be served largely through a direct presence and since protected national markets tend to be extraordinarily profitable for efficient competitors able to gain entry, they are apt to take a low profile with respect to a further opening of the market once they are safely inside. Like other businesses, financial institutions are rent-seekers, and the rents they seek frequently develop because of, rather than in spite of, national protectionist policies—not so different from multinational enterprises in the manufacturing sector and their use of investment incentives to enhance returns.[1] The best evidence for this would be a comparison of returns from the highly competitive offshore activities of financial institutions and returns from a weighted mix of their onshore operations. Moreover, many of the major players do very well indeed by serving markets via correspondent relationships that could be endangered by liberalization efforts and direct market entry.

3. Foreign based financial institutions are vulnerable to the allegation that their very foreignness may compromise prudential and monetary-policy measures in the domestic market. They may be tempted to evade domestic taxes or exchange controls by off-market pricing of interbank foreign exchange in transactions or other financial services, by parking funds in tax havens or by "round-tripping" to avoid restrictive monetary policies. Cases in each of these categories have surfaced in recent years, as has the use of foreign banks as financial conduits by domestic residents to facilitate illegal transactions.[2] In all countries, a domestic focus on the "sensitive" nature and the central importance of the banking and financial services industry will always exist, and foreign based institutions will always occupy a somewhat vulnerable position. With few exceptions, the evidence seems to be that foreign institutions recognize this and attempt to tailor their behavior to minimize such concerns on the part of host governments.

4. Protection in financial services can be easily analyzed in terms of all the standard welfare criteria. The adverse impact in terms of static and dynamic efficiency have already been noted. There are also the effects on the redistribution of income, from the users of financial services to the protected local institutions. Unless protectionism involves discriminatory taxation, no tariff-like revenues accrue to the government. Instead, unearned returns go to domestic players and to those foreign firms fortunate enough to achieve market access—in the latter case much the same as under quotas or "voluntary" export-restraint agreements (VERs) in trade in goods. And, due to the quota-like characteristics of many trade barriers in this sector, such impacts tend to multiply in an expanding domestic financial market where foreign suppliers are locked out.

At the same time, the effects on the terms of trade of the country imposing the restrictions are unclear. On the one hand, the high prices foreign financial firms are able to charge in a restricted market point to a terms of trade deterioration. On the other hand, countries may use entry or operating restrictions to extract concessions in the real prices of financial services supplied by foreign institutions and possibly achieve an improvement in the terms of trade. To all of these effects must be added adverse dynamic impacts via eroded competitive pressure on financial institutions serving domestic markets for continued innovation, cost-control and efficiency gains.

5. Competitive distortions in financial services have unusually serious implications for "effective protection." Except for retail business, all financial services are essentially inputs to be used in the production of other goods and services. Protectionist measures that raise the cost, erode the quality, or reduce the availability of credit or other financial services in the market clearly serve to undermine the international competitiveness of the prospective users of these services, with broad adverse implications through time. Limited availability of venture capital, for example, can have dramatic effects on the future structure of a national economy and its international trade performance.

6. It seems clear that (with a few rather notable exceptions) protection in financial services as defined here has been of concern mainly to commercial banking organizations. Most countries have nonexistent or poorly developed stock and bond markets. This has made them of limited interest to foreign based investment banks and securities firms concerned with origination, underwriting, and dealing in securities. Some countries that do have major securities markets, such as Switzerland and Germany, have in the past "reserved" leadership in the new-issues business to local houses. Others, such as Canada, Japan, and the United Kingdom, have severely restricted the activities of foreign based securities firms, including membership in local stock exchanges. And the prevalence of exchange controls and other restrictions has impeded distribution of foreign securities in many countries.

On the other hand, countries concerned with the development of viable indigenous capital markets have actively sought foreign involvement in investment banking, as in the case of Australia. Moreover, various kinds of merchant-banking services, such as corporate financial advice and asset management, can be effectively marketed without a direct presence in the country concerned, often with the government itself as a major client. So, with some notable exceptions, departures from national treatment in nonbanking wholesale (but not retail) financial services may have had rather limited distortive effect thus far.

Finally, economic growth and changes in the financial environment periodically prompt countries to reassess their national policies toward foreign based financial institutions. We can again mention Australia as well as Sweden and (earlier) Chile in this context.

Another such case is Canada, a country that has traditionally been hostile to foreign based financial institutions but that has also been under heavy domestic as well as external pressure to liberalize its treatment of foreign players over the years.[3]

The traditional fear of domination by U.S. banks has come up against the reality of Canada as the home of several of the largest and most powerful banks in the world, some of which have done extremely well in the U.S. domestic market. Foreign commercial banks, so-called Schedule B banks, have been limited in terms of the proportion of total banking assets they are allowed to hold, and in 1986 this amounted to about 16 percent. Moreover, since 1971 foreigners, as well as Canadians outside the securities industry, have been prohibited from owning more than 10 percent of securities firms in the Province of Ontario, the country's financial center with two-thirds of all securities trading being done in Toronto. Established foreign securities houses were also limited in growth to the average of the Canadian securities industry as a whole. After the restrictions were imposed, the number of foreign securities dealers with branches or subsidiaries in Canada dwindled from twenty-six to four.

One result: In a period of rapid securitization, Canadian institutions were increasingly left behind and Toronto was in danger of losing its position as the fourth largest capital market in the world. The capitalization of the entire Canadian securities industry in 1986 (under $1 billion) was well below the capitalization of some of the major securities firms operating in international markets. The consequence was that an increasing share of Canadian securities business was being transacted outside Canada. During the first half of 1986, Canadian issuers raised almost $10.6 billion in the Euromarkets, nearly 80 percent of it through foreign institutions. Salomon Brothers, for example, became one of the leading traders in Canadian bonds serving the market from New York without any presence in Canada itself—selling high-quality paper and dealing with sophisticated investors without the need for government approvals. Moreover, Canadian securities houses had virtually no chance of competing internationally.

In December 1986, Ontario announced that it would permit foreign securities dealers to register for the first time since 1971. They would also be permitted to own 50 percent of local securities dealerships after June 30, 1987 and 100 percent after June 30, 1988. At the same time, Canadian banks and investors were allowed to own and operate securities dealerships as well. The announcement triggered plans by numerous foreign firms to set up securities activities in Ontario, as well as a loosening of federal restrictions of bank ownership of securities houses, in part to prevent foreign domination of the industry.

Sometimes called by Canadians the "Little Bang," deregulation was expected to attract growing numbers of Japanese and European as well as American firms to a hitherto highly compartmentalized and sheltered industry. Advocates of liberalization noted that Toronto "was overdue for an injection of innovative, hard-nosed management. With barely 100 Canadian securities firms and the bulk of the business centered on the Toronto exchange, critics contend that the industry has been guilty of featherbedding, with high commissions and high profits, and a slowness to introduce some of the new financial products that have become popular elsewhere."[4] Even so, unlike the bilateral Canadian-American trade negotiations proceeding simultaneously, financial deregulation and the prospective market penetration by foreign players seemed to arouse relatively little opposition from the indigenous industry. This was evidently attributable to the industry's realization that Canada's role in international capital markets would continue to dwindle in the absence of serious liberalization. In addition, local firms expected large gains as foreign players bid for acquisitions in the Canadian securities industry.

Foreign based securities firms are allowed to increase equity participation in Canadian houses to 50 percent as of June 30, 1987 and 100 percent as of June 30, 1988. Ownership had been restricted to 10 percent since 1971 under the traditional Canadian policy of economic nationalism, and foreign firms that were grandfathered (mainly Merrill Lynch and Prudential Bache) were strictly constrained in terms of capitalization. The delay was apparently aimed at giving local firms first crack at acquiring Canadian houses, including local insurers and banks that have already established a worldwide presence in their own industries and could benefit substantially by moving aggressively into the securities business.

The Canadian banking crisis of 1985–86 eliminated virtually all of the country's smaller banks, a number of which were taken over by foreign institutions. Lloyds Bank, for example, took over Continental Bank of Toronto (renamed Lloyds Bank Canada), with fifty-five branches and C$5.4 billion in assets. Hong Kong and Shanghai Bank of Canada took over the Bank of Columbia, with C$3.1 billion in assets, as well as (through acquisition of London Stockbroker James Capel & Co. and Toronto investment dealer Brown Baldwin Nisker) a significant securities operation. In mid-1987, Deutsche Bank sought to add to its commercial banking presence in Canada by acquiring a 50 percent stake in McLean McCarthy, a Toronto stock brokerage represented on the Toronto and Montreal stock exchanges. Other banks active in Canada were Citibank, Morgan, Manufacturers Hanover, Bank of America, Chase Manhattan, and Chemical Bank from the United States; Swiss Bank Corporation and Crédit Suisse; Midland Bank, National Westminister, and Barclays of the United Kingdom; Banque Nationale de Paris, Crédit Lyonnais, and Société Générale of France; and Bank of Tokyo. Together, the fifty-five foreign-owned banks booked about C$40 billion in assets at the end of 1986.

In the securities business, Shearson Lehman Brothers increased its stake in McLeod Young Weir, a major Toronto securities house, from 10 to 30 percent, while Merrill Lynch, Goldman Sachs, and Salomon Brothers each initiated or expanded its commitment to the Canadian market. All four major Japanese securities houses—Nomura, Daiwa, Nikko, and Yamaichi—purchased seats on the Toronto stock exchange and increased their Canadian efforts. Nippon Life and Sumitomo Life set up offices to monitor their Canadian assets.[5]

In March 1987 the French authorities announced that foreign banks and brokerage firms would henceforth be allowed to buy equity stakes in French brokerage houses, gradually eliminating a monopoly accorded to sixty domestic stockbrokers by Napoleon in 1807. Foreign firms can own 30 percent shares in French brokerage houses beginning in 1988, rising to 49 percent in 1989 and 90 percent in 1990, with a complete phase-out of the brokers' equity trading monopoly scheduled for 1992. France also extended stock exchange trading hours and opened an over-the-counter market to facilitate the raising of share capital by small firms, as well as a futures market and a market for commercial paper. "Le petit bang" paralleled similar moves in the United Kingdom and Canada, designed to make the Paris bourse and the six regional stock exchanges in France competitive with equity markets abroad, as well as to promote market-making ability via adequate capitalization through foreign investments in French brokerage firms. The alternative was to have large equity deals bypass the French market entirely, in favor of Euroequity deals out of London. Speculation was that the major French banks, as well as foreign banks and securities houses such as Morgan Stanley, Salomon Brothers, and Nomura Securities would move to take advantage of the opportunity.

On a regional level, it was acknowledged by Jacques Delors, president of the European Commission, that free trade in financial services within the EC would not be possible without considerable reinforcement of the European Monetary System (EMS), including participation by the United Kingdom. This includes harmonization of banking regulations, taxation of financial institutions, control of speculative financial flows, liberalization of remaining exchange controls, and the right of establishment for banks and other financial institutions. The interdependence of these diverse aspects of financial integration bore particularly on the United Kingdom and Germany.

Britain has been in the forefront of pressing for liberal international trade in financial services, yet reluctant to join the EMS. In Delors' view, the role of London as Europe's premier financial center is incompatible with the absence of the United Kingdom from a regional arrangement on exchange rates and macroeconomic policy that has existed in its current form since 1978. "I cannot conceive of the achievement of a common financial space without the entry of the pound into the EMS exchange rate mechanism. It is a big currency with a large market, not like the Greek drachma or the peseta."[6]

At the same time, Germany's support of freedom of international capital movements was deemed incompatible with its reluctance to harmonize banking regulations throughout the EEC, opening its own financial services sector to outside competition, and ceding some degree of independence on the part of the Bundesbank.

ELEMENTS OF LIBERAL TRADE IN FINANCIAL SERVICES

Given the existing vacuum with respect to internationally agreed rules on trade in financial services and the clearly significant costs of protection in this sector at the global and national levels, what policy "benchmarks" would seem to be appropriate?

First, there should be a clear recognition that financial services reflect the underlying principles of comparative advantage, like any other industry. There is no greater justification for protection (appropriately defined) in financial services than there is for steel, automobiles, or telecommunications equipment. We have emphasized that countries with an international competitive advantage in financial services are also those pursuing an open domestic competitive environment in this sector—although it could also be that countries following free trade principles in financial services develop the most competitive players in global markets. In any case, countries that have a competitive advantage in this sector have the *right* to seek access to foreign markets as a matter of general reciprocity, in return for access to their own domestic markets for goods or services in which they have a competitive disadvantage.

Second, the principle of "national treatment," shorthand for "equality of competitive opportunity," should be universally accepted as governing international trade in financial services. With appropriate safeguards, this principle can fully provide for the legitimate concerns addressed by prudential controls and the role of the financial system in the execution of monetary and economic policies. In this sector, as noted, national treatment is the generic equivalent of liberal trade, even in the presence of highly regulated financial markets.

If a country wants to adopt *dirigiste* financial policies in order to implement a particular strategy for growth or certain structural goals, that is its sovereign prerogative. It is not necessarily incompatible with the principle of national treatment, although it may well be more difficult to achieve in the presence of international financial integration and offshore financial markets.

Much more difficult are cases where the entire domestic financial system is nationalized, as is the case in a large number of developing countries and essentially all centrally planned economies. National treatment in such cases raises a family of problems that are not dissimilar to state trading issues in commercial policy generally. The presence of private banks may be ideologically unacceptable, as may a situation where the only remaining private banks are foreign owned. Nationalized banks may be managed in ways that have little to do with profit based criteria, and any foreign banks present could be forced to behave similarly (possibly to their great dismay) and still be afforded full national treatment. Even in such cases, an appropriate role for foreign financial institutions may be found, albeit a highly restrictive and individually negotiated one, as the case of China shows.

It thus seems likely that an appropriate version of the principle of "national treatment" will become the main objective of trade liberalization in the financial-services sector. It combines a nondiscriminatory most-favored-nation component with a nonprotectionist, market access component and is thus a robust and consistent goal. The same principle may well be equally appropriate in other service sectors, so that banking and financial services would fit quite well into the structure of international negotiations of an "umbrella" agreement to deal broadly with the services issue (see Chapter 9).

BENCHMARKS

If equality of competitive opportunity is to be the standard by which market access must be measured with respect to the international financial services industry, then this can be viewed as comprising the following components:

Freedom to establish branches, agencies, subsidiaries, representative offices or other affiliates within a national market on a basis identical to that applying to locally owned financial institutions. Referring once again to the client-arena-product matrix, reproduced in Figure 8–1, this freedom of establishment is critical to competitive equality in serving the client and product cells lying within a national arena, and maximizing the positive linkage effects to cells in the rest of the matrix. National antitrust and other policies relating to establishment would bear on foreign players identically to domestic players.

Regulatory symmetry, insofar as possible, with respect to domestic and foreign competitors. This includes the incidence of prudential controls such as capital requirements, asset ratios, lending limits, and reserve requirements. It also involves equality of access to the domestic securities markets, including lead-managing local-currency issues in the local and offshore markets,

Figure 8–1. International Financial Services Activity Matrix Once Again (C-A-P) Model).

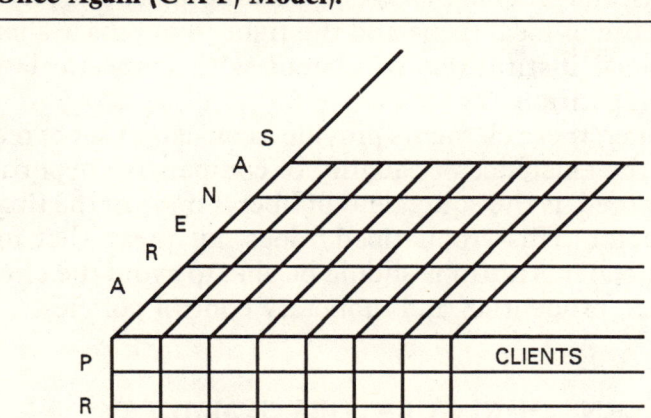

as well as equal access to the national payments clearing system, money markets, and central bank discount facilities, and trust and investment businesses.

Freedom to import critical resources, including travel and resettlement of professional staff, subscriptions of capital in the case of certain nonbranch affiliates, data processing and telecommunications equipment on the same basis as local firms. Included is equality of access to transborder communication and data transmission.

Symmetry with respect to the application of exchange controls, if any, as between foreign and local players. This bears on capital outflows such as foreign borrowing in the local markets and local investments abroad, as well as remittances of earnings.

193

Equality of access to domestic client groups, financial institutions, and product markets, including branching privileges equal to those of local firms and the right to purchase shares in local financial institutions consistent with domestic laws regarding competition.

Together, these elements provide a consistent set of requirements for the existence of equality of competitive opportunity, which, as noted, is the equivalent of liberal trade in the financial services sector. This emphatically does *not* mean that foreign based financial institutions should be able to avoid the effects of national tax, prudential, and monetary control policies.

PATTERNS OF REGULATORY SYMMETRY

National treatment is perhaps best defined generically as "equality of competitive opportunity." This should be distinguished from *strict* national treatment in which identical laws and regulations are rigidly applied to foreign and domestic banks. A government moratorium on bank branches, for example, would qualify as strict national treatment, yet exclude foreign banks that are wholly new to the market or have not yet developed viable branch networks, thus violating equality of competitive opportunity.

Besides questions of monetary control and prudential supervision and regulation, another reason for government intervention in the entry or operations of foreign based financial institutions relates to competitive structures in domestic markets. Countries have widely differing antimonopoly policies and enforcement procedures, and the acquisition of domestic financial institutions by foreign buyers could run afoul of antitrust arrangements. "Horizontal" acquisitions, within the country, once a local presence has been established, could do so as well. The same concerns about the competitive structure also apply to domestic financial institutions. Again, if the same standards are imposed on all prospective purchasers of existing banks (whether based abroad or domestic), this would be considered national treatment and would not in any way represent protectionist intent. Antitrust issues can, however, be raised as a pretext for action that is in fact protectionist.

To repeat, given the need for financial regulation and control per se, regulating foreign based players on precisely the same basis as domestic players is broadly equivalent to the principles of free trade applied to the financial services sector. Anything beyond this which has the effect of discriminating against the competitive position of foreign financial institutions in the relevant domestic markets may be defined as protectionism and can be shown to have many of the same economic implications as protection in international trade in goods.

Appendix 8–1, at the end of this chapter, summarizes financial regulation in eight major industrial countries. It is clear that even among these countries significant regulatory distortions can arise, despite a persistent trend toward financial liberalization in recent years. It is equally clear that the precise regulatory and control motives of the authorities are often difficult to sort out.

Banking and other financial services, increasingly conducted on a global basis, constitute an industry that is characterized by the presence of some large and sophisticated players. That they should become targets for protectionist measures in various countries is hardly surprising. Nor are the very real economic losses entirely attributable to protection. Each country's regulatory profile is unique and, beyond the sort of taxonomy of distortions offered here, further generalization is difficult.

PROBLEMS OF CAPITAL ADEQUACY

It should be obvious that the implementation of a truly level playing field in this sector is made vastly more complicated because of the regulatory and prudential considerations just discussed. Countries differ with respect to capital requirements, statutory and "hidden" reserves against loan losses (in the form of deliberately undervalued assets), regulation of domestic deposit rates, deposit insurance, domestic competition policies, and

195

a variety of other dimensions that can affect an institution's competitive positioning internationally. While it is similar in nature to the competitive effects of subsidies and governmental participation in other industries, it is perhaps more serious in this sector. Moreover, in no other industry have uniform global standards been attempted.

For example, Japanese commercial banks have long been alleged to possess an artificial competitive advantage in international markets as a result of home-country regulations permitting exceedingly low capitalization. This has permitted them to be exceedingly aggressive in competing for various kinds of lending around the world. Indeed, in 1986 representatives of the Federal Deposit Insurance Corporation and the Federal Reserve System renewed pressure for greater coordination of prudential controls within the context of the Bank for International Settlements, with the intent of leveling the playing field.

Bank regulators have discussed this issue for years, confronting time and again the fact of national sovereignty in banking supervision and monetary control and the entrenched interests of banks themselves. At a meeting in Amsterdam during October 1986, for example, banking supervisors resolved to work toward the same minimum capital standards for all banks that do business across national borders, as a matter both of competitive fairness and prudential soundness. That minimum most probably also represents the maximum capital standards that countries will impose if their banks are not to suffer in international competition. Supervisors also agreed to work toward a uniform definition of capital—which in many cases includes not only equity but also long-term debt, as well as greater commonality in loan loss provisioning. Some progress has been achieved, but regulatory coordination must also involve agreement on sanctions (including exclusion from specific businesses and markets) for institutions that violate or circumvent the rules.

In a major breakthrough on this issue the United States and the United Kingdom in January 1987 announced agreement on almost identical standards with respect to bank capital requirements. The purpose was to improve the resilience of the multinational banks and the international financial system as a

**Figure 8–2. Off-Balance-Sheet Commitments of U.S.
Money-Center Banks (September 1986).**

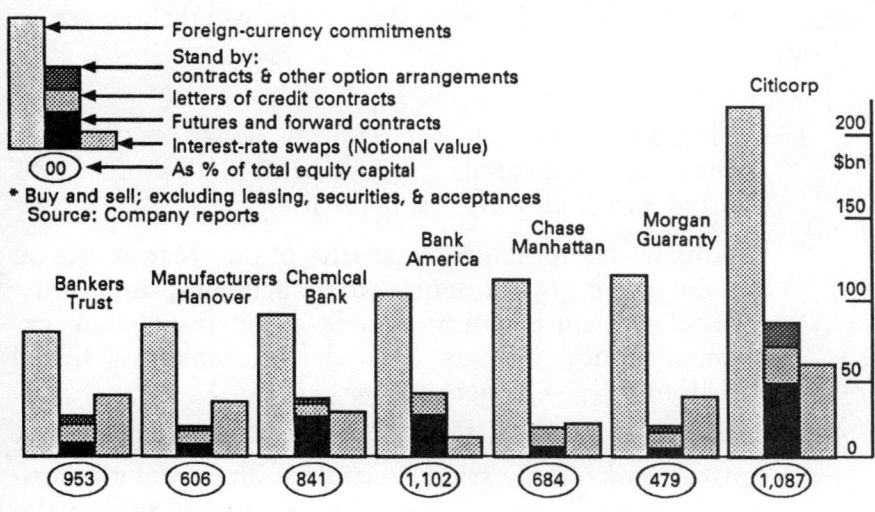

Source: The Economist, March 9, 1987.
Copyright 1987, *The Economist*, distributed by Special Features

whole to future shocks, including those related to off-balance-
sheet exposures (see Figure 8–2), *and* to ensure equitable competitive conditions with respect to capitalization. The
"risk-based capital standard" that was agreed upon links future
capital requirements to exposure risk categories, particularly
credit card obligations, off-balance-sheet commitments and international lending. Liquid assets, government-guaranteed loans,
Treasury securities, and other low-risk/high-liquidity assets
would serve to reduce capital requirements.

The agreement does not create *uniform* capital requirements, but rather sets out firm principles that are responsive to
institutional differences between the two countries. It does
mandate levels of primary capital and introduces the concept of
risk-based capital requirements. This involves assigning a
"weight" to each type of instrument involving potential exposure
to loss, with higher weights (and therefore greater capital back-

197

ing) assigned to exposures assessed to have greater embedded risk. Mandated levels of capitalization of banks are then based on the weighted total exposure of each institution, whether or not that exposure appears on the balance sheet. The weightings are as follows:

1. Cash and claims on the central bank, as well as government-guaranteed export and shipping loans (United Kingdom only)—0 percent.

2. Claims with a remaining maturity of one year or less on the domestic government and its agencies, and short-term claims on discount houses and certain stock exchange money brokers and market makers (United Kingdom only)—10 percent.

3. Short-term claims on domestic and foreign banks, foreign central banks, domestic government and agency securities in excess of one year remaining maturity, and similar domestic government-backed debt, as well as local-currency claims on foreign central banks—25 percent.

4. Direct claims on multinational development institutions in which the domestic government is a shareholder or contributing member—50 percent.

5. All other assets—100 percent.

6. Off-balance-sheet items involve applying a credit conversion factor that translated the credit risk embedded in each to a credit-equivalent, to which the above percentages are then applied. Commitments that are direct substitutes for credit, suchas financial guarantees, are assigned a 100 percent conversion factor. Other commitments such as swaps and revolving underwriting facilities are assigned conversion factors between 10 and 50 percent, depending on maturity.

The intent was that riskier instruments become more costly to hold, lessening the chances of excessive exposure and the prospect that regulators will have to step in to provide support in a crisis. It was expected, for example, that the requirements would limit underpricing of off-balance-sheet commitments. Given the high rate of financial innovation and the deluge of new instruments, this approach for the first time gives regulators a coherent framework into which to slot new types of exposures as they evolve. The risk-based capital standards would be applied beginning in 1988, and banks would have several years to bring their financials into compliance with the new rules.

The risk-based capital accord was expected to put greater pressure on U.S. banks to increase still further their capitalization levels. This could place them at a further disadvantage against the securities firms with which they are increasingly in competition. Nor are the provisions of the accord uniform. For example, it continues to permit British banks to count "silent" reserves (which do not exist in the United States) as part of capital, under the presumption that they will be phased out over time as part of the harmonization of EEC banking regulations. The question remained open whether the accord could readily be extended to the other main home-countries of multinational banks, in particular Germany, the Netherlands, France, Switzerland, and Japan in order to further level the competitive playing field and reduce chances of financial instability through interbank exposures. Likewise, there was the question whether free-riders may emerge among the smaller countries to give their banks a competitive edge through less rigorous capital requirements.

Japanese reaction to the U.K.-U.S. accord centering on a 5.5 percent capital requirement was initially less than fully supportive; the average capital ratio of Japanese banks in 1986 was 2.7 percent, less than half this level. The banks argued that differences in the way they operate, as well as interbank support and protection from the Bank of Japan, do not require the same level of capitalization in order to ensure stability—in effect acknowledging the existence of a de facto public subsidy. They also implied that the accord was aimed at impairing their competitive performance in penetrating foreign markets and acquiring foreign financial institutions.

Equity-to-asset ratios have indeed differed dramatically among countries in which some of the major international financial institutions are home-based. In 1985 the ratio was 4.0 in Belgium, 4.2 in Canada, 4.8 in France, 1.8 in Germany, 8.8 in Italy, 1.1 in Japan, 1.7 in the Netherlands, 8.1 in Spain, 5.6 in Sweden, 3.2 in Switzerland, 5.7 in the United Kingdom, and 3.8 in the United States. At the same time, hidden reserves are acceptable in some countries—such as Germany, Japan, and Switzerland—which seriously distorts equity-to-asset ratios as a measure of capital adequacy. Nevertheless, even taking hidden reserves into account, there have been allegations that Japanese banks are able to operate with significantly lower capital and thus possess an unfair competitive advantage over banks home-based in other countries.

By October 1987 indications were that Japan was basically in agreement with the U.K.-U.S. initiative on risk-based capital requirements, with 6 percent set as the basic level, following months of task force negotiations under the auspices of the Bank for International Settlements. Resistance on the part of the Japanese banks centered on the argument that part of their undisclosed holdings of securities (specifically, 70 percent of their average unrealized capital gains over the previous five years) should be counted as part of capital. Non-Japanese banks were said to have argued that less than 30 percent would be more appropriate, and a final figure of 30–50 percent appeared to be emerging.

Wide international differences also exist in the availability of information on bank performance, which may influence their relative competitive positioning and certainly affect the ability to determine whether the international competitive playing field is in fact fairly even. Transparency in U.S. accounting for banks is assured by the regulatory structure, and any disclosure problems are generally quickly remedied, including cross-border exposures and off-balance-sheet exposures in such transactions as swaps. In other countries disclosure is far less extensive, and in some cases nearly meaningless. Disclosure of off-balance-sheet risks in many cases is altogether absent, and many home countries of multinational banks fail to disclose their worldwide operations on a consolidated basis.

It is clear that the U.K.-U.S. accord on capital requirements must be extended to other countries if it is to have the desired effect on competitive and prudential conditions under which banks operate internationally. Similarly, coordination with authorities regulating the securities industry is essential if competitive rules under which firms in the two sectors of the financial services industry operate are not to act as further distortions to competitive conditions.

On the other hand, it has also been argued that coordinated risk-based capital requirements can actually be counterproductive, since assets categorized in the same risk class may have vastly different risk profiles. Moreover, since different assets and off-balance-sheet exposures require different levels of capital, the result may well be distortions in banking decisions (for example, loading up on highly interest-sensitive U.S. government securities, which require less capital backing than perhaps less risky alternative asset deployments). Such distortions ultimately may lead to increased, rather than decreased, vulnerability of individual institutions. It could also reduce financial innovation and place banks at a competitive disadvantage against nonfinancial institutions operating in the securities markets that are not subject to similar requirements.[7]

In mid-December 1987 twelve major industrial countries finally published a specific set of risk-based capital proposals based on the U.K.-U.S. initiative — the other countries were Japan, Germany, France, Canada, Italy, Sweden, Belgium, the Netherlands, Switzerland and Luxemburg. The proposals are summarized in Tables 8–1 and 8–2. The compliance deadline was set at 1992, although interim standards were to take effect in 1990. While still subject to some controversy, the proposals represented a major step in the direction of a level playing field in international banking.

As part of its mandate to regulate British wholesale markets under the Financial Services Act, the Bank of England in July 1987

201

Table 8–1 Global Capital Standards — Transitional Arrangements

	Initial	End-1990	End-1992
Minimum Standard	Level at year-end 1987	7.25%	8.0%
Measurement	Tier I capital plus 100% supplementary elements	Tier I capital plus 100% (3.625% plus 3.625%)	Tier I capital plus 100% (4% plus 4%)
Tier II Capital Included in Tier I	25% of Tier I capital	10% of Tier I capital (0.36%)	None
Limit on General Loan Loss Reserve in Tier II Capital	No limit	1.5%, by exception to 2%	1.25%, by exception 2%
Term Debt in Tier I Capital	No limit	No limit	Maximum of 50% of Tier I
Deduction of Goodwill	Deducted from Tier I capital	Deducted from Tier I capital	Deducted from Tier I capital

Source: Comptroller of the Currency, Federal Deposit Insurance Corporation, Federal Reserve Board, and Goldman, Sachs & Co., 1987.

Tier I Capital includes: – Tangible common equity (common equity less goodwill)

Tier II Capital includes: – Undisclosed reserves
– Unrealized securities and fixed asset gains (limited to 45% of gains)
– Hybrid debt capital instruments (including perpetual debt, fixed charge preferred stock, and the mandatory convertible securities of U.S. banks)
– Subordinated term debt (limited to 50% of Tier I)
– Loan loss reserves, not directly ascribed to particular assets (limited to 1.25% of risk-adjusted assets)

Table 8–2 Risk Weights by Category of On-Balance-Sheet Asset

Percentage	Asset Category
0%	Cash
	Balances at and claims on domestic central bank
	Loans to domestic central Governments
	Securities issues by domestic central Governments
	Loans and other assets fully collateralized by cash, domestic central Government securities, or fully guaranteed by domestic central Governments
0% or 20%	Claims on IBRD and regional development banks
20%	Claims on domestic and foreign banks with an original maturity of less than one year
	Claims on domestic banks with an original maturity of one year and more and loans guaranteed by domestic banks
	Claims on foreign central Governments in local currency financed by local currency liabilities
	Cash items in process of collection
0%, 20% or 50%	Claims on the domestic public sector (excluding the central Government) at national discretion and loans guaranteed by such institutions
50%	Loans for owner-occupied residences fully secured by mortgages
100%	Claims on the private sector
	Cross-border claims on foreign banks with an original maturity of one year and more

Source: Comptroller of the Currency, Federal Deposit Insurance Corporation and Federal Reserve Board, 1987.

issued a "grey paper" outlining a regulatory framework for gold bullion and large sterling and foreign currency deposits, spot and forward foreign exchange commercial transactions, and various other wholesale instruments, as well as a code of conduct for market participants. Institutions covered by the rules must be "fit and proper" according to the criteria laid down by the Bank of England, specifically with regard to capitalization, management and operational capability, and standards of businessconduct. The intent of the risk-based capital requirements for nonbanks was to be as close as possible to those agreed under the U.K.-U.S. accord in order to avoid competitive distortions between banks and nonbanks active in the same financial markets. The so-called London Code of Conduct is designed to cover a specific set of financial instruments that would adhere to the Code wherever they are traded, thus representing a uniform level of quality. These include swaps, sterling and foreign exchange deposits, gold and silver bullion, options, and futures. The Code also governs relationships among market participants and between them and their customers.

The purpose of the Bank of England initiative was to provide a simple, straightforward structure that would embody acceptable levels of safety and soundness, without significantly impairing efficiency and competitive performance, for those transactions and market participants not covered by banking regulation or the self-regulatory Securities and Investment Board in the retail sector.

ROLE OF THE GENERAL AGREEMENT ON TARIFFS AND TRADE

In moving from the present, highly distorted playing field superimposed on the client-arena-product matrix, reflecting actual competitive conditions in the global financial services industry, to conditions approximating equality of competitive opportunity, the role of the GATT as a prospective vehicle for liberalization needs to be examined.

The General Agreement on Tariffs and Trade originated in the late 1940s as part of a grand design for a set of rules to govern the postwar international economy. The economic chaos of the 1930s and the war provided an outstanding opportunity for the exercise of economic statemanship, particularly by the United-States, which found itself in a position of economic hegemony.

Rule-making had to cover international monetary affairs, inter-governmental transfers of resources and foreign aid, international trade, and international private capital flows including foreign direct investment.

Given the high stakes and conflicts among national interests involved, the institutions that emerged from these efforts, while by no means a true grand design, have proved remarkably durable and adaptable to changing circumstances: the IMF in international monetary affairs, the World Bank family of institutions in project and program financing, and the GATT in international trade.

The principal omission was an institution to set rules governing private capital and technology flows, and this gap has contributed to the kinds of conflicts that have characterized the relations between multinational enterprises, governments, and interest groups over the years. The central issue in this area is the symmetry of rights and obligations of countries, governments, and other players. The unwillingness to acknowledge this symmetry, particularly by the American business community in the early years and by governments of developing countries later on, has prevented creation of an agreed set of rules in this critical area—an omission that turns out to be particularly important in the financial services sector.

As of 1985 the GATT covered 122 countries, of which 90 were full signatories, 31 had not yet become signatories but in fact substantially complied with GATT rules and accordingly were afforded trade treatment by signatories as if they were members, and one country applied the Agreement on a provisional basis. Countries outside the GATT included the Soviet Union and other Eastern European countries, Iran, Saudi Arabia, and China, although many were given trade treatment by members as if they were indeed GATT signatories and several have expressed interest in eventual membership. In all, it is estimated that about 80 percent of world trade takes place under the GATT rules.

GATT PRINCIPLES AND FINANCIAL SERVICES

The GATT Articles of Agreement essentially consist of a set of rules covering trade matters that have been voluntarily accepted by signatories. These rules have evolved considerably over the years through modifications and supplements, interpretation and precedent, and are anchored in a rather complex legal document. Several basic principles, however, can be identified as forming the core of the GATT, and can be examined in terms of their applicability to international trade in financial services.

Unconditional MFN Treatment

First is unconditional most-favored-nation (MFN) treatment of imports (Article I). In the case of tariffs, this means that imports from any other GATT signatory country, as well as any others afforded MFN treatment, are subject to identical rates of duty. Any tariff reductions negotiated with any other countries will immediately and unconditionally be extended to all other GATT signatories as well.

This principle of nondiscrimination in the application of tariffs is subject to two important exceptions. One is that members of trade blocs or common markets that have agreed to extend more favorable tariff treatment to each other than they extend to nonmembers may do so, as long as they do not raise new barriers to outsiders and are working toward substantially free trade among the members themselves (Article XXIV). The second is the Generalized System of Preferences (GSP) which since 1979 has allowed GATT signatories to grant more favorable tariff treatment to developing countries than they do to other GATT signatories, as part of an effort originating in the United Nations Conference on Trade and Development (UNCTAD) to promote LDC export performance in manufactured goods.

While unconditional MFN treatment in the case of tariffs is relatively clear-cut and has shown itself to be a valuable contribution to an open international trading system, the same cannot be said of quotas and other quantitative restraints of international trade. In principle, unconditional MFN treatment applies to import quotas as well, with the additional stipulation that any quotas imposed should be removed as soon as practicable (Article XIX). In practice, however, quantitative trade restrictions have become increasingly selective through the use of "voluntary" export restraints (VERs) individually negotiated between pairs of countries, leading to a serious erosion of the relevance of the GATT. In the case of garments, these arrangements have indeed been largely negotiated under GATT-sanctioned rubrics: the Short-Term Arrangement on Cotton Textiles (STA) of 1961, successively replaced by the Long-Term Arrangement on Cotton Textiles (LTA) in 1962, and the Multifibre Arrangement (MFA) in 1974.

Unconditional MFN treatment in financial services would mean that institutions from all signatory countries could participate in the national market on an equal basis. This clearly precludes the application of reciprocity in the treatment of foreign based financial services firms.

Broad-Gauge Reciprocity

A second cornerstone of the GATT system is trade liberalization on a "reciprocal and mutually advantageous" basis. Reciprocity was recognized from the outset as being both necessary and desirable to assure a balanced opening of markets and competitive opportunities to all players. Since trade liberalization under the GATT has proceeded over the years in a reciprocal manner, the levels and structures of trade barriers that exist have embedded in them the results of decades of mutual concessions. This means that countries choosing to accede to the GATT must alter their trade policies in a way that conforms to the GATT Articles of Agreement and achieves broadly the same degree of liberal market access as GATT members, the so-called admission fee. A number of the countries choosing to remain outside the GATT have found this trade policy adjustment politically or economically difficult, although many are nevertheless afforded GATT treatment by signatories. In effect, there is an exception made for developing countries, which are not expected to reciprocate in full when that would not be consistent with their development needs.

Reciprocity in the GATT context is thus defined in the generic, broad sense, applying across the full spectrum of internationally traded goods. This emphatically does not mean reciprocity with respect to a specific product or market, but rather reciprocal market access reflecting the structure of each country's comparative advantage.

The GATT principle of broad-gauge reciprocity would appear to strongly support trade liberalization in the financial services sector, since countries such as the United States and the United Kingdom—with a presumed competitive advantage in this industry—are among the most important importers of manufactured goods from countries with a presumed competitive disadvantage in this sector. The GATT exception for the developing countries, however, could be a major stumbling block in view of the central role of the financial services sector in the process of economic development. The "special and more favorable treatment" anchored in the GSP and codes of conduct with respect to nontariff barriers negotiated during the Tokyo Round would presumably not apply in the case of financial services.

Protection via Tariffs

The GATT recognizes tariffs alone as a legitimate way of protecting domestic industries, which in turn are "bound," with quantitative restrictions to be used only for balance-of-payments reasons, for development purposes, and to protect the agricultural and fisheries industries.

As we have seen, tariffs are essentially not used to protect the financial services industry, with virtually all protection being applied in the form of quantitative restrictions on entry and operations. Since these are prohibited under the GATT, a strong case can be made for trade liberalization in this sector. Only the "development" exception would lend legitimacy under the GATT to financial services protection, under Part IV of the Agreement, and even here the case can be made that protection is often self-defeating.

National Treatment

The principle of "national treatment" is anchored firmly in the GATT Articles of Agreement, and is supposed to govern the application of all national policies affecting internationally traded goods and services. This GATT principle is highly relevant to the financial services industry, as we have seen, since this is essentially what trade liberalization is all about in this particular sector. Unfortunately, it also appears to be one of the GATT principles that is regularly violated by countries around the world.

Fair Trade

The fifth major principle underlying the GATT involves "fair trade" rules governing subsidization and dumping (Article VI). This is difficult to apply in the financial services sector. Banks and other firms in the industry frequently practice market segmentation and price discrimination as a normal part of doing business. They also "buy into" certain cells in the client-arena-product matrix through cross-subsidization from other cells, the equivalent of "dumping" in this sector. When coupled to the fact that a significant number of players in the international financial services industry have government equity participation or benefit from the lender-of-last-resort function of their home central bank (or from deposit insurance that is actuarially unsound), and in many cases have been subject to differing capital requirements and other prudential controls imposed by their home governments,it is not certain precisely how the GATT "fair trade" rules can be directly applied to this sector. The U.K.-U.S. agreement on

209

capital standards, noted above, makes notable progress in this direction.

Dispute Settlement

It is equally uncertain whether the GATT surveillance and dispute settlements procedures (Article XXIII) are fully applicable to the financial services sector. Surveillance suffers from the complex character and incidence of measures affecting competitive conditions in the financial services industry, which makes definition of "nullification and impairment" of benefits under the GATT difficult—as is true of many nontariff barriers in the goods sector as well. Dispute settlement, particularly when alleged trade distortions have to do with the incidence of monetary-policy and prudential measures, will potentially conflict with the mandates of national monetary and supervisory authorities.

Transparency

An overriding principle of the GATT is transparency, meaning that the terms and conditions under which suppliers are afforded market access should be clear and precisely stated. Tariffs, for example, represent competitive distortions that meet the transparency criterion. They can be analyzed in terms of their competitive effects, incorporated into business planning, and subjected to international negotiation on the basis of reciprocity. The same is decidedly not true of many types of nontariff barriers, such as health and safety standards and government procurement, and this is one element that has made the NTB negotiations and their implementation so much more difficult.

The transparency principle certainly applies to financial services. Many of the market-access barriers we have described in Chapter 7 are anything but transparent in terms of their effects on competition in the marketplace. Prudential and regulatory aspects makes transparency even more difficult to achieve in this sector, and implies the need for substantial cooperation on the part of the competent authorities in each country. Nevertheless, transparency remains a highly relevant objective in any trade liberalization affecting the financial services industry.

Right of Establishment

Finally, the GATT says nothing about the right of establishment or the rules governing foreign direct investment, both of which play a critical role in this industry.

SUMMARY

Taken in its present form, therefore, the GATT presents a decidedly mixed picture as a vehicle for bringing about the benchmarks of liberal trade in financial services, cataloged in the previous section. Some GATT provisions, particularly national treatment, are in full alignment with these benchmarks. But others are either irrelevant or capable of application only with major modifications. In the following chapter, we shall consider the options for negotiating broad-based liberalization of effective market access in the financial services industry within the context of multilateral trade negotiations.

Appendix 8–A.   Highlights of Financial Regulation in Major Industrial Countries.

	Interest Rate Controls	Credit Controls
United States	None on over-30-day maturities; otherwise abolished for individuals in 1983	None
Japan	Being phased out on large time deposits (over $2 million), MMC minimum reduced to about $200,000 as of September 1986	Ad hoc "window" guidance
Germany	Abolished in 1967	None
France	On demand, time, and savings deposits	To be abolished at end-1986
United Kingdom	Abolished in 1971	None since 1982
Italy	None	With varying degrees of formality
Canada	Abolished in 1967	None

Market Structure		Product Structure[b]
Domestic	International[a]	
Separation of commercial banks and securities firms; state banking	No controls since 1974; easy foreign entry	Wide range of well-developed markets in CP, CDs, FRNs, etc., with few restrictions
Separation of banking, securities, trust, and insurance; also of short- and long-term lending	Controls eased in 1980–84; continuing portfolio requirements and difficult foreign entry	CDs (introduced in 1979), BAs (1985), deep-discount bonds; no options; size and maturity limits on corporate issues
Universal banks separate from regional savings banks, real estate banks, and building and loan associations	Controls substantially eased in 1960s and abolished in 1980–81; eased foreign entry in 1985	Zeros and FRNs (May 1985), CD (1986); swaps allowed but discouraged; no CP, futures, options, or MMMFs
Universal banks separate from merchant banks, long-term credit institutions, finance, and specialized credit institutions	Eased in 1986 but still some controls on residents' lending for financial transactions; foreign entry easy in principle	CDs, CP with some restrictions on maturities and amounts (1985), futures (1985); no options
Eroding divisions among commercial banks, merchant banks, and building societies	No controls since 1979; relatively easy foreign entry	Similar to U.S., with CP market new and relatively undeveloped
Separation of specialized banks, and short- and long-term credit institutions	Easing in 1986, but still controls on outflows; easy foreign entry	No futures or CP, undeveloped options and CD markets; zeros possible
Separation of chartered banks and securities dealers, under review	No capital controls; limitations on foreign entry and ownership of financial institutions	Wide range of well-developed markets with few restrictions

Appendix 8–A. (continued).

	Interest Rate Controls	Credit Controls
Switzerland	None	None

Source: Morgan Guaranty Trust Company, *World Financial Markets*, January 1987.

a. It should be noted that even countries that have abolished cross-border controls generally regulate insurance and pension portfolios.

b. The acronyms are: commercial paper (CP), certificates of deposit (CDs), floating rate notes (FRNs), bankers' acceptances (BAs), zero-coupon bonds (zeros), and money market mutual funds (MMFs).

NOTES

1. Stephen Guisinger and Associates, *Investment Incentives and Performance Requirements* (New York: Frederick A. Praeger, 1985).

2. Ingo Walter, *Secret Money* (London: George Allen and Unwin, 1985).

3. William Ollard, "Foreigners Still Find Canada Chilly," *Euromoney*, November 1986.

4. John F. Burns, "Canada Opens Market's Doors," *The New York Times*, January 13, 1987.

5. F.N. Burton and F.H. Saelens, "The European Investments of Japanese Financial Institutions," *Columbia Journal of World Business* (Winter 1986), and "Deregulation Starts Buying Spree," *Financial Times*, July 22, 1987.

6. "Problems in European Financial Integration," *The New York Times*, March 8, 1987.

7. Lowell L. Bryan, "Capital Guidelines Could Weaken Banks," *The Wall Street Journal*, April 23, 1987.

8. Bank of England, *The Regulation of the Wholesale Markets in Sterling, Foreign Exchange Bullion* (London: Bank of England, 1987).

Market Structure		Product Structure[b]
Domestic	International[a]	
Universal banks separate from cantonal and local savings banks	Controls abolished in 1979–80; no SF Eurobond market; foreign entry with reciprocity	Undeveloped money and short-term bill markets; no options, CP, or CDs

9

TOWARD TRADE LIBERALIZATION IN FINANCIAL SERVICES

The purpose of this book has been fivefold. The first intent is to give an accurate portrayal of what the international financial services industry is all about—the products that are being supplied, and the client groups that comprise the market, and the offshore and onshore markets in which the products are sold and the clients are supplied. The Client-Arena-Product model has been used for this purpose. It is consistent with the standard structure-conduct-performance model of industrial organization and lends itself to the analysis of competitive dynamics of individual markets as well as market linkages. Extreme complexity, and the difficulty of pinning down precisely the relevant product attributes and competitive variables, makes such a structure essential in any attempt to make sense out of this increasingly global industry.

With respect to the players, we have considered the sources of institutional competitive power, how they apply to different aspects of the international financial services business, and how they help to explain rather dramatic variations in performance among institutions in individual markets and around the world. With respect to countries, we have examined the sources of national competitive advantage or disadvantage in this sector after making clear precisely what is being traded internationally. This discussion, again, was placed in the context of accepted theories of international trade.

Third, we have examined the nature of competitive distortions in this sector: their origins in the political economy of protection through rent-seeking behavior, their characteristics as tariff-like and quota-like entry and operating barriers to market access, and their relationship to regulatory and prudential controls. The structure of market-access barriers in this sector was linked to the basic Client-Arena-Product model to show their effects not only on individual market characteristics but also on the linkage effects through the entire matrix. It was thus made clear that access barriers to any particular market can have competitive consequences for the affected players that reach well beyond that market itself. Similarly, it was made clear that protection in this sector can have severe adverse international competitive implications for other industries.

Fourth, the principal dimensions (benchmarks) of trade liberalization in this sector were established and were related to the national interests of countries as well as the imperative of broad-guage reciprocity in international trade relations. A strong statement was made in favor of national treatment, defined in this sector as "equality of competitive opportunity" in the light of possibly differential incidence of regulatory and prudential controls, as the operative target for trade liberalization in this sector. Given the link between competitive distortions and institutional performance in an industry where excess returns can be quickly eroded by incremental competition, it is apparent that the vested interest even of the most competitive international players is "optimal" deregulation and liberalization of market access rather than "maximum" liberalization.

Fifth, the general principles of sectoral trade liberalization in financial services were related to the existing institutional structure in the form of the GATT and other relevant organizations. Most of the GATT principles were found to be consistent, given appropriate adaptation, with the imperatives of trade liberalization in the financial services sector.

ISSUES FOR SECTORAL TRADE LIBERALIZATION

It is not surprising that developing countries have resisted including sectors like financial services in the Uruguay Round of GATT trade negotiations, fearing that their sectoral competitive disadvantage would yield few benefits from liberalization while their protectionist policies could, under the broad rubric of reciprocity, endanger trade concessions in other areas of vital interest to them. Indeed, a strong case can be made that any GATT arrangement covering financial services will not be honored by a large number of countries, and that this will further weaken an already fragile structure of international trade rules. Yet even here, the more successful LDCs will eventually come to see the inconsistency and economic "drag" that is the product of the combination of a highly competitive industrial sector, export-led economic growth, and a "retarded" financial services industry. Since these will usually be the more interesting LDC markets for the major international players in this industry, some of the differential problems of market access between developed and developing countries should eventually fall of their own weight.

Meanwhile, bankers themselves in many cases appear lukewarm to the idea of including their industry in broad-based GATT discussions. They appear to view the industry as too complex and "special" to be thrown into general trade negotiations. They are sensitive to the possibility that concessions will be wrung, on their behalf, out of industries that include important clients. They consider it possible to penetrate the really important foreign markets without fundamentally changing the overall rules of the game, either on an *ad hoc* basis or by leading clients into offshore and foreign financial markets. And given our conclusion that competitive distortions may be the *cause* of supernormal profits in an industry where differential competitive advantages are hard to come by, a truly level playing field may be against the interest even of major global players. Of course, the self-interest of bankers is not what trade liberalization is all about, so that some of these views should not be taken too seriously—although they obviously influence the political pressure (or lack thereof) behind liberalization in this sector.

Financial services have already played an important role in the negotiations for free trade between the United States and Canada, as they did in the earlier free trade arrangements between the United States and Israel. The U.S.-Canadian talks covered services, investments, and intellectual property rights and were viewed by governments as a possible model for the Uruguay Round of trade negotiations. On the other hand, bilateral trade agreements are certainly against both the spirit of the GATT and most-favored-nation treatment, and it was not clear whether the issues arising between the United States and either Israel or Canada would be representative of those arising in the far broader framework of the Uruguay Round.

One such issue was national treatment versus reciprocity. Acceptance of reciprocity would mean that Canadian and Israeli banks could establish nationwide branches as well as commercial and investment banking operations in the United States, thus gaining exemption from the Glass-Steagall, McFadden, and Bank Holding Company Acts that apply to American institutions. This is because no such restraints apply to American banks in either of these countries. National treatment, on the other hand, would mean that American banks would have far greater powers in Canada and Israel than banks from these two countries would have in the United States. Under reciprocity, Canadian and Israeli bank access to the complete American markets for financial services is worth far more than American bank access to their respective markets. Yet under national treatment, American banks would have much wider powers in their markets than Canadian and Israeli banks in the United States.

Perhaps an alternative to the GATT model for liberalizing competitive conditions in the financial services sector focuses on the OECD decisions governing the treatment of foreign direct investment on the basis of a fundamental symmetry of rights and obligations on the part of governments and companies. This encompasses many of the trade liberalization benchmarks proposed in Chapter 8, although it too is silent on the right of establishment.

Given the complexity of the international financial services industry, and its interrelationship with important national objectives such as financial safety and stability, monetary policy, economic structure, and external balance, it is likely that significant progress can be made only by applying the existing broad GATT principles through the negotiation of a specific code of conduct. There is a precedent in the NTB codes negotiated during the Tokyo Round, where the issues were also sufficiently complex in each case to warrant a highly specific approach based on broad principles already embedded in the GATT.

The specifics of the 1986 Ministerial Declaration on the Uruguay Round, setting the parameters for the multilateral trade negotiations beginning in 1987, remained largely concerned with merchandise trade. Part II of the Declaration concerned itself with the services sector. The entire wording is as follows:

> Ministers also decided, as part of the Multilateral Trade Negotiations, to launch negotiations on trade in services. Negotiations in this area shall aim to establish a multilateral framework of principles of rules for trade in services, with a view to expansion of such trade under conditions of transparency and progressive liberalization as a means of promoting economic growth of all trading partners and the development of developing countries. Such framework shall respect the policy objectives of national laws and regulations applying to services and shall take into account the work of relevant international organizations.
>
> GATT procedures and practices shall apply to these negotiations. A Group on Negotiations in Services is established to deal with these matters. Participation in the negotiations under this Part of the Declaration will be open to the same countries as under Part I. GATT secretariat support will be provided, with technical support from other organizations as decided by the Group on Negotiations in Services.[1]

A GATT financial services code would have to deal specifically with each of the benchmarks identified earlier, although it would be rather difficult to incorporate even limited special and differential treatment for developing countries (see below). Surveillance and dispute resolution mechanisms would have to be designed. The code would have to be incorporated into a broad system of international obligations encompassing the services sector, and would no doubt have in common many elements of relevance to other services industries. The real question is whether these commonalities are sufficiently strong to permit successful negotiation of an "umbrella" agreement covering substantially all trade in services. The uniqueness and complexity of the financial services industry and its highly regulated character make for a difficult "fit" under an umbrella that also covers shipping, air transport, telecommunications, insurance, and other types of internationally traded services, each of which has its own specific attributes. Still, certain common threads such as national treatment do run through the issue of trade liberalization in all of these industries. And assured market access for financial services is connected to freeing up international markets in other services industries as well, most particularly insurance and telecommunications.

As of early 1987, the Group on Negotiations in Services had been set up, and a list of elements to be considered had been identified. These included:

1. Definitional and statistical issues

2. Broad concepts on which principles and rules for trade in services, including possible discipline for individual sectors, might be based

3. Coverage of the multilateral framework in services

4. Existing international disciplines and arrangements

5. Measures and practices contributing to or limiting the expansion of trade in services

Item 5 includes specifically any barriers perceived by individual participants, to which the conditions of transparency and progressive liberalization might be applicable. A review at the end of 1987 was then to set the stage for actual negotiations.

At its meeting in April 1987, the group focused on the collection of statistics on international trade in services, and participants agreed that it would be a long time before such data reached the quality of international trade statistics. Participants differed, however, on the necessity for reliable data as a prerequisite for successful negotiations on services. In addition, participants put forward such terms as mutual advantage, transparency, national treatment, increasing international competition, and progressive liberalization—often used in international trade negotiations in the past—as having potential significance in the services sector as well.[2]

WHAT TO NEGOTIATE?

As we have seen, the objective of trade liberalization in the financial services sector must be built on several similar but not equivalent concepts:

- Equality of competitive opportunity
- Right to establish and invest in a viable commercial presence
- National treatment
- Effective market access

Each is a rather "plastic" concept that is subject to differences in definition and interpretation. That these concepts are not identical becomes clear if we review once again the nature of competitive distortions as they arise in this particular sector, and classify them in terms of the underlying intent:

Type I. Measures that are intentionally used to discriminate between foreign based and domestically based suppliers of financial services to national client groups. These may be tariff-like if they impose differential costs on the two sets of players or quota-like if they restrict one group at the expense of the other through some form of licensing. That is, Type I measures conform to the standard techniques of commercial policy applied in the goods sector and generally covered by existing GATT codes and agreements.

Type II. Measures that prescribe certain areas of activity (client groups and product groups) for different types of financial

223

institutions, whether domestic or foreign. There is no intention to discriminate explicitly against foreign players, but foreign based firms may nevertheless be severely constrained relative to conditions in their home markets or in third markets. These are quota-like constraints that are not amenable to liberalization in the context of international trade negotiations as conventionally defined.

Type III. Domestic measures that are not explicitly designed to protect domestic suppliers against competition from foreign based financial institutions, but that have the effect of making market access more difficult or more costly than faced by indigenous competitors.

Clearly, Type I measures are fully amenable to negotiations among countries in their classic form. They are trade distortions that intentionally discriminate between domestic and foreign players and therefore have a great deal in common with conventional nontariff barriers in the goods sector.

Type II measures are based on domestic policies that have the *effect* of discriminating against foreign based firms even in the absence of any intent to do so (although "intent" is often impossible to identify). Here foreign players seek changes in domestic policies which will improve their effective market access without thwarting the ostensible national aims of the policies themselves. They lend themselves in part to the negotiation of codes of conduct that are not designed to remove specific impediments, but rather set standards for aligning domestic policies with the objective of removing competitive distortions in the process and making it more difficult to use such measures with protectionist intent.

Type III measures have effects on competitive positioning that is purely collateral in nature. It is doubtful that such policies lend themselves to alteration in a trade negotiations context. They do, however, lend themselves to harmonization in a bilateral and multilateral context among the regulators, as was done in the case of the U.K.-U.S. agreement of risk-based capital requirements.

UMBRELLA, SECTORAL, AND
SUBSECTORAL ISSUES

There are three distinct levels involved in thinking about international trade negotiations as they affect the financial services industry.

Umbrella Parameters. What basic principles appear to make sense with respect to all types of services entering the channels of international trade—that is, where value added is created using factors of production resident in one country and sold to residents of another? The focus here would be on the definition of effective market access and the maintenance of a viable commercial presence.

Sectoral Parameters. What are the specific implications of each umbrella parameter for the financial services industry in terms of its impact on effective market access, commercial presence, and equality of competitive opportunity? What additional rules may be necessary to advance trade liberalization in in financial services that are uniquely applicable to this sector?

Subsector Implications. What are the specific implications of each of the umbrella parameters and sectoral parameters for effective market access and equality of competitive opportunity with respect to each of the principal types of financial services supplied internationally?

RELEVANCE OF AN UMBRELLA
AGREEMENT ON SERVICES

At least a dozen main elements of an umbrella agreement on services have been identified.[3] Their applicability to the financial services sector and to its various subsectors varies widely among the various principles that might be embedded in an umbrella agreement.

225

Nondiscrimination. Under this principle, most-favored-nation treatment would be extended to the services sector. Strictly, any signatory of the umbrella agreement (open to all GATT signatories) would be accorded MFN treatment under all of the sectoral codes. Given free-rider behavior and the sensitivity of the financial services sector, particularly in developing countries, it is doubtful that full MFN treatment is feasible in this context. *Code-conditional* treatment would appear to be more appropriate, whereby only the signatories of a financial services code would be afforded its benefits. This would follow the pattern set in the various nontariff barrier codes established in the Tokyo Round of multilateral trade negotiations, and would be subject to "unilateral choice": any GATT signatory of the umbrella agreement would be entitled to sign the financial services sectoral code subject to meeting agreed signatory criteria anchored in the code.

National Treatment. The principle of national treatment would govern international trade in all services, to include the right to establish a commercial presence and to be subject to a regulatory environment identical to that of locally based suppliers of services. An umbrella principle of this sort would clearly have to be tailored to the specifics of the financial services sector, where fiduciary and monetary policy considerations play a major role. It would also have to recognize that certain functions may be allocated to government entities as a matter of national sovereignty. Equality of competitive opportunity is the key objective of liberal cross-border delivery of financial services, so that the national treatment concept would be a critical component of any code negotiated for this sector.

Reciprocity. An umbrella code should focus on the notion of broad-gauge reciprocity, so that access to markets for certain services can be negotiated in return for reciprocal access to foreign markets for *other* services, as well as for goods. This, of course, has been the traditional view of reciprocity for international trade negotiations in the goods sector. If comparative advantage is to be allowed to work, then all tradable goods and services ought to be captured under the principle of reciprocity.

Limiting reciprocity to individual sectors thwarts this goal and facilitates the formation of intergovernmental cartels and market-sharing agreements. However, it seems unlikely that broad-gauge reciprocity is practicable, although it could in fact be captured in the pattern of mutual and balanced concessions that may develop in the course of negotiations. Moreover, as we have noted, sectoral reciprocity has a long history in financial services, and the sector itself may be sufficiently broad that sectoral reciprocity may represent a viable second-best objective.

Transparency. The objective here would be to ensure adequate reporting, publication, and dissemination of any rules covering the supply of services on the part of foreign based firms. Annual reporting requirements might be set for the competent government authorities to the GATT secretariat, with the purpose of producing published reports. Transparency is clearly of relevance for a sectoral code on financial services. Although information on rules and regulations governing access by foreign based firms to national financial services markets exists in most countries, there has been no systematic collection, translation, classification, and dissemination at the international level. This represents an important shortcoming in relation to the degree of transparency that has been achieved in the goods sector, particularly with respect to tariffs.

Consultation Requirement. This principle would require any signatory of the umbrella code to consult with any other signatory on matters pertaining to market access in any services sector. It is clearly of relevance to the financial services sector and should be incorporated in any sectoral code.

Regulatory Due Process. The point here is to assure "the right of any signatory and its business entities to fair procedures in the government regulatory processes of any other signatory, including fair notice and available information about regulations and their application, right of appeal, right of the signatory government to take up matters under consultation requirements with [the] other signatory on behalf of citizens/business entities."[4] An umbrella principle along these lines would clearly be relevant to the financial services sector. It would formalize and facilitate bilateral consultations that have traditionally been the focus of efforts to achieve market access in this sector, thereby reducing the potential for friction.

Dispute Settlement. In the tradition of the GATT, provision for dispute settlement would be incorporated in an umbrella code for services. This would include mandatory bilateral consultations, use of professional conciliators, creation of impartial panels to deal with disputes that cannot be resolved through bilateral consultations (determination of rules and rule applicability, but no recommendation or conciliation functions), approval of panel determinations by a competent sectoral committee, and provision for sanctions or retaliation in the event appropriate relief is not forthcoming. Such machinery is clearly relevant to the financial services sector, particularly the use of professional conciliators and impartial expert panels. As noted earlier, conditions under which competition takes place in this sector are sufficiently specialized that such shifting of disputes to "lay" forums can be highly damaging and lead to retaliation. Expert involvement, if impartial, can significantly reduce this danger. Such dispute settlement machinery could be unified and cover all sectoral codes, which would not inhibit bringing to bear financial expertise in the case of disputes affecting that sector.

Waiver. Countries would be permitted to lift applicability of any provision in the umbrella agreement or a specific sector agreement for a limited time in order to resolve disputes or damage caused by the provision. Dispute settlement machinery would apply to the use of waivers as well, with opportunity for damaged countries to seek redress. A waiver provision in an umbrella agreement would be fully applicable to the financial services sector, and should be incorporated in a sectoral code, particularly in view of questions about the ultimate impact of specific code provisions to subsectors and individual suppliers and services in this highly complex sector.

Special and More Favorable Treatment for Developing Countries. Since the early 1970s the developing countries have argued for special and differential treatment under the GATT. Most prominent among these is the Generalized System of Preferences (GSP), designed under a GATT waiver to provide reduced-rate or duty-free access of the markets or most industrial countries for many manufactured goods. Such treatment is then withheld if a country breaches a certain threshold, indicating that it no longer "needs" GSP treatment for a given product or has "graduated" into the category of major suppliers of broad groups of products.

It is doubtful that preferential treatment could be successfully incorporated into a financial services code. For one thing, most market-access barriers are quota-like rather than tariff-like, and therefore do not lend themselves easily to the traditional form of special treatment. Nor is it acceptable to subject financial institutions home-based in developing countries to regulatory requirements that are more lax. Perhaps the one form of special treatment that may be applicable involves a delayed phasing-in of obligations under a financial services code for developing country signatories that need time to prepare their domestic financial systems for increased competition. This could avoid foreign domination of the sector by locking-in the superiority of foreign based financial services firms.

As noted, many countries have created "retarded" financial sectors through excessive protection, which in turn have impaired international competitiveness of other sectors of the economy, as well as national economic growth. For this reason alone, developing countries ought to be looking forward to financial deregulation within the structure of a clear set of rules anchored in GATT umbrella and/or sectoral agreements.

Exceptions. Any umbrella agreement would presumably include exceptions for national security, political sovereignty, and safeguards (covering for example "excessive" competitive damage to the domestic industry as a result of foreign penetration) that would have to be specifically invoked and would presumably carry over to a code covering the financial services industry.

229

Standstill. Countries subscribing to an umbrella agreement should be committed to refrain from introducing new barriers to market access. This could be applied in a relatively straightforward manner to measures classified as Type I distortions, above, but would be impractical for Type II and Type III distortions. To impose a standstill across the board to the financial services sector would represent regulatory paralysis, which no country would tolerate. At the same time, a standstill must not be interpreted as an endorsement of existing competitive distortions.

Administrative. In addition to its substantive provisions, an umbrella agreement would cover funding for the GATT secretariat to carry out its mandate under the sectoral agreements, voting rules, rules covering ratification, amendment, and so forth for both the umbrella itself and the various sector codes.

The umbrella agreement thus would not amend the GATT, but rather would be negotiated "in the context of the GATT," as would each of the sectoral codes.

In the financial services industry, the question remains how relevant even a sectoral code would be for each and every product supplied in national markets by foreign based competitors—the *relevance* factor. If not, there may be a need for subsector codes, either negotiated separately or developed as part of the sectoral negotiations. There is also the question whether sectoral codes for licensed and unlicensed professional services (accounting, law, consulting), insurance, and perhaps others covering activities that overlap with financial services would be mutually consistent.

A number of additional questions remain open as well. In terms of timing, how would work on the umbrella and sectoral codes proceed, and how effectively will overlapping issues be handled? Can countries readily predict the implications for their national economies and the individual sectors of the various provisions embedded in the codes? If not, would they be willing to become signatories? Would a strict, binding code signed only by the most important countries in global finance be preferable, in terms of furthering liberal trade in financial services, than a more general and nonbinding code that is acceptable to large numbers of countries? How binding could any code be, and how effective the prospective complaints and dispute settlement procedures? How would grandfathering be handled, and are there prospects for retroactive application? Should the umbrella code be a relatively general statement of principles, with the individual sectoral codes much more specific, binding and enforceable? That could result in many countries signing the umbrella code but abstaining from the financial services code. If this happens, what are such countries' rights under the latter? All of these are questions that remain for discussion in the years ahead.

NOTES

1. General Agreement on Tariffs and Trade, *Ministerial Declaration on the Uruguay Round* (Geneva: GATT, 1986).
2. *Gatt Focus*, May 1987, p. 3.
3. John H. Jackson, "Potential Umbrella MTN Agreement on Services," Georgetown University Law Center, Washington, D.C., 1987. Mimeo.
4. Ibid.

BIBLIOGRAPHY

Aliber, Robert Z. "International Banking: A Survey." *Journal of ¿Money, Credit and Banking* (November 1984).

American Bankers Association. *The Future Development of U.S. Banking Organizations Abroad*. Washington, D.C.: American Bankers Association, 1981.

Bailey, Elizabeth E., and Ann F. Friedlander. "Market Structure and Multiproduct Industries." *Journal of Economic Literature* (September 1982).

Bank for International Settlements. *Recent Innovations in International Banking*. Basel: Bank for International Settlements, 1986.

Baumol, William, J. Panzar, and R. Willig. *Contestable Markets and the Theory of Industry Structure*. New York: Harcourt Brace Jovanovich, 1982.

Bertrand, Olivier, and Thierry Noyelle. "Changing Technology, Skills and Skill Formation: The Policy Implications of the OECD/CERI Comparative Study of Financial Service Forms." Paris: OECD, 1986. Mimeo.

Bloch, Ernest. *Inside Investment Banking*. Homewood, Ill.: Dow Jones Irwin, 1986.

Boston Consulting Group. *The Future of Wholesale Banking*. Rolling Meadows, Ill.: Bank Administration Institute, 1986.

Bryan, Lowell L. "Capital Guidelines Could Weaken Banks." *The Wall Street Journal*, April 23, 1987.

Burns, John F. "Canada Opens Market's Doors." *The New York Times*, January 13, 1987.

Caves, Richard. "Economic Analysis and the Quest for Competitive Advantage." *American Economic Review* (May 1984).

Caves, Richard, and Michael Porter, "From Entry Barriers to Mobility Barriers: Conjectural Decisions and Contrived Deterrence to New Competition." *Quarterly Journal of Economics* (May 1977).

Channon, Derek F. *Bank Strategic Management and Marketing*. New York: John Wiley and Sons, 1986.

Cohen, Michael, and Thomas Morante. "Elimination of Nontariff Barriers to Trade in Services: Recommendations for Future Negotiations." *International Law Journal* (1981).

Cooper, Kerry, and Donald R. Fraser. *Bank Deregulation and the New Competition in Financial Services*. Cambridge, Mass.: Ballinger, 1986.

Corbet, Hugh. "Prospect of Negotiations on Barriers to International Trade in Services." *Pacific Community* (April 1977).

Cowhey, Peter F. *Trade in Services: A Case for Open Markets*. Washington, D.C.: American Enterprise Institute, 1986.

Crane, Dwight B., and Samuel L. Hayes, III. "The New Competition in World Banking." *Harvard Business Review*, July-August 1982.

Davis, Steven I. *The Euro-bank*, 2d ed. London: MacMillan, 1979.

———. *Excellence in Banking*. London: MacMillan, 1985.

Diebold, William, and Helena Stalson. "Negotiating Issues in International Service Transactions." In William R. Cline (ed.), *Trade Policy in the 1980s*. Washington, D.C.: Institute for International Economics, 1983.

Dunning, John H. *International Production and the Multinational Enterprise*. London: Allen and Unwin, 1981.

Feketekuty, Geza. "International Trade in Banking Services: The Negotiating Arena." Washington, D.C.: Office of the United States Trade Representative, 1987. Mimeo.

Fieleke, Norman S. "The Growth of U.S. Banking Abroad: An Analytical Survey." In *Key Issues in International Banking*. Boston: Federal Reserve Bank of Boston, 1977.

Fraser, Robert D. *International Banking and Finance*. Washington, D.C.: R & H Publishers, 1973.

Galbraith, Craig S., and Neil M. Kay. "Towards a Theory of the Multinational Firm." *Journal of Economic Behavior and Organization* (March 1986).

General Agreement on Tariffs and Trade. *Articles of Agreement*. Geneva: GATT, 1984.

———. *The Scope, Limits and Function of the GATT Legal System*. Geneva: GATT, 1985.

———. *Ministerial Declaration on the Uruguay Round*. Geneva: GATT, 1986.

Gladwin, Thomas N., and Ingo Walter. *Multinationals under Fire*. New York: John Wiley and Sons, 1980.

Goddin, C. Stuart. "Memorandum on National Treatment and Reciprocity." Office of the Comptroller of the Currency, U.S. Department of the Treasury, Washington, D.C. September 12, 1983. Mimeo.

Goldberg, Ellen S., et al. *Off-Balance-Sheet Activities of Banks: Managing the Risk-Reward Tradeoffs.* Philadelphia: Robert Morris Associates, 1983.

Gray, H. Peter. "Toward a Unified Theory of International Trade, International Production and Foreign Direct Investment." In John Black and John H. Dunning (eds.), *International Capital Movements.* London: Allen and Unwin, 1982.

Gray, H. Peter, and Jean M. Gray. "The Multinational Bank: A Financial MNC?" *Journal of Banking and Finance* (March 1982).

Grey, Rodney de C. *Traded Computer Services.* Toronto: Grey, Clark, Shih & Associates, 1983.

Grubel, Herbert G. "A Theory of Multinational Banking." *Banca Nazionale del Lavoro Quarterly Review* (December 1977).

———. "There Is No Direct International Trade in Services." *American Economic Review*, Papers and Proceedings (May 1987).

Guisinger, Stephen, and Associates. *Investment Incentives and Performance Requirements.* New York: Frederick A. Praeger, 1985.

Guth, Wilfried. "International Banking: The Next Phase." *The Banker* (October 1981).

———. "Bank Strategy in the 1990s," *The Banker* (April 1986).

Guttentag, Jack, and Richard Herring. "Provisioning, Charge-Offs and the Willingness to Lend." The Wharton School, University of Pennsylvania, 1986. Mimeo.

Hayes, Samuel, III, A. M. Spence, and D. v. P. Marks, *Competition in the Investment Banking Industry.* Cambridge, Mass.: Harvard University Press, 1983.

Heimann, John. "The Problem of Confidence in Domestic and International Banking Systems." *Journal of Banking and Finance* (September 1982).

Hindley, Brian. *Economic Analysis and Insurance Policy in the Third World*, Thames Essay No. 32. London: Trade Policy Research Centre, 1982.

Hindley, Brian, and Alasdair Smith. "Comparative Advantage and Trade in Services." *The World Economy* (June 1984).

Hirsch, Seev. "Services and Service Intensity in International Trade." London: Trade Policy Research Centre, 1987. Mimeo.

Hislop, Angus. "Making Sense of Capital Adequacy." *The Banker* (February 1987).

Hogan, Warren E., and Ivor F. Pierce. *The Incredible Eurodollar.* London: Allen and Unwin, 1982.

Jackson, John H. "Potential Umbrella MTN Agreement on Services." Georgetown University Law Center, Washington, D.C. 1987. Mimeo.

Kallberg, Jarl S., and Anthony Saunders. *Direct Sources of Competitiveness in Banking Services.* New York: Salomon Brothers Center for the Study of Financial Institutions, 1986. Mimeo.

Khoury, Sarkis J. *Dynamics of International Banking.* New York: Praeger, 1980.

Ladreit de Larrechère, Guy. *The Legal Framework for International Trade.* Geneva: GATT, 1984.

Letiche, J. M. "Dependent Monetary Systems and Economic Development." In W. Sellekaerts (ed.), *Economic Development and Planning.* London: MacMillan, 1974.

Leutwiler, Fritz et al. *Trade Policies for a Better Future.* Geneva: GATT, 1985.

McKenzie, George W. *Economics of the Eurodollar Market.* London: MacMillan, 1976.

Manguno, Joseph P. "Korea Modifies Its Banking Regulations." *The Wall Street Journal*, December 30, 1986.

Martineau, Lisa. "A Long Wait for Foreign Banks." *The Banker* (January 1987).

Mathis, John F. (ed.). *Offshore Lending by U.S. Commercial Banks*, 2d ed. Philadelphia: Bankers' Association for Foreign Trade and Robert Morris Associates, 1982.

Mathur, Shiv Sahai. "How Firms Compete: A New Classification of Generic Strategies." Centre for the Study of Financial Institutions, The City University Business School, Working Paper No. 81, July 1986. Mimeo.

Miles, R. E., and C. C. Snow. *Organization Strategy, Structure and Processes.* New York: McGraw-Hill, 1978.

Miles, R. H., and K. S. Cameron. *Coffin Nails and Corporate Strategy.* Englewood Cliffs, N.J.: Prentice-Hall, 1982.

Monti, Antonio. "Recent Trends in International Banking." *Journal of Banking and Finance* (September 1982).

Morgan Guaranty Trust Company, "America's Banking Market Goes International." *Morgan Economic Quarterly* (June 1986).

Nayyar, Deepak. *International Trade in Services: Implications for Developing Countries*. Bombay: Export-Import Bank of India, 1986.

Neu, C. R. "International Trade in Banking Services." Paper presented at a NBER/CEPS Conference on European—U.S. Trade Relations, Brussels, June 1986. Mimeo.

Newman, H. "Strategic Groups and the Structure-Performance Relationships." *Review of Economics and Statistics* (August 1978).

Office of Technology Assessment, U.S. Congress. *International Competition in Banking and Financial Services*. Washington, D.C.: OTA, July 1986. Mimeo.

Ollard, William. "Foreigners Still Find Canada Chilly." *Euromoney*, November 1986.

Organization for Economic Cooperation and Development. *Trade in Services in Banking*. Paris: OECD, 1983.

———. Working Party of the Trade Committee. *The Elements of a Conceptual Framework for Trade in Services*. Document TC/WP(85)79. Paris: OECD, December 16, 1985.

———. Trade Secretariat. *Elements of a Conceptual Framework for Trade in Services*. Document TC(87). Paris: OECD, January 2, 1987.

Oster, S. "Intraindustry Structure and the Ease of Strategic Change." *Review of Economics and Statistics* (August 1982).

Page, Diane, and Neil M. Soss. "Some Evidence on Transnational Banking Structure." In *Foreign Acquisitions of U.S. Banks*. Washington, D.C.: U.S. Government Printing Office, 1982.

Panzar, John C., and Robert D. Willig. "Economies of Scope." *American Economic Review* (May 1981).

Pastré, Olivier. *Multinationals: Banking and Firm Relationships*. Greenwich, Conn.: JAI Press, 1981.

———. "International Bank-Industry Relations: An Empirical Assessment." *Journal of Banking and Finance* (March 1981).

Pecchioli, R. M. *Internationalization of Banking*. Paris: OECD, 1983.

Porter, Michael E. *Competitive Strategy*. New York: Free Press, 1980.

Roussakis, Emmanuel (ed.). *International Banking*. New York: Praeger, 1983.

Salomon Brothers, Inc. *The Hong Kong Banking System: An Intriguing Financial Services Center*. New York: Salomon Brothers, 1987.

———. "The Regulators' New Risk-Adjusted Capital Ratio Proposal: U.S. and U.K. Perspectives." *Bank Weekly*, February 9, 1987.

Sagari, Sylvia B. *The Financial Services Industry: An International Perspective.* Ph.D. dissertation, Graduate School of Business Administration, New York University, 1986.

Saunders, Anthony, and Ingo Walter. "International Trade in Financial Services: Are Bank Services Special?" Paper presented at the *Symposium on New Institutional Arrangements for the World Economy.* University of Konstanz, 1987. Mimeo.

Schwamm, Henri, and Patrizio Merciai. *The Multinationals and the Services.* Chichester: John Wiley and Sons, 1985.

Swoboda, Alexandre K. "International Banking: Current Issues in Perspective." *Journal of Banking and Finance* (September 1982).

Teece, David J. "Economies of Scope and the Enterprise." *Journal of Economic Behavior and Organization* (March 1985).

Tschoegl, Adrian E. *The Regulation of Foreign Banks: Policy Formation Outside the United States.* New York: Salomon Brothers Center for the Study of Financial Institutions, New York University, 1981.

———. "Foreign Bank Entry into Japan and California." In Allen M. Rugman (ed.), *New Theories of the Multinational Enterprise.* London: Croom Helm, 1982.

———. "Size, Growth and Transnationality among the World's Largest Banks." *Journal of Business* 56, no. 2 (1983).

Tugendhat, Christopher. "Opening-up Europe's Financial Sector." *The Banker* (January 1985).

U.S. Comptroller of the Currency. *Foreign Acquisition of U.S. Banks: Motives and Tactical Consideration.* Washington, D.C.: U.S. Government Printing Office, 1982.

———. *A Critical Evaluation of Reciprocity in Foreign Bank Acquisition.* Washington, D.C.: U.S. Government Printing Office, 1984.

———. *U.S. Banks' Loss of Global Standing.* Washington, D.C.: U.S. Government Printing Office, 1984.

U.S. Department of the Treasury. *Report to the Congress on Foreign Government Treatment of U.S. Banking Organizations.* Washington, D.C.: U.S. Government Printing Office, 1979; updated 1984.

Walter, Ingo. *Barriers to Trade in Banking and Financial Services.* London: Trade Policy Research Centre, 1985.

———. *Secret Money.* London: George Allen and Unwin, 1985.

——— (ed.). *Deregulating Wall Street.* New York: John Wiley and Sons, 1985.

Walter, Ingo, and H. Peter Gray. "Protectionism in International Banking." *Journal of Banking and Finance* (December 1983).

Watson, Maxwell, et al. *International Capital Markets: Developments and Prospects*. Washington, D.C.: International Monetary Fund, 1986.

Wellons, Philip A. *Passing the Buck: Banks, Government and Third World Debt*. Cambridge, Mass.: Harvard Business School Press, 1987.

Wilson, Dick. "Waiting Game for China's Foreign Bankers." *The Banker* (August 1986).

Yannopoulos, George N. "The Growth of Transnational Banking." In Mark Casson (ed.), *The Growth of International Business*. London: George Allen and Unwin, 1983.

Index

Actuarial risk base, 78–80
Admission fees for market access, 207
American Express, 30, 31, 60, 64, 145, 154
Anthony Gibbs bank, 127
Antimonopoly policies, 194
Antitrust policies, 115, 194–195
Arbitrage and market positioning, 21–22
Argentina, 144
Arm's length transactions, 104, 105
Aubrey Lanston and Company, 154, 155
Australia, 124–125
Automated teller machines, 64, 66, 145, 146
Automobile industry, 191

Bahamas, 160, 161
Banco Central (Spain), 153
Bank for International Settlements, 38, 196, 200
Bank Holding Company Act, 76, 133, 220
Bank of England, 126–127, 158, 203–204
Bank of Japan, 141, 200
Bank of Korea, 138
BankAmerica/Bank of America, 125, 153, 188
Bankers Trust, 125, 128, 155
Banks (general discussion), 9–10, 77; branching system, 76, 133, 151–152, 192, 194; capital adequacy, 195–204; competition among, 2, 199, 201, 204; constraints on growth, 143; deregulation of, 129; failure of, 36, 37; funding for, 78; and GATT negotiations, 219; and government policy, 71; hidden reserves, 199, 200; international lending by, 17–18, 87, 103; internationalization of, 10–11, 69, 111; legislation concerning, 118; money center, 11, 77; nationalized, 192; operating restrictions, 143; performance disclosure, 200–201; political power of, 117–118; profitability of, 71; project financing by, 18, 58; regulation of, 78; safety of, 159; and technological change, 20, 43; and trade vs. protection, 114; training programs, 82. *See also financial services listings*; Loans
Banks, commercial foreign, 10–11, 19, 134, 186; control of, 114–115; credit rating of, 78–79; crisis of, 38; protection of, 185; in United States, 6, 10, 11–12, 27, 123, 133–134, 152
Banks, commercial U.S.; 72, 76, 80; expansion by, 181; international activities of, 6, 10, 26–27, 103, 128; megabanks, 76, 77; offshore markets for, 10–12; restrictions on, 133; super-regional, 77
Banks, correspondent, 26, 59–60
Banks, investment: European, 9, 10; international activities of, 6, 11, 26–27; U.S., 19, 80, 103, 129, 133, 185, 186
Banks, Japanese, 6, 67, 141, 157–158, 163, 199; in Britain, 12; capital ratio of, 199–200, 201–203; commercial, 196; deregulation of, 155; in Europe, 126; securities trading by, 80; in United States, 11–12, 126
Banks, merchant, 9, 11, 19–20, 75, 186; British, 9–10, 19, 69, 127; Japanese, 19; U.S., 19, 125
Banks, multinational, 71

ABOUT THE AUTHOR

Ingo Walter is the Dean Abraham L. Gitlow Professor of Economics and Finance at the Graduate School of Business Administration of New York University, and holds a joint appointment as the John H. Loudon Professor of International Management at INSEAD in Fontainebleau, France. From 1971 to 1979 he was associate dean for academic affairs at New York University, serving as chairman of international business from 1980 to 1983, and as chairman of finance from 1983 to 1985. He previously taught at the University of Missouri–St. Louis, where he was chairman of the department of economics from 1967 to 1970. He received his A.B. and M.S. degrees from Lehigh University and his Ph.D. degree in 1966 from New York University.

Dr. Walter's principal areas of research include international trade policy, international banking, environmental economics, and the economics of multinational corporate operations. He has published papers in various professional journals in these fields and is the author or editor of a dozen books, including a widely used textbook. At present, his research interests focus on competitive structure, conduct, and performance in the international banking and financial services industry, and on risk elements relating to international trade and capital flows.

He has served as a consultant to various U.S. and foreign government agencies, international institutions, banks, and corporations. Among them are the U.S. Environmental Protection Agency, Department of Commerce, Organization for Economic Cooperation and Development, International Finance Corporation, British Petroleum, General Electric Company, Philip Morris International, Swiss Bank Corporation, and J.P. Morgan & Company.